Salt, Sweat, Tears

The Men Who Rowed the Oceans

ADAM RACKLEY

PENGUIN BOOKS

PENGUIN BOOKS

Published by the Penguin Group
Penguin Books Ltd, 80 Strand, London wc2r 0rl, England
Penguin Group (USA) Inc., 375 Hudson Street, New York, New York 10014, USA
Penguin Group (Canada), 90 Eglinton Avenue East, Suite 700, Toronto, Ontario, Canada m4p 2y3
(a division of Pearson Penguin Canada Inc.)
Penguin Ireland, 25 St Stephen's Green, Dublin 2, Ireland (a division of Penguin Books Ltd)
Penguin Group (Australia), 707 Collins Street, Melbourne, Victoria 3008, Australia
(a division of Pearson Australia Group Pty Ltd)
Penguin Books India Pvt Ltd, 11 Community Centre, Panchsheel Park, New Delhi – 110 017, India
Penguin Group (NZ), 67 Apollo Drive, Rosedale, Auckland 0632, New Zealand
(a division of Pearson New Zealand Ltd)
Penguin Books (South Africa) (Pty) Ltd, Block D, Rosebank Office Park,
181 Jan Smuts Avenue, Parktown North, Gauteng 2193, South Africa

Penguin Books Ltd, Registered Offices: 80 Strand, London wc2r 0rl, England

www.penguin.com

First published by Viking 2014
Published in Penguin Books 2014
001

Printed in Great Britain by Clays Ltd, St Ives plc

isbn: 978-0-241-96703-4

www.greenpenguin.co.uk

To Alice

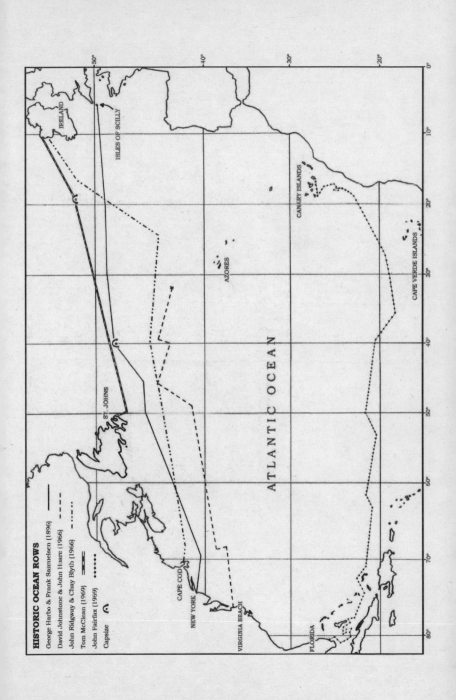

HISTORIC OCEAN ROWS

George Harbo & Frank Samuelsen (1896)
David Johnstone & John Hoare (1966)
John Ridgway & Chay Blyth (1966)
Tom McClean (1969)
John Fairfax (1969)
Capsize

ATLANTIC OCEAN

IRELAND
ISLES OF SCILLY
CANARY ISLANDS
AZORES
CAPE VERDE ISLANDS
ST. JOHNS
CAPE COD
NEW YORK
VIRGINIA BEACH
FLORIDA

50°
40°
30°
20°
10°
0°

10°
20°
30°
40°
50°
60°
70°
80°

Equipment on a Modern Ocean Rowing Boat

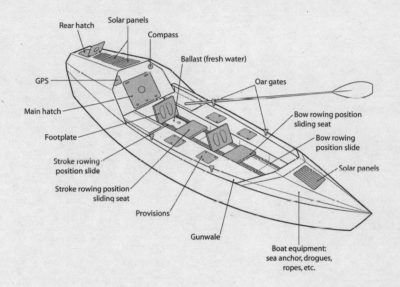

Rear hatch

Solar panels

Compass

Ballast (fresh water)

GPS

Oar gates

Main hatch

Bow rowing position sliding seat

Footplate

Bow rowing position slide

Stroke rowing position slide

Solar panels

Stroke rowing position sliding seat

Provisions

Gunwale

Boat equipment: sea anchor, drogues, ropes, etc.

Contents

Glossary

AIS – Automatic Identification System. A system which shares information between vessels within a short range of each other over the VHF radio system. AIS information can be programmed to display on a vessel's GPS screen.

ARGOS – Satellite beacon-system which can be used to track vessels anywhere in the world.

Autohelm – GPS-controlled steering system.

Backstops – The point at the end of a rower's stroke when the legs are fully extended, shoulders are back and the handles of the oars are pulled back towards the chest.

Beam sea – Waves coming in to the side of a boat. A beam sea may cause a boat to rock violently or capsize.

Bow – The front of the boat. Rowers face away from the direction of travel and so row with their backs to the bow.

Bow rowing position – The foremost rowing position in the boat. The rower in the bow seat steers the boat using a footplate which is linked to the rudder by steering lines.

Cam cleat – Spring-loaded mechanism which uses friction to stop a rope pulling through in one direction, but allows the rope to move freely when being pulled in the opposite direction.

Cleat – Fitting onto which a rope can be tied off.

Dory – Small, flat-bottomed fishing boat.

Draught – Vertical distance between a boat's waterline and the keel.

Drogue – A funnel-shaped device deployed underwater from the bow or stern of a boat to keep her facing into the weather, reducing the likelihood of capsizing and slowing her drift.

EPIRB – Emergency Position-Indicating Rescue Beacon. A small device mounted on the outside of a boat that is activated manually or after prolonged submersion in seawater in order to request a rescue. The EPIRB sends a satellite message and emits a radio signal, allowing rescuers to pinpoint the boat's location.

Gunwale – Top edge of the side of a boat. On a rowing boat this is a flat surface for sitting on, jumping off, or pulling yourself back into the boat after a swim.

Keel – 'Spine' of a boat, running along the length of its hull. A deep keel reduces the effect of the wind and swell, allowing the boat to hold its course more easily, while also making the boat more stable by lowering its centre of gravity.

Knots – A knot is one nautical mile per hour.

Nautical mile – A measure of distance used by mariners equivalent to one minute of arc at the equator. (There are sixty minutes of arc in one degree.) One nautical mile is equivalent to 1.15 land miles.

Port – The left-hand side of the boat when facing in the direction of travel.

RIB – Rigid Inflatable Boat.

Sea anchor – Parachute that opens under water to keep the boat facing into the oncoming weather. This reduces the likelihood of capsizing and slows the boat's drift.

Slide – Narrow track that the rower's sliding seat rolls along. The seat runs on four small wheels.

Starboard – The right-hand side of the boat when facing in the direction of travel.

Stern – The back of the boat. Rowers face away from the direction of travel and so row facing the stern.

Stroke rowing position – The rearmost rowing position in the boat. Called the 'stroke' position because the rower in the stroke seat sets the tempo of the rowing stroke for the rest of the boat.

Two-up – Both members of an ocean-rowing pair on the oars at the same time, as opposed to one crew member rowing and the other resting.

Prologue

The packet contains fifty-six jelly beans in six different flavours. I remove a bean and inspect it closely. I try to imagine what it will taste like, before putting it in my mouth. There is a tightening along the inside of my jaw and the bottom of my tongue as my taste buds respond to the tanginess of the sweet. I roll it around my mouth, savouring the flavour and the changing texture as the hard, smooth shell dissolves, leaving the soft, thick centre. For a while this sticks to my teeth and the roof of my mouth, but soon the residue has dispersed and I am left with a lingering sweetness. I repeat this exercise fifty-five times.

In an hour the jelly beans are gone and I feel a sense of loss. In my hand is the empty packet, which I now consider closely. I reread the list of ingredients and look at the branding and the manufacturer's address. I study the picture of each flavour of jelly bean and try to remember what it tasted like. I become aware that I am running my tongue across my teeth and in the cracks between them, looking for a crumb to savour.

From the angle I am lying at, it is possible to look out through a thin opening in the main hatch at a slice of cloudless, ethereal blue. My mind leaves the stimulation of the last hour behind and drifts in the empty sky. I'm reminded of a line from a book I once read. 'Whither are we moving? Are we not straying as through an infinite nothing? Do we not feel the breath of empty space?'

Every few seconds I feel the gentle, rhythmic acceleration as Jimmy drives on the oars. My ears are filled with the trickle of water on the hull of the boat, the splash of the oars, the roll of the sliding seat and the occasional creak of an oar gate. My view of the deck, through the perspex hatch, is blocked by a towel, which serves to keep the sun out of the cabin. But the air inside is still and the heat is oppressive.

I look at my watch. It reads 15:51. My watch is set to GMT, which means it is nearly 1 PM local time. This is the hottest part of the day. There are less than nine minutes until my next shift. I think through the things I must do before I am ready to take over from Jimmy on the oars. A muffled gasp from the deck reminds me that he is in a great deal of pain.

I shuffle around so that I am now sitting up, with my feet in the footwell, in front of the hatch. I slide my feet into a pair of red Crocs and open one of my water bottles. It is almost full. I pour in the remaining half of my isotonic powder packet. From the netting on my right I pull out my white legionnaire's hat. Inside the hat are my sunglasses. I put both on. I pull the towel off the hatch and stow it in the overhead netting. Sun streams into the cabin and almost immediately I start to sweat. I unwind the cord which has been keeping the hatch ajar, and swing the hatch open.

Jimmy is sitting five feet away, facing me. He is wearing a hat and sunglasses that match mine and a pair of fingerless yellow DeWalt gloves. Black hair and a thick black and reddish beard of almost the same length cover his head and much of his face. When he sees me he pulls his right earphone out, without breaking his stroke.

'How's it going, Jim?' I ask.

'Feels like good rowing conditions, but the mileage isn't great. I think there's a current. We've done three miles. Is it hot in the cabin?'

The water is flat. There is a momentary hint of movement in the air, then it is still again. I shield the GPS monitor from the glare of the sun and look at the current speed and bearing and our remaining miles to destination. The monitor tells me that Antigua is 1,011 nautical miles away.

'It's really hot in the cabin. There's just no breeze at all. How's your bum?'

'Bum's OK. PvK's lube is working well. But I'm having problems with my crotch.'

I nod, but I'm short of anything helpful to say. Jimmy has been working through the medical kit, looking for solutions to his crotch chafing. He has also been cutting his seat padding into smaller and smaller pieces to try and reduce the rubbing.

'Ready when you are,' I say.

'Let's do it.'

I lean through the hatch, take Jimmy's water bottle and pass him mine. Then he hands me his seat padding. It consists of three layers of dense foam and a neoprene rowing seat pad, held together with Velcro strips. This padding sandwich is topped with a wool cover, which is thick with Sudocrem and Vaseline. I lay Jimmy's seat padding in the cabin and hand him mine, which he places on the wooden seat. Then he gets up and moves down the starboard side of the deck, while at the same time I move up the port side. We are well practised and in a few moments we have swapped places. Jimmy is standing in the footwell inside the main hatch and I am sitting in the bow rowing position, adjusting the foot straps around my Crocs.

We have performed this routine every two hours for the last forty-seven days.

The American Dream, 1896

On a crisp January morning in 1883, Howard Blackburn and Tom Welch stepped off their schooner and into a twelve-foot fishing dory. After a week of fishing by the Grand Banks off the coast of Newfoundland, the schooner's hold was almost full and soon she would be making the journey back to the busy fish market in Gloucester, Massachusetts. While Welch pulled in and rebaited the cod lines, Blackburn sat at the oars, keeping the dory clear of drifting sea-ice. All the while the pair chatted about how they would spend their wages back on dry land.

That afternoon Blackburn and Welch missed the tell tale signs of an approaching winter storm and, while the more experienced crews cut their day short and returned to the schooner, the young dorymen worked on. Soon the storm was upon them, accompanied by a thick, disorientating mist. Separated from the safety of the schooner, there was nothing they could do but spend the night bailing and knocking off the ice that was forming around the hull and threatening to sink their little boat. When dawn came and the weather finally cleared, Blackburn and Welch took to the oars and made for Newfoundland, but on the second day Welch stopped rowing, lay down in the bottom of the boat in despair, and died. Blackburn continued to row and after five days with no food, water or sleep, he carried Welch's frozen body ashore. Blackburn had lost all his fingers and thumbs and most of his toes to frostbite.

Blackburn's story was the talk of the town when George Harbo arrived in the New Jersey fishing village of Nauvoo. The stocky young Norwegian had just landed on a steamer from Brevik, where he had studied at nautical school. Norway had a proud naval tradition, once boasting the third largest merchant fleet in the world after Britain and America, but she had been left behind in the race to build bigger and faster steam vessels, and now the fleet transported only low-margin bulk commodities. Demand for Norwegian timber and fish was also in decline and, over the last twenty years, a fifth of Norway's population had emigrated in search of a better life.

By contrast a million people were arriving in America every year, looking for that better life. The country was rapidly industrializing, jobs were plentiful and land was cheap. From the Old World of Europe, America was seen as a land of opportunity. Many of the Norwegians who arrived in New York made their home in the New Jersey fishing communities just across the bay. So it was for Harbo, who, after a brief stay in Brooklyn, made his way to Nauvoo, an informal collection of rough wooden huts built on sand dunes at the water's edge. Shanty towns such as this one each housed a few hundred dorymen. Conditions were basic, but they provided a sense of community and an honest living.

The dorymen worked the waters around Sandy Hook Bay and sold their produce at Fulton Fish Market, at the foot of the newly opened Brooklyn Bridge. Harbo joined a crew and had soon made enough money to pay for a ticket to bring his wife, Anine, over from Brevik. The following August, their son, Andrew, was born and Harbo took his young family to Brooklyn to watch the unveiling of the Statue of Liberty. The sense of occasion gave Harbo confidence that he had been right to bring Anine to America. Here, with hard work, anything was possible.

But in some ways the New World was not so different from the Old. The New York metropolitan area, which encompassed a large part of the New Jersey shoreline, had hierarchies of its own, controlled by the Irish community through a political body called Tammany Hall. At local elections, their strategy was blunt and effective. In those wards that were predominantly Irish, the ballot often returned more votes than registered voters, while ballot boxes from other wards were stolen and thrown in the Hudson, or returned nearly empty, with voters having been prevented from attending the polling stations.

With their men in power, the bosses of Tammany Hall extended their grip across city life. Most notorious amongst them were Richard Crocker and Bill Tweed, both of Dublin stock, who controlled appointments to the city's police force and access to lucrative contracts, such as refuse collection and public works. They created self-serving monopolies, like the licence to supply ice to the New York Harbor, and this in turn allowed them to amass huge personal fortunes.

For many of those outside the patronage of Tammany Hall, life was a struggle. In Manhattan, one and a half million people lived in dilapidated tenement blocks run by petty gangs who controlled pickpocketing, prostitution, extortion and murder in their respective areas. Having a trade and the benefit of an education, Harbo was in a better position than most of these unfortunates, but still he dreamed of something more than a simple fisherman's life.

His hero was Henry Stanley, a Welshman who, like Harbo, had come to America as a young man in search of his fortune. While working as a reporter at the *New York Herald*, Stanley was sent to Africa to find David Livingstone. The expedition was a success, and Stanley became a household name. Harbo owned a copy of the book *How I Found Livingstone*, and knew that Stanley's lectures had filled theatres on both sides of the Atlantic. In recounting the stories of his adventures, Stanley had become rich. If Harbo could accomplish something as notable as Stanley had, he would be able to give his family the life they deserved.

As time passed, and Harbo continued to bring home the same wage from the same hours of toil in the New Jersey surf, a creeping sense of failure grew within him. Anine had left her family in Norway to help him make something of himself in America, and this was not the future he'd had in mind for her. Anine respected her husband's choices, but she never felt at home in America; a Lutheran upbringing in Brevik had not prepared her for the squalor and violence of New York.

Harbo's nautical training and experience of the tides and currents around the channel into Manhattan meant that he was well qualified for a position as a harbour pilot. The law required all ships entering New York Harbor to be under the command of a licensed pilot, and the rate paid depended on the size of the vessel. The sighting of a transatlantic steamer would spark a race amongst a dozen pilot boats, competing for the generous fee. Successful pilots often became rich and well respected, like Captain Richard Brown, who was a well-known figure in Sandy Hook Bay. Captain Brown had skippered the *America* to victory at the Royal Yacht Squadron's first annual regatta around the Isle of Wight in 1851. In his honour, the trophy was renamed the America's Cup.

The opportunity to become wealthy, and perhaps one day earn a reputation like old Dick Brown's, convinced Harbo to leave the dorymen and join a piloting company. He worked hard and was soon earning good money. For the first time since moving to America, he could afford to make life more comfortable for his family, moving them into a New Jersey suburb and buying Anine a small piano. The sound of her playing reminded him of their good fortune, and to add to their blessings Andrew was joined by a baby sister, Louisa.

But Harbo had become part of an industry that was poorly regulated, and the race to bring in the next ship encouraged excessive risk taking. Six months after Louisa was born, tragedy struck the New York pilots when seventeen of them drowned in a storm in a single night. The deaths shook the community and prompted Anine to question Harbo's choices; she would rather have a fisherman for a husband than have no husband at all. For months the couple argued, in their own restrained way. Eventually, Harbo relented and by the time their third child, Grace, was born he was back where he had started at Nauvoo. It was a painful blow for the proud young man and it left a seed of sadness in his marriage. Every morning, as he ran his dory through the surf, he was reminded that he had failed.

Meanwhile, in the summer of 1888, Norwegian explorer Fridtjof Nansen led the first crossing of the Greenland ice cap. Nansen rejected the traditional 'siege' approach to polar exploration, which involved setting up resupply positions along the expedition route in advance of the main party, and instead adopted a fast, lightweight, self-sufficient philosophy, designing his own sledges, sleeping bags, stoves and wolfskin clothing. The Norwegian press predicted that the expedition would be a disaster, ensuring that Nansen received no public funding. But the young explorer was already known to his countrymen as a national skiing champion, and he used his charisma to pay for the expedition through private donations. Despite terrible weather conditions, the party successfully crossed the ice cap in seven weeks. The team then had to spend a long winter in the small, isolated town of Godthåb, and it wasn't until the following spring that a ship was able to make the journey to the west coast of Greenland to bring Nansen and his companions home. On his return to Kristiania (now Oslo) in May 1889, he was greeted by a crowd of 40,000. Nansen's reputation – and his fortune – were made. Because Nansen was Norwegian and of a similar age to Harbo, the explorer's story struck a chord with him and rekindled Harbo's ambition to make a name for himself.

Anine was growing homesick for her old life in Brevik, and the changing attitudes in New York towards immigrant communities made her increasingly anxious. Then, in May 1891, eleven Italian immigrants were lynched by a mob as a reprisal for the murder of an Irish police chief. It was the final straw. Despite Harbo's pleas, she made arrangements to take the three children back to Norway, leaving in August 1891 on a steamer bound for Brevik.

Four days into the Atlantic crossing, a small funeral party gathered on the stern deck of the steamer. At the front stood Anine, gripping Andrew and Louisa tightly, her thick black hair tied in a bun over her head. After the captain had said a few words, the crewman dropped a small canvas bag containing Grace's body into the sea. She had died suddenly from pneumonia. In a bag weighted with sand, Harbo and Anine's youngest daughter quickly sank beneath the waves.

Alone in New York, the grieving Harbo buried himself in his work. He found a niche picking molluscs from the tidal mudflats around Sandy Hook. Emptying his catch onto the deck, Harbo would sort the soft-shell clams from the mud and other debris. During long, lonely hours on the mudflats he began to think seriously about how he might follow in Nansen's footsteps.

Clamming was hard work, but soon he was making enough money to hire another doryman. Frank Samuelson was a fellow Norwegian, a few years younger than Harbo. He had been working on a merchant vessel and at a stopover in New York had asked the skipper for permission to leave. As Harbo had, he soon arrived in Nauvoo. Samuelson was 6'3", broad shouldered, and powerful on the oars: he could row a dory out past the breakers faster than any of the other fishermen. Harbo knew that he could do with the help of a man like this on the voyage that was beginning to come together in his mind.

In 1893, Nansen left Norway on another expedition, this time in a bid to be the first man to reach the North Pole. This was the catalyst Harbo needed to make a decision that he'd been considering ever since Anine had left him. One afternoon, while they worked the clam beds, he explained that he planned to row across the Atlantic Ocean and wanted Samuelson to join him.

Samuelson looked at the older man in silence. They had met only a few months earlier, but he knew Harbo well enough to tell that he wasn't joking. He wondered instead if he had gone mad. No one had ever rowed across the Atlantic before. As far as he knew, no one had even attempted it. Samuelson gently reminded him of the story of Howard Blackburn, who had lost his dorymate and all of his fingers rowing from the Grand Banks back to Newfoundland ten years earlier. The vicinity of the Grand Banks was perilous, foggy, and iceberg-ridden, and eighteen years later would become notorious as the final resting place of RMS *Titanic*.

In order to reach Europe from New York, Harbo and Samuelson would have to row past the Grand Banks and then on for a further two thousand miles. But Harbo was adamant. A winter crossing would indeed be suicide, but a summer crossing should be possible given the right conditions. He began to explain to Samuelson about the seasonal weather and the importance of riding the Gulf Stream; it was a relief to finally be sharing his thoughts with someone.

The Gulf Stream was well known to mariners of the time. Benjamin Franklin had named it in 1770 when, as Postmaster General of the British American Colonies, he was asked to investigate why mail ships took so much longer to reach America from Britain than those on the return journey. With the help of his cousin, a Nantucket whaling captain, Franklin produced the first chart of the Gulf Stream. With the benefit of this current, Harbo believed that a crossing could be completed by two men in a dory, under the power of oars alone, in less than sixty days.

The pair usually worked in silence, but that afternoon Harbo spoke excitedly about his plan. He explained the size of the boat they would need, the quantity of fresh water and the type of provisions. Samuelson interrupted occasionally with a question, but it was clear that Harbo had thought the project through in detail. Samuelson promised to consider it, and lying in bed that night he could think of nothing else. The next morning, as they carried their boat down to the beach, he agreed to join Harbo's expedition. They put down the dory and shook hands, and then Harbo made him promise to keep their plans a secret. More than the ridicule of the other dorymen, Harbo feared that word would get back to Anine.

In the winter of 1894 Harbo returned to Norway to see his family and during his stay there Anine became pregnant again. Harbo knew that he should use their time together to explain his plan to her but, afraid she would make him promise to abandon the idea, he avoided the subject. To keep his mind from it, he chatted instead about Nansen's latest polar expedition. He spoke about Nansen so much that, in October 1895, when their second son was born, Anine sent word to Harbo that she had named him after the explorer.

Harbo and Samuelson used their modest savings to commission William Seaman, a respected New Jersey boat builder, to construct a boat which could handle the conditions they expected to encounter in the North Atlantic. Seaman built an eighteen-foot dory with a double-ended hull which would surf comfortably in the waves and, using the best materials available, sheathed the boat's sturdy oak frame with white cedar planks.[1] He made a canvas cover which could be fixed across the gunwales in rough seas to help prevent the dory getting swamped. Watertight metal lockers would keep documents and sensitive equipment dry, while also providing buoyancy to prevent the boat sinking in the event that it was swamped. As an added precaution, Seaman installed grab rails along the hull that would allow the crew to right the boat if it capsized.

Only when preparations were at an advanced stage did Harbo write to Anine to tell her of his plans. He explained how their crossing would be assisted by the warm currents of the Gulf Stream, and how Samuelson's experience and his power on the oars made him the perfect crew. He described Seaman's pedigree as a boat builder and all the safety features that had been built into the boat. He reminded her of the crowds that had greeted Nansen on his return to Kristiania, and tried to explain that the fruits of the expedition would finally provide them with the life he had always promised her. In desperate letters Anine begged Harbo not to go. It was clear to her that the expedition was suicidal, and almost everyone agreed with her, particularly those with experience of the open ocean. But Harbo was already finalizing his preparations, and would not be put off. In fact, he was looking for a publicist.

From Sandy Hook Bay it was possible to see across the water to Coney Island, which was known to the locals as 'Sodom by the sea'. Behind the promenade entertainments, illegal drinking houses jostled with opium dens and brothels for custom, and unlicensed prizefighting was a popular crowd-pleaser. This was the world of Richard Fox, a fight promoter and media man who published a monthly boxing journal called *The Ring* and also the *Police Gazette*, a daily tabloid. No one had done more than Fox to promote bare-knuckle boxing in America, and he was a man who got his way. When John Sullivan, America's unofficial prizefighting champion, refused to fight in a bout that Fox proposed, Fox taunted him by awarding the challenger a diamond encrusted title belt and announcing him in *The Ring* as the Heavyweight Champion of the World. Goaded into a response, Sullivan reluctantly agreed to fight on Fox's terms, and beat the challenger to claim the belt.

Fox had arrived on a boat from Dublin twenty years earlier and scraped together the money to buy *Police Gazette*, a failing newspaper. He had a keen nose for stories that would appeal to popular tastes, and he filled the *Police Gazette* with scandal, crime and sensation, making a small fortune in the process. When there was little to report, Fox created news by offering gold medals to people who broke bizarre and dangerous records. With ruthlessness and charm, Fox had made it in America.

The media mogul was the obvious person to approach for help in publicizing the expedition, and at his offices the dorymen outlined their plan to row from New York to the French port of Le Havre. Fox was intrigued, and after listening to their plans he agreed that if they named the boat after him, his newspaper would raise the profile of their expedition and award them gold medals on their return.

On Saturday 6 June 1896, Harbo and Samuelson cast off from the Battery, on the southern tip of Manhattan. True to his word, Fox had given the expedition good publicity, and curious locals gathered to watch the pair load *Fox* with equipment and supplies. Based on Harbo's estimate that it would take sixty days to row to Europe, they provisioned with sixty gallons of water, a hundred pounds of tinned meat and fish, hard tack biscuits and jam, coffee, wine and a wooden box full of raw eggs, carefully wrapped in seaweed.

By the time everything was stowed and the pair were happy that *Fox* was correctly balanced in the water, over a thousand people were watching from the quay above the pontoon, and the crowd was starting to get impatient. Two men and a small wooden boat were not quite the spectacle that the *Police Gazette* had promised them, nor were Harbo and Samuelson used to being the focus of all this attention. As people began to shout and jeer, Harbo tried to tell them about the terrible conditions they would face in the North Atlantic. But the crowd wasn't in the mood for a lecture and Harbo's thick accent only encouraged them. Just before 5 PM, the tide turned and the dorymen cast off, relieved to finally be free of the mob and on their way.

Adopting their usual rowing positions, Harbo sat in the bow, from where he took charge of steering the boat, while Samuelson sat in front of him in the stern position. Filled with nervous excitement, they rowed hard through the long summer evening, building up a sweat under their woollen shirts. By sunset they were off Coney Island, with the lights of the promenade obscured by a thick mist. These were familiar waters and, dropping anchor in the shallows just outside the main channel, the pair went to sleep listening to the ring of the Sandy Hook fog bell and thinking of their warm beds only a few miles away.

Samuelson woke before sunrise and pulled himself out from under the canvas cover to make a pot of coffee on the kerosene stove. The dorymen shivered through breakfast in the rain and, despite the headwind, they were glad to get back on the oars. Occasionally they heard a vessel pass, but with a visibility of only twenty yards, they saw no one. Harbo's calculations put them south of the shipping lane, which they hoped would keep them safe from a collision. Late in the morning they stopped for biscuits, jam and a drink of water. By now visibility had improved enough for Harbo to confirm their position with a compass bearing. Samuelson suggested that they make coffee, but Harbo reminded him that there was only enough kerosene to use the stove once a day.

Sunday June 7th. Lifted anchor 4 AM. Wind north-east moderate with rain and fog. Started to row out to sea. Passed Sandy Hook lightship 11 AM, bearing west, distance 5 miles. This is the last bearing.[2]

After rowing two-up through the day their plan was to row alternate three-hour shifts at night and, after a dinner of hard tack biscuits and tinned ham, Harbo returned to the oars. In the stern of the boat Samuelson pulled the wool blanket and the canvas deck cover over himself and curled up on the mattress, which was made of reindeer hair and would stay soft and warm, even when it got wet.

A stiff southerly wind arrived with the dawn, but the fog remained. Now well beyond their old fishing grounds, it felt to Harbo as if the adventure was starting in earnest. By midday the fog had lifted enough for him to take a sight on his brass quadrant. By aligning the instrument with the sun at its highest point, a reading of latitude could be taken. Harbo and Samuelson would know how far north they were, but without an expensive chronometer there was no way of accurately measuring longitude. To know the distance they had covered across the Atlantic relied on dead reckoning, which was based on Harbo's estimates of the currents, wind and their rowing speed.

They rowed on, making good progress for two more days. On 11 June dawn broke with a fresh westerly breeze, but throughout the day the sea blackened as the sky clouded over, and the wind grew stronger, until by nightfall they faced a full-blown storm. The wind tore the tops off the waves and dumped water into the boat. Harbo and Samuelson battled to keep *Fox* stern to the waves, while the churning, chaotic sea threatened to spin her around and throw them overboard. They rowed on through the night, leaving the oars only to bail out the boat. While he bailed, Samuelson thought of

Blackburn and Welch and how much worse things would be if this were January. Despite the conditions, it was exhilarating to know that, even as it battered them, the storm was sending *Fox* in the right direction.

By daybreak the storm had blown over and the sea was back to a long, rolling, ocean swell. After bailing the last of the water from the bottom of the boat, Harbo pulled the sodden reindeer hair mattress out from under the canvas to air, then checked their provisions and repacked the boat, while Samuelson prepared the stove for a hot meal. Exhausted from the night's ordeal, he didn't notice the oily sheen of the kerosene on the stove housing and, when he lit the wick, the whole stove burst into flames. He shouted and jumped back, shielding his face. Harbo grabbed the bailing bucket and doused the flames. Apart from a few singed hairs Samuelson was fine and they laughed off the incident over a breakfast of hard tack, cheese, jam and eggs served with tinned beef and washed down with a pint of coffee.

Friday June 12th. Both of us rowed all night . . . This morning the oil stove set fire to its house. Looked like danger for a few minutes but was soon put out.

After a few hours of rest, Harbo took a sight to confirm their latitude and the pair started rowing again; that night a clear sky made it easy to stay on course. Again they rowed in shifts and, despite the sodden bedding, sleep came easily. The following day they attracted the attention of a passing schooner. After overcoming his surprise at finding a fishing dory 350 miles out to sea, *Jossey*'s skipper confirmed their position and promised to report *Fox* to the harbour master when he arrived in New York. Five days later, *Fox*'s paper noted wryly that the Norwegians were 'not yet' drowned.

After waving off the schooner, Harbo and Samuelson rowed on as the swell grew short and choppy. The wind swung round to the east, gradually building until the pair found that, despite rowing two-up, they were being driven backwards. They had planned for conditions like this and their drills were well practised. While Samuelson kept the boat facing into the weather, Harbo deployed the sea anchor off the bow. The heavy canvas parachute was caught by the westerly currents and opened quickly. It was an eerie shape, hanging thirty feet below the surface, like the body of a giant squid.

The line from the sea anchor quickly snapped tight and swung the bow of the boat directly into the oncoming weather. This would reduce their drift west and prevent *Fox* from being spun side-on to the waves (a position likely to cause a capsize). Dawn passed, but the wind continued to strengthen, whipping the sea into twenty-five-foot breakers. After tying-in to a safety line both men turned to the task of bailing. Soon they could barely bail fast enough to keep the gunwales above water. They were fighting for their lives.

By late afternoon, cold and weak, but with the storm starting to subside, they ate a couple of hard tack biscuits and shared a bottle of wine. In all their years at sea neither of them had endured suffering like this and, huddled together for warmth under the canvas sheet, they wondered if they would have the strength to face another storm like that. Their conversation was slow and disjointed. Harbo thought of his family back in Brevik and wondered if Anine had been right to call this expedition suicidal.

Checking through the inventory, Harbo found that they were missing a can of kerosene, which meant there was now only enough fuel to eat a hot meal every second day. Instead of coffee, they began to drink condensed milk mixed with water and they ate the eggs raw from their shells. One afternoon *Fox* was surrounded by a pod of inquisitive whales and, although Harbo worried that the merest flick of a tail might destroy their little dory, the animals glided past without incident.

The following day *Fox* was spotted by a German steamer, the *Fürst Bismarck*. The skipper commented on the terrible state of the pair's hands and faces, which were peeling and scabbed from exposure to the elements. He asked if they needed anything. There were many things they would have liked to ask for. In particular Samuelson thought that with a few canisters of kerosene they would be able to make life a little more bearable with hot food and coffee. But Harbo turned down the skipper's offer of assistance, reminding Samuelson of the principle of self-sufficiency that they had agreed to before setting off. As they cast off from the steamer, the crew lined up on the deck to cheer and wave. Soon the ship had disappeared over the horizon and *Fox* was alone again in the North Atlantic.

After three weeks at sea, *Fox* was somewhere south of Newfoundland, perhaps a few hundred miles from the Grand Banks. A night of sharp, icy rain marked the start of a storm that lasted for several days, forcing the dorymen back into a routine of bailing and rowing, occasionally deploying the sea anchor for long enough to snatch a moment's rest and some food. By 1 July conditions had improved sufficiently for Samuelson to light the stove. By the time Samuelson had cooked their meal, Harbo was fast asleep. Samuelson woke him and, after they had eaten, they huddled together on the soaking mattress and fell into a deep, blissful sleep, with the gentle sound of lapping water in their ears, and the morning sun warming their faces.

Harbo woke soon after midday and stood up to stretch his back and legs. The air was still and the blue sky was streaked with a thin wisp of cloud. On the horizon he saw a sail. He watched it for a while and, when he had worked out its speed and direction, he woke Samuelson. They made a course to intercept the vessel and, as they drew near, Harbo identified it as a fishing schooner. The storm must have carried *Fox* right onto the Grand Banks.

The skipper of *Leader* naturally assumed that *Fox* was a fishing dory that had been separated from its ship, but the state of the two men and a glance at the equipment on board verified Harbo's story. The pair declined the skipper's offer of a meal, but the position he gave put them on the south-eastern edge of the Grand Banks. Harbo did a quick calculation before sharing the good news with Samuelson. They had rowed a thousand miles from New York and were now more than a third of the way across the Atlantic. That afternoon they came across another fishing schooner and retold their stories about the adventures of the last few weeks. As the sun set, Harbo and Samuelson shared a meal of tinned fish and hard tack, washed down with condensed milk and water. They agreed that it had been a good day. Chatting with fellow dorymen had raised their spirits and, having reached the Grand Banks from New York, the pair knew that they had already accomplished something remarkable. To mark Independence Day they allowed themselves a small luxury.

> *Saturday July 4th. This day we celebrated by washing ourselves in soap and fresh water. The first day our faces have seen good fresh water since leaving New York.*

Although there were only damp, salty shirts and oilskins to put back on afterwards, it felt wonderful to be clean.

For the best part of a week conditions were kind to them, but soon enough the bad weather returned and Harbo and Samuelson were back to the now familiar routine of rowing and bailing. One evening Harbo was rowing while Samuelson bailed when the howling wind suddenly cut out and the sea became as flat as if they had entered the shelter of a harbour. Through the darkness, Harbo thought he could hear the sound of waves breaking on a beach. He wondered if exhaustion was causing him to hallucinate, but his dorymate could hear the same thing. Samuelson stood up in the stern of the boat and tried to make out where the sound was coming from. He could think of no other explanation than that they had made land, but Harbo reminded him that they were little more than a week east of the Grand Banks. Europe was still two thousand miles away.

Suddenly, out of the darkness, a cliff face emerged, less than sixty feet away. Harbo saw Samuelson's expression and turned in his seat to look. It was an iceberg. In silence both men craned their necks to gaze up the wall of ice, which rose into the starless night. Around them everything was still, except for the gentle breaking of waves and, in the distance, the wind's muffled roar. There was something majestic about the iceberg and resting in its calm lee they felt cocooned from the harsh ocean around them. Harbo tried to preserve the image in his memory as the iceberg slipped past and into the night. A few moments later and they were again at the mercy of the storm.

With first light it became clear that things were about to get much worse for Harbo and Samuelson. To the east, the cloud base was starting to fall, a sign that the weather was closing in, but the men were more alarmed by the view to the west, where the sky was a wall of black. *Fox* was in the path of a hurricane.

They made ready by lashing their equipment, supplies and finally themselves to the boat. While they still could, they ate a little food. At Harbo's signal, Samuelson spun the boat into the weather, so that he could deploy the sea anchor. As the wind picked up it blew the rain horizontally into their eyes, making it hard to see the next wave. Soon the wind was gusting to seventy knots and both men turned their attention to bailing out the boat. Again and again the angry breakers knocked Harbo and Samuelson onto the deck, or into each other. At one point Samuelson had to grab Harbo by the rope around his waist to stop him being washed out of the dory. The seas were bigger than anything they had experienced before. Then, from a dangerous angle on the starboard side, both men saw a wave coming in fast. They knelt low on the deck and braced themselves for its impact. *Fox* tilted as she rose up the face of the wave and for a moment Harbo and Samuelson's world hung at ninety degrees, until the dory was caught in the violent, churning crest, which overturned her, spinning her over and over. Harbo tried to hold on, but was torn from the rolling dory and thrown into the sea. For a second there was an eerie peace. The line around his waist wrenched tight and, with his lungs bursting for air, he kicked and fought his way to the surface to find himself alongside the upturned hull of the boat. Samuelson was already there, clinging on to the handrail.

In the calm waters of Sandy Hook Bay the dorymen had practised their capsize drill and now they set to work righting the boat. Neither of them felt the freezing water as they struggled on the upturned hull, with the hurricane raging around them. Eventually they pulled *Fox* over and hauled themselves back in. With their sea anchor lost in the capsize there was now no chance of rest and, coursing with adrenalin, Harbo and Samuelson immediately set about rowing and bailing to keep the boat afloat. As the night drew on, the fight against the storm became a battle against exhaustion. After three days and nights wrestling with the sea all the dorymen wanted to do was lie down in the bottom of the boat and sleep.

> *Friday July 10th. It has been blowing a gale for 2 days, and the sea is bigger than we have ever seen it on this trip. At about 8 PM a big sea struck us partly side-ways, upsetting the boat and us into the water. In a few minutes we got into the boat again. We lost many things this time . . . Everything we have in the boat soaked with water . . . This is the 3rd night without sleep.*

A dull thud brought Samuelson back to his senses; Harbo was lying unconscious on the deck. Samuelson jumped up and shook the older man, who woke and gazed blankly up at him through heavy, swollen eyes. There was no chance of starting the kerosene stove in these conditions, but Samuelson sat Harbo in the stern of the boat and wrapped him as best he could in their sodden bedding. He gave him food and wine and returned to the oars.

By the afternoon the weather had started to clear and Samuelson was able to get the stove going for the first time in five days. The two men sat together and took stock of the situation. In the capsize they had also lost the replacement sea anchor and much of their food, water and kerosene. There was now no question of their crossing the ocean without assistance. With careful rationing the remaining supplies might last ten days, but with over a thousand miles to go, their only chance of survival was to be spotted by a ship.

Four days of light winds allowed them to eat, sleep and recover their strength, but their predicament weighed heavily on their minds. Although they had perhaps six days of food left, there was nothing to do but keep rowing. Then, on 15 July, *Fox* was seen by the Norwegian merchant vessel *Cito*, en route to England with a cargo of Canadian timber. Harbo and Samuelson cheered and hugged each other when they saw *Cito* change direction to intercept them.

From the state of the two men on board, Captain Clausen could see that the little boat had been at sea for some time, and at first he thought he had misunderstood when Harbo explained that they did not need to be rescued. As Harbo retold the story of the last six weeks, culminating in the capsize, Clausen was filled with emotion at the strength and courage of his countrymen. He invited them on board. Both men struggled on the rope ladder, but at the top many helping hands pulled them onto the deck and steadied them.

Wednesday July 15th. Spoke to barque CITO of Laurvig, Norway, Capt. Clausen. Received from the CITO water and provision to last another 5 weeks and had dinner on board. Could hardly walk when we got on her deck. We were treated like Lords. Left the CITO again 5 PM.

The captain gave Harbo and Samuelson a fix on their current position; they were almost two-thirds of the way across the Atlantic. At their request, he also inspected *Fox* and signed their log to confirm that the oars were the only form of propulsion on board. The dorymen were soon underway again and, with their provisions stowed safely away, success seemed within their reach for the first time since the hurricane.

Over the course of the next fortnight Harbo and Samuelson settled back into the rhythm of life on *Fox*. With the sense that their journey was entering its final stage, they even started to enjoy it. The dorymen had experienced the North Atlantic in all her moods, and although for now she was kind to them, they remained vigilant, and kept the empty freshwater tanks topped up with seawater. They knew first hand that a stable boat was more important than a light one.

Tuesday 21st July. Frank's watch stopped today. Main spring broke. We feel the loss of time very much.

Samuelson's pocket watch had done well to survive that long. Samuelson's father had given him the watch when he left the family farm to join the merchant navy. It was now impossible to measure their three-hour shifts. Minutes sometimes seemed like hours, and in their dream-like daze, an hour on the oars could pass in the blink of an eye.

On 24 July, *Fox* was spotted by *Eugen*, another Norwegian merchant vessel carrying timber to England. The pair enjoyed the same generous welcome as they had been given on *Cito* and shared their stories over a meal at the captain's table.

As they approached the English Channel, Harbo and Samuelson

agreed that they would make first landfall at the Isles of Scilly before completing the final 300 miles to Le Havre. The approach to the Scillies was notoriously dangerous, but Harbo was desperate to send the world news of their successful crossing. As they got closer to land, precise navigation became vital and Harbo was nervous, repeatedly checking his sights. He told Samuelson how careless navigation had wrecked the British fleet off Bishop Rock in 1707, with the loss of 2,000 lives. Despite the urgent need for a lighthouse, the ferocious conditions and the scale of the engineering challenge meant that it was another 150 years until Bishop Rock's lighthouse was finally completed.

In the early hours of 1 August Samuelson spotted a light to the north and woke Harbo, who confirmed that it was the Bishop Rock lighthouse. They were now less than twenty miles from the Isles of Scilly. Harbo took to the oars and guided them on a north-easterly bearing. While the pair rowed, they chatted and joked about what they would eat when they reached land, and about having a wash and wearing a clean shirt.

What excited Harbo most was the prospect of returning to New York with Anine and their children. He wanted to share with her all his experiences on the ocean, the magic of the iceberg and the terror of the hurricane, and he longed to hold his baby son for the first time. His new-found fame and the fortune that it would bring on the lecture circuit would allow him to give Anine the life she deserved. He thought of Nansen's return to Kristiania from the Greenland ice cap and imagined the crowd that would meet them as they stepped ashore in Manhattan. Through the hunger and exhaustion of the last eight weeks at sea, through near death from hypothermia and their battle with the hurricane, Harbo had never forgotten why he had chosen to row across the Atlantic.

It was a clear, calm morning, and as they passed Bishop Rock they saw teams of masons and huge blocks of granite being ferried out to the lighthouse; work was underway to strengthen the existing tower. Harbo took a bearing for St Mary's, the largest of the islands, and as they got closer the indistinct haze of land formed into the outline of buildings, fields, beaches and the harbour of Hugh Town.

From the entrance of Hugh Town harbour, a few final strokes brought *Fox* up onto the white sandy beach. This was a moment that they had thought about often during the last eight weeks. Slipping off the gunwale, Harbo and Samuelson took their first tentative steps on to dry land, steadying each other on their unstable legs.

Finally, it was over. They had rowed across the Atlantic.

Before anyone else arrived, there was one last thing that Harbo wanted to do. He turned to Samuelson and thanked him for that time when they had stood together on the New Jersey shore and Samuelson had agreed to partner him in the expedition. The world had called it a suicide mission, but Samuelson had stood by Harbo, and his belief that the Atlantic could be rowed.

Their arrival in the Scillies was met with curiosity by local fishermen, who called for the harbour master. His officious manner evaporated after he had looked at their log book and inspected *Fox* and realized they were not crazed castaways but had in fact rowed from New York. A small group quickly formed around Harbo and Samuelson and in answer to their questions Harbo told them the story of the crossing. At the office of the American Consul their messages were sent by telegram to London and from there to New York and Kristiania. Back in Sandy Hook Bay, the other dorymen would read the news in the afternoon edition of *The New York Times*:

London, Aug 1. – A dispatch from the signal station on the Scilly Islands states that the rowboat Fox passed there at 11 o'clock this morning after a passage of fifty-five days from New York. The two occupants of the boat were well but somewhat exhausted from the effects of their long row.

With news of their arrival in the Isles of Scilly broadcast across the world, Harbo and Samuelson were eagerly awaited at the busy port of Le Havre. There, fellow seamen looked at the little fishing boat in awe; the idea of taking to the Atlantic in any vessel under a thousand tons seemed absurd. After a brief stop in Le Havre, the pair rowed up the Seine to Paris, where *Fox* was to go on display.

Harbo and Samuelson had expected a hero's welcome, but their arrival in Paris went largely unnoticed, and any interest in the small wooden fishing boat quickly waned. It was now clear to the dorymen that fame and fortune would not come as easily as they imagined, and they left for London with plans for a stage performance that they hoped would find a better reception. They set up a show at the Royal Aquarium in Westminster, an actor narrating their crossing while Harbo and Samuelson acted it out on board *Fox*. Although the show ran for two months, the ticket sales barely covered their costs.

Meanwhile the public's interest had shifted to a more glamorous enterprise: three years after leaving Kristiania, Fridtjof Nansen was finally on his way back from the Arctic. Although the explorer had failed to reach the pole, he was honoured around the world, and returned to Kristiania flanked by a naval escort. Nansen's procession through the city included a triumphal arch of 200 gymnasts and ended at the Royal Palace, where he stayed as the king's guest.

The contrast between Nansen's welcome and their own was not lost on Harbo and Samuelson. The dorymen shared the explorer's courage and tenacity but they were also modest men, and lacked Nansen's flair and charm. The pair took *Fox* to several more cities in Europe, with little success, and eventually Harbo and Samuelson decided to cut their losses, and boarded a steam liner for the voyage back to America. In New York they performed one final show for Richard Fox, who presented them with gold medals emblazoned with the logo of the *Police Gazette*.

Back in Nauvoo, friends noticed that Harbo seemed more at ease; perhaps he no longer felt haunted by failure. Anine soon returned to New York with the children and Harbo moved their growing family into a comfortable house in Brooklyn. He settled back into work on the mudflats and occasionally took jobs navigating for the Sandy Hook Harbor Pilots Association. At the end of a day at sea he would make his way home, over the Brooklyn Bridge and south through the suburbs. Along the way, the smart townhouses and grand mansions gave way to more suburban dwellings, as the streets opened out. After twenty minutes he would turn onto a street where whitewashed wooden houses stood in wide, well-kept plots.

One evening, as he swung open the gate, the sound of a piano became audible from the front room and, stepping onto the veranda, he was surrounded by children, with the maid carrying the youngest. He greeted each of them, then turned to Anine, who had appeared in the doorway, heavily pregnant. Tonight there was a mood of general excitement around the house; Uncle Frank and his wife Anna were coming to dinner, which meant there would be plenty of opportunity for the children to ask again about the time he and their father rowed a small fishing dory across the Atlantic Ocean.

2.

Hope

Date: 26 July 2008
Location: St Neots, Cambridgeshire

We approach the start line with calm confidence. Along the west bank of the Great Ouse, rowers and spectators sit in groups on the grass enjoying the late July sunshine. As we near the top of the 1,000m course we get a cheer of encouragement from the Globe Rowing Club camp. At our cox's instructions, we spin the boat round behind the stake-boat, which is anchored close to the east bank and marks our starting position. I look across at the other novice men's four. After six months of training together on the rough tidal waters of the Thames, the Great Ouse is like silk under our blades and we feel pumped and ready. This is our first race and we want to do ourselves and Globe proud.

Before the race can start we need to row backwards for a short distance so that our stern is within reach of the boy sitting on the stake-boat; he will hold us in position until the starting call. We have never backed-down onto a stake-boat before and on the first attempt we veer off and the stern of our boat rubs roughly on the stake-boat's submerged anchor line. We take a few strokes, reposition ourselves, and on our second attempt the boy is able to grab the stern. Now our cox drops her hand to indicate that we are ready to start. I take a deep breath and behind me my team mate, Eze, repeats our starting strategy: 'Half, half, three-quarters, three-quarters, lengthen.'

'Attention.'

There's a moment's pause. We're sat halfway up the slide, bodies primed, blades buried in the water.

'GO.'

I punch my legs straight and snap my hands into my chest. As we gather momentum the cox calls the strokes to us.

'Half, half, three-quarters, harder on stroke side . . .'

Something isn't right. The cox is pulling desperately on the steering line.

'. . . Easy on bow side. *Easy on bow side*. STOP!'

Before I can slam my blade into the water the boat comes to a sudden halt. I turn in my seat to see that we are lodged firmly in the reed bank. We all sit in silent embarrassment, except for the cox, whose feelings about us, the boat and the situation generally are clearly articulated.

We back ourselves out of the bank and as we sheepishly limp down to the finish line, back past our club, the other teams and the amassed spectators, I remind myself why I am here.

From: Adam Rackley
Sent: 28 December 2006 14:22
To: Arnold, James (London)
Subject: Up for a challenge?

Jimmy,

Hope you've had a good break. Saw you at Simon & Dave's do in Balham last month but was rather inebriated & didn't have a chance to catch up.

I'm writing because I know from Simon & Dave that you're a man who likes a challenge. I've been talking to a couple of similarly minded individuals about the idea of putting together a team for the 2009 Woodvale Atlantic Rowing Race. The event takes place every 2 years around November/December and the record for a 4-man team is 35 days. Crossings typically take 6–8 weeks.

This would be a serious commitment (training/couple of months off work/serious fundraising – £70k including all fees, transport, boat, equipment, food for a 4-man team). I'm planning a meeting towards the end of January to get everyone who's interested together to see what people think.

Food for thought! Let me know what you think & whether you're interested in meeting up towards the end of Jan.

Adam

Why would anyone want to spend months at sea in the sweltering heat, living on a tiny, cramped boat, with nothing to look forward to but blisters, boils, chafing, salt sores, seasickness, sharks, storms, sleep deprivation, dehydration, hunger and twelve hours of rowing every day? Why would anyone want to spend their savings and years of their life, to exhaust the generosity of friends and the understanding of loved ones, just for the opportunity to endure disappointment, frustration, isolation and terrible, grinding boredom?

For me it was about taking something that seemed impossible and proving that it wasn't, and learning something about myself and those around me along the way. When I pressed 'send' on that email to Jimmy I had no idea of the impact that it would have on the next three years of my life. If I had known then what I know now, this particular chapter in the history of ocean rowing may well never have been written.

I didn't know Jimmy well, but what little I did know made him an obvious candidate for my team. In a recent marathon, Jimmy had pushed himself as hard as he could to beat his previous time. At the halfway point, the friend he was running with had pointed out that they were well ahead of the planned pace and suggested slowing down. But with a three-hour marathon now in sight, Jimmy had no intention of dropping the pace; he kept it up until a few miles from the finish, where he passed out. For a lesser man, waking up in the paramedic's tent would have marked the end of his race, but Jimmy wouldn't let a small thing like that get in the way of his goal and, after swigging an isotonic drink, he ran on to the finish. Jimmy would still have beaten his previous time if a zealous race marshal hadn't stopped him within sight of the finishing line because the paramedics had removed his race number, resulting in disqualification.

Here was someone who would never allow himself to give up, or to give less than everything. Someone with deep reserves of mental strength and physical toughness. Over the years to come, Jimmy never disappointed me. But it was only later that I came to properly understand Jimmy's complete and uncompromising focus. He would accept any amount of pain rather than make concessions to the ocean.

We met in The Fine Line on Cheapside, near where we worked in London. I introduced Jimmy to the Woodvale Atlantic Rowing Race and outlined the kind of commitment it would require; even getting to the start line would be a considerable challenge. Although Jimmy had come along only to humour me, our meeting convinced him that, despite having never rowed before, and lacking any experience of the ocean, I was committed and serious. Suddenly the idea of rowing across the Atlantic seemed not only achievable, but also compelling. A week later Jimmy emailed to let me know that he had been unable to think about much else since we had spoken. Jimmy was in.

The following month Jimmy came to my flat to meet the other two team members. Nick was an old friend with whom I had shared adventures in the past, and who was now an officer in the Royal Welsh, based in Chester. Ben was my girlfriend's cousin, and was always involved in one challenge or another, which he juggled with the pressures of running a start-up in Manchester.

We ate and drank and speculated excitedly about what it would be like on the ocean. A bottle of port eased the evening along and by the time it was finished we were a team. Before they left, I gave each of my new crew members a copy of mountaineer Chris Bonington's *Quest for Adventure*. It was in the pages of this book, many years before, that I had first read of the ocean rowing adventures of Ridgway and Blyth, Johnstone and Hoare and John Fairfax. Inside the cover of each, I had jotted down a few lines of T. E. Lawrence:

All men dream, but not equally. Those who dream by night in the dusty recesses of their minds wake in the day to find that it was vanity, but the dreamers of the day are dangerous men, for they may act their dream with open eyes, to make it possible.

The next morning, through the haze of a port hangover, I considered that we had completed a significant step towards rowing across the Atlantic. Now only practical matters remained, like learning to row and taking courses in sea survival, navigation, radios and seamanship, raising the necessary funds to buy and kit out an ocean rowing boat and developing 'ultra-endurance'. That hangover

marked the start of a period in which our lives would become consumed by a single goal.

But before attending to all these things our team needed a name.
Wikipedia provided a long list of explorers and scanning through it
I came upon Pytheas, a Greek explorer who had 'discovered' Britain
circa 320 BC. The name had a nice ring to it. After emailing round the
suggestion I learnt that Jimmy's mother, like Pytheas, is from Marseilles. His statue overlooks the old harbour there. With this good
omen the Pytheas Club was formed.

Jimmy and I joined Globe Rowing Club in Greenwich, where we
were welcomed onto a beginners' course and paired up with two
other novices, Fred and Eze, to make a four. Our introduction began
with Monday evenings in the gym, or in the training 'tank' at nearby
Poplar Rowing Club. During these early weeks we were taught how
to move up and down the 'slide'; the track that the rower's seat rolls
along. We learnt to maximize the power that we put through the
oars by driving with our legs at the beginning of the stroke, and
rolling our shoulders and flicking our wrists at the end, all while
keeping our backs straight and pivoting at the hips. We learnt about
teamwork and timing; ensuring that every oar entered and left the
water at the same moment. There was a lot to remember.

As we became more proficient, we joined the club's Saturday
morning outings on the river. We started in a heavy, broad-beamed
wooden training boat, which was well suited for beginners.
Although the training boat was stable relative to other rowing boats,
we felt like we could be tipped into the water at any moment. While
our evenings at the gym and in the tank had been about power and
rhythm, once we were on the water it became clear that these
meant nothing without balance.

After a couple of months, and with the coaches finally happy
with our performance in the training boat, we graduated into a
lightweight but tippy 'fine boat'. Fine boats are racing vessels
designed purely for speed, with no compromises made for the
experience of the crew. At first we found it almost impossible to
keep the boat balanced. Despite our months of training it felt like
we were starting at square one.

To save us from taking a 'bath' in the Thames, we were mixed in with experienced rowers, but eventually our beginners' crew, now whittled down to four, was allowed to venture onto the river alone in a fine boat. We were accompanied by Phil, our old-school, gold-sovereign-ring-wearing coach, who barked orders from behind the wheel of his small motor launch.

'Hands, body, slide. Hands, body, slide. Hands, body, slide.'

Phil's mantra was like a meditative chant.

'Hands, body, slide. Hands, body, slide.'

Over and over again.

Suddenly the boat was jolted by the wash of a passing clipper, causing the person sitting in front of me to 'catch a crab'; the paddle of his blade digging deep into the water, throwing the whole crew off balance. Now it was my turn to catch a crab; the water snatching the blade from my hands, hitting me in the chest, and throwing me back. With a sharp stab of pain, the handle of Fred's blade struck me in the lower back.

'EASY THERE. Easy there!' screamed Phil.

The boat stopped and we composed ourselves. All eyes were on Phil, who sat in the aluminium tub beside us, effervescing.

'What the bloody hell do you think you're doing? *What the bloody hell do you think you're doing?* You've got to control the blade. C-o-n-t-r-o-l the blade.'

Phil gestured aggressively, bringing an imaginary handle into his sternum and tapping down with an exaggerated action.

'It's – not – the blade – that's the problem.' Phil's staccato speech in time with his hand actions.

'The problem is the bloody monkey on the end of it. C-o-n-t-r-o-l the blade,' he repeated. 'C-o-n-t-r-o-l the blade. You need to get a grip. All of you. Get a grip of your monkey.'

For a moment there was a hint of a snigger in the boat, but Phil was serious. Deadly serious.

The following summer Jimmy and I were ready to race in a novice four. While our first regatta at St Neots ended inauspiciously in the reed bank (we later discovered that our steering problems resulted from the rudder having sheared off on the stake-boat's anchor line), we enjoyed some small successes. That season our crew was joined by a second coach, Gus, a young Chilean rower who had raced in the Athens Olympics. Gus was excited by our ocean rowing project and met us at Globe every week to offer encouragement and monitor our progress. Some weekends he would meet me at the Regatta Centre at Albert Docks to help with my migration from rowing (using one oar in a relatively stable four- or eight-man boat) to sculling (using two oars in a much less stable one- or two-man boat). Gus put together a training plan designed to help us develop endurance and put on weight. At his instruction I descended into the hot, airless free-weights basement at my gym. Down here the sound of pop music was drowned out by a chorus of grunts and yells and the rhythmic clink of weights being stacked and pumped.

Jimmy took to rowing more quickly than I did, which was no surprise given his sporting pedigree. After university Jimmy had initially followed the path to becoming a professional footballer. Taking a job at an investment bank had meant giving up that dream. His childhood and early adult years had revolved around football and cricket training. He reminisced about matches at which he had played badly only to learn later that a professional club's scout had been watching. By contrast, my rugby career always featured more determination than ability and on the football pitch I earned the nickname 'Rhino' (I could charge and little else).

The same summer that Jimmy and I started racing, the Pytheas Club was reduced to two. For Ben the pressures of running a start-up business, for Nick a tour of Afghanistan, had replaced the dream of rowing across the Atlantic.

The race had categories for four-man, two-man and solo entries, and in practical terms being a two-man team made things easier. Jimmy and I lived and worked near to each other. We rowed together on Wednesday evenings and weekends and we often met for lunch in the little Italian sandwich bar behind Moorgate Tube station. But I was sad to lose Nick and Ben. I had imagined that Nick's humour would break the tension of difficult situations at sea and I related most closely to Ben's perspective on physical challenges; we shared a need to test ourselves in this way. Nonetheless, with the division of responsibilities now more clear-cut, Jimmy and I pressed on with our preparations.

With less than eighteen months until the race start we became increasingly selfish with our time. Friends, families and girlfriends all suffered from our single-mindedness. I began to row 125km per week, putting in training sessions early in the morning and late at night. I became the last one to arrive at the office and the first to leave. I had been a keen long-distance runner but the energy this burnt meant that, despite weight training and eating 5,000 calories per day, I was still struggling to bulk up, and so I had to give up running, too. As our preparations intensified, every waking hour was absorbed by training, planning, courses and work on the boat.

After putting in a few hours on the river, the rest of our Saturdays and Sundays were spent with Peter Jackson, a long-retired merchant seaman, who taught us about tropical revolving storms and celestial navigation for our Ocean Yachtmaster exam. I struggled through seven-day weeks, missed occasions and missed holidays. I craved a week off, a Sunday morning lie-in, but I knew that wherever I was, whatever my training plan for the day, when I was giving my all, Jimmy was giving even more. I had to keep up.

My girlfriend, Alice, was always supportive, but there was one nightly ritual to which she objected. I'd taken to keeping a bag of cotton wool and a bottle of surgical spirits on my bedside table, and every night I doused the areas which would be in contact with the oars and the sliding seat, gradually toughening up my hands, bum and crotch. Once we were on the ocean these areas of skin would suffer dampness, friction and the abrasive rubbing of dried salt for twelve hours every day, and while the surgical spirits weren't fun, the alternative was far worse.

Colleagues at the small firm where I worked had taken a friendly interest in my new hobby, and eventually Jimmy and I felt ready to share our plans beyond a close circle of friends and family. Without hesitation my boss, Charles Montanaro, agreed to a six-month sabbatical and gave us money for a boat, making Montanaro Asset Management our title sponsor. There were three options for getting our hands on an ocean rowing boat. We didn't have the time or know-how to build one from a plywood kit, and we didn't have the budget to commission a boat yard to custom-build one, which led us to the third option, to buy one second-hand.

We spoke to Simon Chalk, the race organizer, and looked through the 'For Sale' section on the Ocean Rowing Society website. After talking to a number of people and comparing the prices and specifications of the various boats that were for sale, we settled on *Gemini*, a composite boat, built of wood and fibreglass, at Rossiter's boat yard in Christchurch, Dorset. She had crossed the Atlantic the previous year rowed by Alan Lock and Matt Boreham.

Our surveyor reported back that *Gemini* was 'built like a tank'; her joints were double-laminated and the aft cabin was built from inch-thick plywood. Having done an independent crossing, the boat lacked most of the compulsory Woodvale race equipment, and although she came at a knock-down price, what we thought we had saved in cash up front, we ended up paying for in time and money later.

Gemini had not been touched from the moment she had landed in the Caribbean, and we spent a whole weekend emptying the detritus of the previous expedition; half-eaten ration packs littered the deck; the hatches were full of algae and stagnant seawater, tea bags, toilet paper and sachets of isotonic drinks. We built new rowing positions and sliding seats from plywood, aluminium, rollerblade trucks and marine-grade ball bearings. Galleons Point Marina near London City Airport became our second home. We even slept there, in our bivi bags, taking two-hour shifts as we layered on coats of epoxy-based Coppercoat anti-fouling, which would prevent barnacles and algae from building up on the hull.

Four months before the race start most of our work on the boat was complete and we lifted her off the hardstanding and onto a mooring. Now our time was spent in the Royal Albert Dock, which was adjacent to the marina, getting used to the weight and feel of the boat. One weekend we took her out onto the river and rowed from Galleons Point Marina up to Teddington Lock and back. Rowing the boat under Tower Bridge and through central London, with the tide, in the early hours of the morning, was magical. Along the picture-postcard stretch from Richmond to Teddington we attracted a lot of interest from the club rowers who passed us. We stopped for the night on the pontoon at Mortlake and cast off at dawn for the journey back to the marina. We rowed through the capital enjoying the eerie silence until, passing under Southwark Bridge, there was a sudden commotion on the South Bank. I looked up and saw one of my flatmates with a group of his friends on their way home from a night out, waving and shouting. Their world and mine couldn't have been more different.

Our next objective was an overnight row and for this we decided to head east, out into the estuary, where conditions would be rougher. We set off from the marina on a Saturday morning in late August. We told Keith, the lock-keeper, that we would be back in twenty-four hours, having completed a round-trip to Southend. We passed Tilbury Docks and rowed on through the decaying industrial wasteland of disused pontoons and chemical storage facilities.

Approaching the mouth of the estuary the swell started to pick up. Although the waves were only a metre high, they seemed to tower above the boat. Our trip was beginning to feel like a 'proper' adventure; little could we imagine the ten-metre swell we would soon encounter in the Atlantic. With the current of the river behind us, the rechristened *Spirit of Montanaro* ripped through the water, and we made our turning point, opposite Southend, within twelve hours, as planned. With large container vessels and dry bulk ships running at twenty knots down the estuary, we waited for the all-clear over the VHF radio from Gravesend Vessel Traffic Services before crossing to the north side of the channel for the return trip. We turned back towards London just as the tide changed. We had rowed against the tide without too much difficulty on the way out, but now the wind and the river current were also against us. We took it in turns to row through the night. Gauging our progress against the lights of Southend, which were half a mile off our starboard side, we covered no ground over the course of six hours and caught our rudder on a sandbank at low tide.

The tide turned again and soon after that morning broke. We were very tired and had almost run out of food. We called the marina to say we would be back that afternoon. We knew that if we arrived any later than 4 PM the tide would recede beyond the entrance to the marina and we would be stuck until Monday morning. By midday we couldn't row against the quickening tide any more and we dropped the anchor. We relaxed on the hot deck for three hours, eating the last of our food and mulling over our next move. There was no longer any chance of getting to the marina on time. If we carried on rowing we might get there by late evening and we could anchor up at the entrance until the lock-keeper returned on Monday morning. Alternatively we could try to moor up somewhere en route. Without a firm plan we pulled up the anchor and rowed two-up into the back-breaking tide.

With evening approaching and hunger playing on our minds, we decided to drop anchor at a point from which we could scramble, climb or swim to dry land for food. In the distance we saw a group of small boats on floating moorings. As we got closer the clubhouse came into view. Thurrock Yacht Club looked deserted. There was no pontoon, so we decided to pull up the rudder and beach the boat, then walk to the nearest town. Beaching the boat was easy enough. Next I lowered myself off the gunwale onto the beach. Except that it wasn't a beach. By the time I was in it up to the hip, I concluded that the thick estuary mud was, in fact, bottomless.

Having watched our plan unravel with some amusement, a figure came out of the clubhouse and indicated to us to take a floating mooring – someone would come out on a launch to pick us up. Freeing the boat from the heavy, stinking mud, in which I was now covered from the waist down, was easier said than done, but with industrious use of our small folding grapnel anchor and some frantic stroke work, we dislodged ourselves and took the floating mooring.

Twenty minutes later the launch appeared. They could only take one of us, because someone had to stay aboard to manoeuvre the boat round to the slipway should the launch be unavailable for the return journey. I volunteered to stay and Jimmy jumped on the launch with strict instructions to buy a lot of food. An hour later the buzz of a small outboard heralded Jimmy's return.

That evening we feasted on cold baked beans, bananas and chocolate biscuits. After thirty-six hours of hard rowing every inch of our bodies ached and even with two of us crammed together in the cabin, which was about the size of a single bed and had just enough headroom to sit up, we relished the prospect of a night's sleep.

We woke just before dawn, bade farewell to Thurrock Yacht Club and rowed out into the rising tide. We passed under the huge span of the Queen Elizabeth II Bridge at Dartford in the early hours of the morning and, rowing two-up, with the tide in our favour, broke seven knots. Rested and recharged, we were back at Galleons Point Marina in a couple of hours.

It was Bank Holiday Monday and once we had moored up and cleaned out the boat, we headed off to enjoy the rest of the weekend. I met Alice and a friend of hers at Westminster pier; they wanted to take a boat trip down the Thames. I sat on the top deck, enjoying the sunshine and the sensation of effortless speed.

In mid-October Jimmy and I joined a handful of other ocean rowers at a marina on the Hamble, where we learnt the basics of sea survival and first aid. The weekend was a chance to chat with the other crews about their final preparations. We all had similar stories to tell; although it was still six weeks until the race, even getting this far had been a huge strain on time, energy, money and relationships.

The following week we took *Spirit of Montanaro* to Tilbury Docks, where she was loaded onto a container for shipping to the Canary Islands. After all the hours that we had spent working on the boat it was a relief to finally see her go, and for now we had one less thing to worry about. But the pause in activity was momentary, and we would soon be reunited with her in La Gomera.

3

The First Race, 1966

Reporters had fallen over each other to predict Samuelson and Harbo's certain demise when they departed from New York in June 1896, but few wrote about their safe return to the city later that year. In fact, their accomplishment and the very idea of rowing across the Atlantic soon disappeared from the public imagination completely. For almost seventy years little changed, until in August 1965 a chain of events began that would pit two rival crews, very publicly, against each other. That month an advert appeared in *The Times*:

> *Will five fortitudinous oarsmen over 28 join me and engage in the second ever transatlantic rowing voyage?*

The advert had been placed by David Johnstone, a thirty-three-year-old journalist with a restless imagination. At 6'3", he was a physically imposing figure, his face framed by a thick black beard. Johnstone lived between his mother's and brother's homes in Farnham and the bedsits and shared flats of his friends in London. Easy laughter and a gift for telling stories made him popular within this close circle, who happily made allowances for his peripatetic lifestyle, but amongst acquaintances he was often quiet and reserved. Johnstone delighted in confounding people's expectations; to offer him advice was to be sure that he would take a different approach entirely. His passions were for travel, books and adventure, and for huge quantities of food to sustain his seventeen-stone frame. A favourite recipe involved lining a casserole pot with ham and filling it with the parson's noses of chickens, which he stewed in a rich sauce.

Generous with money when he had it and dependent on the charity of friends when he did not, Johnstone had little interest in a career, financial security or commitment of any sort. He would arrive at friends' homes unannounced and rarely agreed to any firm social plans. Although smart and creative, Johnstone had abandoned higher education and instead gone travelling across Australia, where he worked at a fruit-canning factory, on sheep stations, as a carpenter and driving a lorry. He enjoyed physical work the most, and even spent some time employed as a gravedigger. He would stick at a job until he either became bored or was fired for insubordination. Back in England he worked at a law firm, then an insurance company, and later ran a coffee bar.

It was typical of Johnstone's contrarian attitude that he only became a journalist after his father, who worked on Fleet Street, had died. Rather than buckle to the demands of the national press, Johnstone opted for the relaxed environment of a provincial paper, leaving his job when adventure beckoned, to work for a publisher in Kenya, sail in the Indian Ocean, and travel overland across East Africa. He sometimes spoke of buying a house in Farnham or the south of France and settling down, but any money he earned was spent on his mother, or the upkeep of his boat on the Hamble, or went towards buying cars which he thrashed around racing tracks and on the road until they were scrap.

Behind Johnstone's carefree lifestyle was a tendency to depression. He had attacks of self-doubt which stemmed from the feeling that he had never really fulfilled his potential. He believed he was destined for great things and yearned for an opportunity to prove this to the world.

The news that an American journalist had just landed in Falmouth after sailing single-handed across the Atlantic started the discussion that evening at Johnstone's local pub in Farnham. Sailing was one thing, but the Atlantic had actually been *rowed*, he explained, by two Norwegian fishermen in the nineteenth century. Suddenly it occurred to Johnstone that rowing the Atlantic was the test he had been looking for, the chance to show the world what he was capable of. He immediately announced his intention to his friends and the following morning sent an advert to *The Times*.

Amongst the hundred-odd replies was one from John Hoare. Hoare was also a journalist, a few years younger but with the same physical presence and adventurous spirit. He shared Johnstone's love of fast cars and also raced at track days. Their differences were significant too. Hoare's appetite for adventure was more romantic than existential, in that it stemmed from a fascination with wartime heroics and a love of Hemingway. He was in the process of writing the biography of a World War I flying ace.

Hoare was naturally easy going and a keen sportsman. He had done National Service with the Parachute Regiment and now served in one of their Reserve units. Johnstone and Hoare quickly became friends, but they did not enter into the project as equals. Rowing across the Atlantic was Johnstone's idea and, even as his judgment became clouded by self-doubt and the spectre of competition bore down on him, the key decisions would remain his alone.

Six months after Johnstone's advert in *The Times*, John Ridgway, a twenty-eight-year-old officer in the Parachute Regiment, announced his intention to race Johnstone and Hoare across the Atlantic. He planned to join the journalists at the start line in ten weeks' time, but, at the time of the announcement, had neither a boat nor a rowing partner.

Ridgway's challenge was grave news for Johnstone. The men had met twice before. The first had been a chance encounter in Bahrain where Johnstone had written on the Parachute Regiment for the army's public relations office. The second had been in Farnham, the Surrey town where they both lived, after Ridgway approached Johnstone about joining his expedition.

Ridgway had heard of Johnstone's plan the previous year and it had immediately captured his imagination:

> I was shaving one morning and listening to the radio. Jack de Manio, the BBC personality, was interviewing a journalist called David Johnstone about some project he had in mind. I was only half listening. But suddenly I began to understand. This incredible man Johnstone was actually proposing to row across the Atlantic.[1]

After Ridgway had tried, unsuccessfully, to contact him, Johnstone appeared, typically unannounced, at his door. They spoke about the project, but Johnstone recognized immediately a character clash between himself and this steely young officer. He explained to Ridgway that he and Hoare would be undertaking the crossing as a pair, rather than as part of the team of six he had originally advertised for. Finding himself in a race affected Johnstone deeply, adding pressure to what was already becoming an extremely stressful situation.

Johnstone's project was by this point well advanced. With sponsorship from the *People* newspaper, Colin Mudie, a respected naval architect, had been commissioned to design a boat, and *Puffin* was now in the latter stages of construction. Johnstone and Hoare had received lectures on seamanship and sea rowing at the Royal Naval School for Safety Equipment and Survival Training. They had consulted dietary experts and oar makers, and commissioned a special pair of folding oars. Johnstone had studied meteorology and celestial navigation and the workings of all of the mechanical and electrical equipment on board the boat. He had immersed himself in research to identify the best rowing positions and oar gates, and most suitable type of bearings for those gates. But as preparations progressed, Johnstone became increasingly overwhelmed by what he had now, very publicly, committed himself to. He found himself wishing that he might be overcome with some illness which would give him a way out of a situation that had now gathered its own momentum.

Feeling alone in his predicament, and distant from Hoare, who lived in Leicester and to whom he had given only a supporting role in the planning of the project, Johnstone often thought of Ridgway, sometimes even longing for his adversary's companionship.

In many ways I wish I could talk to Ridgway and compare notes. He is the only other man in this world, with Blyth, who is preparing anything like this. We are few and should be together, but I have been made nervous and unhappy at times by Ridgway and his behaviour has in some respects put him out of reach.[2]

To someone with Johnstone's sensitive disposition, Ridgway projected a cool, intimidating confidence. But Ridgway's upbringing was not so different from his own; both came from a comfortable middle-class family, with a hard-working, often distant father. Like Johnstone, Ridgway enjoyed his own company, spending his summers fishing, swimming and rowing alone along the Thames, by his family home near Windsor.

Although his family never discussed it, Ridgway was always conscious that he had been adopted. He was also flat-footed, suffered from bronchitis and showed little aptitude for either sport or studies. From an early age these handicaps made Ridgway determined to try harder than anybody else and it was through sheer grit and determination that he made the First XV rugby team at school. Without the grades to continue his education, he left school at seventeen and joined the merchant navy. He soon grew bored of life at sea, though, and, narrowly avoiding his father's wishes that he become an insurance underwriter at Lloyd's, went on to join the army. Ridgway thrived at Sandhurst, found exciting new friends, and became a popular figure through his involvement in the boxing team there.

As with rugby, Ridgway was not a natural boxer and, although he captained the academy's boxing team in his final term, it was in recognition of his tenacity, rather than any notable competitive success. At Sandhurst's annual inter-company boxing finals Ridgway went into the ring with a broken nose from his previous fight. Throughout the match he was dominated by a skilled opponent who took full advantage of his weak nose and Ridgway spent most of the third round crawling around the canvas on his hands and knees, covered in his own blood. Despite the beating he was taking, Ridgway became hysterical when the referee called a halt to the fight. He had to be pulled from the ring by his corner men as he begged to be allowed to fight on. Reeling from injured pride, he sat in the changing room, sobbing, only coming out at the end of the evening to accept the 'Best Loser' award. The tag stuck, and although Ridgway had been distraught at the disgrace of it at the time, it soon became a badge of honour. It was this reputation for determination that meant he was the only Sandhurst cadet offered a position in the 3rd Battalion of the Parachute Regiment that year.

In 1959 Ridgway joined his battalion and was put in charge of

9 Platoon, to which he became much attached. The platoon included one particular lance corporal, a rebellious young Scot, whom Ridgway found it difficult to manage and repeatedly tried to have demoted to the rank of private. But the rebel defied his platoon commander by progressing swiftly through the ranks and by Christmas 1961, aged twenty-one, he had become Ridgway's platoon sergeant. His name was Chay Blyth.

The following spring Ridgway and Blyth found themselves the favourites to win the Parachute Brigade Reading to Westminster overnight canoe race. Early in the evening they lost thirty minutes in a capsize. Frozen and demoralized, with little prospect of making up the lost time, Ridgway suggested they call it a day. Blyth would not entertain the idea. Suddenly Ridgway saw the contrast between the two of them. He had spent his life being a good loser, but losing was not something Blyth accepted quite so readily.

> For the first time I really saw Chay; the youngest of a family of six children, he had had to fend for himself since leaving school at sixteen . . . I was with someone to whom winning meant progress, who wanted and, indeed, was used to progress. I was twenty-four and he twenty-one. He knew we would win, I knew we wouldn't.[3]

Blyth's attitude won Ridgway over and ten hours later they crossed the finish line, winning the race by eleven minutes.

In 1964 Ridgway left the army to start a new life with his wife, Marie Christine, on a croft in the north-west Highlands. Unable to find a way of making ends meet, he was back with his regiment by the end of the year. Now assigned to a tedious office job, Ridgway immersed himself in physical training, running every day, and all the time thinking of how he and Marie Christine would one day return to the cottage they had bought in Ardmore. He also dreamed of adventure beyond the confines of his desk in Aldershot. A newspaper article about a journalist who planned to row across the Atlantic reminded Ridgway of the radio interview he had heard six months earlier and prompted him to get in touch with Johnstone.

Johnstone's put-down did not deter Ridgway, but two significant obstacles stood in his way. Firstly he could find no way of raising the

£2,000 – about £45,000 in today's money – needed to buy a boat like *Puffin*, which Johnstone had commissioned specially for the crossing. Secondly, and perhaps most pressingly, he had no rowing partner. Despite having only ten weeks to resolve these issues, and arrange much else besides, he made it publicly known that he would be entering into a race against Johnstone to cross the Atlantic.

Two weeks later a solution to the first problem appeared when a friend mentioned a company called Bradford Boat Services in Yorkshire that made a sturdy fishing dory which might be suitable for the task. Ridgway called and learnt that the yard had one left in stock from the Earls Court Boat Show. With his bank overdraft extended, a cheque for £185 was in the post the following day. Another fortnight passed before Ridgway's old platoon sergeant, Blyth, strolled into his office. Ridgway was looking for a rowing partner only amongst the unmarried men, but Blyth had already asked his wife, Maureen, who had agreed. With a month to go before leaving for Cape Cod, Ridgway had both boat and crew.

Ridgway's challenge panicked Johnstone into a series of poor decisions. He called the boat yard in Cowes, on the Isle of Wight, and explained that the tight schedule he had set them to finish the boat would now be cut shorter still. He cancelled the extensive sea trials that he had planned and made arrangements for *Puffin* to be shipped to America in April, to allow for a mid-May departure. All these new arrangements were made in absolute secrecy. Johnstone felt that if they could steal the march on Ridgway and Blyth by setting to sea before their announced departure date, there was a good chance that they could still beat the Paras across the Atlantic.

The new plans had several consequences. The first was that when Johnstone came to collect the boat a number of things remained unfinished. *Puffin* had originally been specified with external buoyancy bags which would reduce the chances of capsize, but these had not yet been fitted. Secondly, rather than the weeks of rowing training and sea trials that they had planned, the sum of their experience of rowing *Puffin* before setting off into the Atlantic would now amount to one afternoon at Cowes.

On 27 April 1966 Johnstone, Hoare and *Puffin* boarded the *United*

States at Southampton, bound for New York. From there they planned to head north to Cape Cod, from where a few hundred miles of rowing would take them out into a corridor of favourable currents that would sweep them east across the Atlantic. Although the strength and direction of the individual currents in the Gulf Stream vary significantly, Johnstone figured that on average it would add a knot to their speed. Day and night, whether they rowed or not, it should take them steadily closer to their destination. But despite their careful research and detailed plans, Johnstone was by now so anxious that a conversation on board the *United States* caused him to change their starting point completely.

The recommendation of the ship's navigator to leave from Cape Hatteras was probably a sound one, for here the Gulf Stream ran at great speed and from close inshore. Although the route from Cape Hatteras would add 500 miles to the 3,000-mile journey from Cape Cod, the opportunity to get into the Gulf Stream quickly from this more southerly start point would make for a faster crossing. Indeed, the advice to start from Cape Hatteras was confirmed by the US Coast Guard when Johnstone and Hoare arrived in New York, along with a very strong warning against attempting the crossing at all. The Coast Guard gave them a 5 per cent chance of survival.

If Johnstone had taken the navigator's advice, or indeed if he had ignored it and stuck to his plan, their crossing may have turned out very differently, but in his mind this new information provided a further opportunity to gain an advantage over Ridgway and Blyth. Johnstone picked a new start point a couple of miles south of the mouth of Chesapeake Bay, neither at Cape Cod nor at Cape Hatteras, but somewhere between the two. He believed that this part of the coast provided the best compromise between total crossing distance and access to the Gulf Stream. In reality, Chesapeake Bay had the disadvantage of adding over 400 miles to their journey and also put them at the mercy of difficult, shifting currents that eddied and swirled with the changing tides, and ranged up to sixty miles off-shore. It was the worst possible compromise.

In the paranoia that now governed Johnstone's decisions, only a very small number of people were told of the new start point. None of them were experts on the currents off Chesapeake Bay and no

advice was sought on the matter. Secrecy was of utmost importance. Thanks to the change of departure point it would take
Johnstone and Hoare two weeks to reach the Gulf Stream and, despite their head start, they would still have further to go than Ridgway
and Blyth when the Paras finally departed on 4 June.

Johnstone and Hoare spent a fortnight in and around Chesapeake
Bay, buying equipment, ballasting *Puffin* with bags of fresh water
and stowing their provisions. Despite the generosity of their hosts
and the keen interest of the public and the gathered press, this
period of relative inactivity depressed Johnstone. His lead on Ridgway was slipping away and he became desperate to get to sea, but at
the same time felt increasingly unsure of the whole project. He was
still fighting his own doubts when the local mayor led the launching
ceremony, and *Puffin* cast off from Long Creek Marina, Virginia
Beach on the morning of 21 May 1966.

With Hoare pulling on the oars and Virginia Beach fading
from view, Johnstone wrote in his diary, *Suddenly very depressing
the thought of the trip – wished we could be rammed, unable to go on,
anything.*

Ridgway was battling his own demons that day. He heard of *Puffin*'s
departure from his bed in a Boston hospital, where he was laid up
with a septic foot, having cut it during a training run in Aldershot
the previous week. He had arrived with Blyth on an RAF aircraft
and, on being released from the hospital, hurried to join his crewmate, who was already in Cape Cod. Together they acquired
last-minute provisions, loaded the *English Rose III* ('*Rosie*'), and
supervised last-minute alterations to her. Local fishermen, who had
been using flat-bottomed, clinker-built dories like *Rosie* for gener-
ations, gave them rowing lessons on Pleasant Bay and taught them
to use short strokes to maintain the boat's momentum. Their new
friends also recommended that they reinforce the boat with thick
oak. Ridgway and Blyth gladly took the fishermen's advice.

The reason behind Ridgway's decision to leave from Cape Cod
was simple. It had been Johnstone's planned departure point and
Ridgway intended to compete on equal terms wherever possible.
Now, though, with the boat already delivered to Cape Cod when

the news of Johnstone's change of plan reached them, the Paras simply could not afford to move it.

As in their choice of boat, Ridgway and Blyth favoured simple equipment that was tried and tested. In Cape Cod they asked the dorymen for advice on oars, and picked up six pairs at the local chandlery. They had brought sixty days of army rations, without flinching at the thought of eating beef curry every day.

By contrast, Johnstone meticulously researched each aspect of his food and equipment, agonizing over every detail before making a decision. At the advice of Archie de Jong, the nutrition expert at Horlicks, who had provisioned countless polar and desert expeditions, he prepared a varied selection of dried-meal plans, with further 'wet' options for days when they couldn't cook. The changing sea conditions they would face prompted Johnstone to bring five different lengths of oar, including a specially commissioned twelve-foot pair that folded in half to pack more easily on *Puffin*, which was only sixteen feet long.

Puffin was a sophisticated vessel; the plywood construction, self-righting design, square racing oarlocks and enclosed aft cabin are all features of modern ocean rowing boats. *Rosie* had only a canvas cover to protect her crew from the elements, but there were advantages to the simple dory design. Being five feet longer than *Puffin*, she was quicker in the water, while a flat bottom allowed her to slide easily off the waves. The Cape Cod fishermen talked Ridgway and Blyth out of adding a keel, pointing out that a keel on a small boat could create a 'tripping effect', by offering just enough resistance below the waterline to cause a roll in heavy beam seas.

On board *Puffin*, Johnstone and Hoare soon realized that the last-minute change of departure point had been a costly mistake. Caught in infuriating onshore currents, their first week at sea was spent drifting in circles, never more than a few miles from the blinking light of Chesapeake lighthouse. Johnstone had felt sick with nerves when they left Virginia Beach, but as he settled in to life at sea, his mood turned to one of resignation; *Puffin* was at the mercy of the wind and the currents and there was very little they could do about it. Perhaps this is why Johnstone and Hoare rarely stuck to a fixed rowing schedule.

The pair also found a number of problems with their equipment. On the morning of their second day at sea, Hoare set about making ham and eggs for breakfast from one of Archie's dehydrated packets. It took him three hours to get the stove started and Johnstone mulled over the option of rowing back to land to pick up a replacement. They also had an instrument called a Harrier, which showed speed and distance through the water. This new technology would soon become standard on ocean-going vessels, and Johnstone had installed one on *Puffin* at great expense. Unfortunately, the Harrier didn't work. After Johnstone took it apart and rebuilt it, readings appeared only intermittently and he doubted their accuracy. He soon stopped using it. By cancelling the sea trials, they had forfeited the chance to iron these issues out before setting off.

In the haste to get a lead on Ridgway and Blyth, the external buoyancy bags were left unfitted, but now that *Puffin* was fully laden with supplies and freshwater ballast her stability was significantly improved, and Johnstone hardly gave the buoyancy bags a second thought. After twelve days at sea they had covered only sixty miles, but Johnstone and Hoare had noticed a change in the colour and clarity of the ocean. The thermometer showed an increase in water temperature; they were finally entering the easterly currents of the Gulf Stream. On 4 June, Johnstone took a sight and calculated *Puffin's* mileage. The results were a shock, and he double- and triple-checked his numbers before giving Hoare the news. In the last thirty hours they had covered seventy miles. They were now on their way across the Atlantic.

Late that same afternoon, 400 miles to the north, Ridgway and Blyth were taking their first strokes out of the harbour of Orleans, Cape Cod. Ridgway wondered if their inexperience on the oars was obvious to the well-wishers watching from the quay. He stared at the small brass plaque that a doryman had mounted on their boat.

OH GOD, THY SEA IS SO GREAT
AND MY BOAT IS SO SMALL

As the last of the boats accompanying them to sea turned back, he was struck by the enormity of their undertaking and turned to Blyth.

'How are you feeling?'

'Champion! How are you, sir?'

Ridgway paused for a moment. 'Since you first volunteered for this expedition we've been equal partners in it. Now we're at sea it seems appropriate to break with the formalities of rank, don't you think?'

Blyth shook his head. 'It's our military training – I couldn't bring myself to call you by your first name.'

'But you calling me "Captain Ridgway" all the time is going to become rather ridiculous after a while with no one else here.'

The pair rowed a few strokes in silence before Chay replied. 'Given you've experience of being at sea, and I'm a novice at this kind of thing, perhaps I could call you Number One instead?'

Ridgway pondered the suggestion and then started chuckling to himself, which set Blyth laughing too.

'Number One it is!'

The pair rowed into the night before dropping anchor and cooking dinner. The feeling of seasickness struck Ridgway the moment they stopped rowing and lasted through until the next morning. Blyth woke from a cold and uncomfortable night's sleep to find Ridgway already awake, sat at the other end of the boat, green-faced and bleary-eyed.

'Are you all right?'

Ridgway turned and was sick over the side. Despite being an experienced sailor, he would take a few days to get his sea legs.

On their third day at sea, *Rosie* was hit by the first of a series of storms. As the breaking waves rose twenty feet and more, Ridgway and Blyth tried to weatherproof the boat by drawing their canvas sheet over the cockpit. For a moment they imagined that they would ride out the weather by huddling together under it. This wishful thinking was dispelled by the next breaker, which filled the boat with water, and the pair were soon bailing for their lives. The weather they faced that night and over the days that followed confirmed their confidence in *Rosie*'s seaworthiness, but made them question their own ability to hold out against the punishing conditions. The first period of bad weather culminated in Hurricane Alma, which hit Ridgway and Blyth on 14 June. Only a night-long vigil on the bilge pump kept the boat afloat.

But the Parachute Regiment had trained Ridgway and Blyth to tackle adversity with discipline and, as they became accustomed to the conditions, their thoughts turned from simply surviving to racing.

We decided we had been messing about too much, not spending enough time at the oars. We had lost the drive we needed to con- quer the Atlantic. So we worked out a routine. Both of us would row from eight each morning until half an hour before last light. One would make the grub and eat and switch around when the other fellow's turn came up. That would mean that the boat would always be driven through the water. At night we would sleep separ- ately, two hours' sleep, two hours' row and so on.[4]

As the pair grew more confident in handling the boat, they took delight in surfing the waves which appeared with the following winds. Sometimes these would grow to thirty or forty feet in height. The boat would race down one wave before rising up to the crest of the next. Ridgway and Blyth would speed along all day, shouting in excitement and pulling harder on one oar or the other to keep *Rosie* on course. At night, though, the sea took on a different character. The huge waves, which had been so exhilarating during the day, became terrible and frightening. Hunkering down in their little dory, Ridgway and Blyth felt as if they might, at any moment, be thrown into the deadly churning waters.

On board *Puffin*, Johnstone and Hoare were struggling to motivate themselves. In bad weather Johnstone found it hard to summon the energy to take to the oars. In good weather, with the wind and the currents of the Gulf Stream behind them, the extra miles gained by rowing hardly seemed worth the effort. On 7 June, while Ridgway and Blyth battled with storms 400 miles to the north, Johnstone and Hoare, who had just been resupplied by a passing vessel, the *Orient City*, spent the day drinking beer, smoking, catching a Portuguese man-of-war in a bucket and watching empty bottles sink into the deep blue.

I oiled the Swiss Army penknife John gave me, put glassier cream on my nose and got out the stove, while John lay back in the cabin with Doris Stenton's 'English Society in the Middle Ages'. [5]

After their hurried preparations to get to sea ahead of the Paras, Johnstone and Hoare now had little inclination to race them. They made life on board as comfortable as conditions allowed, each rowing for around eight hours per day and resting when it got dark. They fished, concocted imaginative meals out of their provisions and discussed the books they were reading. By contrast Ridgway and Blyth were each rowing for sixteen hours and manning the oars continuously through the day and night. On board *Rosie* there was time only to eat, sleep and row.

Despite their limited resources and preparation time, the simple equipment that they had chosen served the Paras well. They ate a hot meal from the gas stove every day, whatever the conditions, and Ridgway commended Blyth, the cook, on never spilling a drop of food. By contrast, Johnstone's custom-built gimbal stove was virtually unworkable, a problem compounded by the boat's increasing tendency to whip and roll in even a light swell. It took hours to prepare a meal and this usually involved covering the stove, deck and cook in stew, boiling water and paraffin. They often abandoned the exercise altogether and ate their food cold.

Blyth took advantage of the period of good weather following Hurricane Alma to repack their provisions. He opened a few of the sealed boxes to check everything was in order but saw that seawater had found its way into some of the supposedly waterproof packaging. He opened another box, and another, to find the same and worse. Eventually he turned to Ridgway to break the bad news: a third of their rations had been spoilt in the storm.

Rosie had left Cape Cod with ten days of fresh food and sixty days of dried army rations. Carefully counting what was left, Ridgway and Blyth reduced their daily intake to 2,000 calories, nowhere near the 6,000 that each of them burnt during the course of sixteen hours on the oars every day. Weakened by hunger, they started to suffer from what Blyth termed 'mental plonk'. Thoughts and reactions slowed and even while they pushed on with the punishing rowing schedule, they slipped into a state of semi-awareness, dangerously indifferent to what was happening around them. Blyth would ask Ridgway a question and minutes would pass before Ridgway was able to make sense of it and summon a response. Then they would turn their heads towards each other, struggling to digest the meaning of the conversation that had just passed, as they carried on rowing in silence.

They took it in turns to sleep at night under a thin foil survival blanket, which kept them warm, but offered no reprieve from the constant wet. The salt meant that they were always itchy and when they tried to sleep the itching could become almost unbearable. Often a two-hour rest period would be interrupted by a wave crashing onto the boat, or a call from the man rowing to pump the bilge. The harsh conditions took their toll and Ridgway in particular suffered from boils, salt sores and chafing.

After five weeks at sea, Ridgway and Blyth were only 1,000 miles into the crossing and it was clear that they would take much longer than the original estimate of ten weeks. This meant further reducing their daily ration to 1,200 calories and even sucking their boiled sweets with the wrappers on to make them last longer. Despite this, Blyth noted in his diary, *To date it's been great. No problems at all. I hope the future is the same.*[6]

Johnstone and Hoare had now been at sea for seven weeks and, in the time since their disastrous fortnight travelling in circles near the mouth of Chesapeake Bay, had been averaging fifty miles per day. In fact *Puffin* had briefly been ahead of the Paras during their fourth week at sea. Now that *Rosie* was also in the Gulf Stream, about 150 miles to the north and travelling on a similar bearing, Ridgway and Blyth had retaken the lead, but the difference was small and both crews had learnt how changeable the ocean can be.

With the extra supplies they had been given by the *Orient City* a few weeks earlier, Johnstone and Hoare ate well, ending each day with a large and varied dinner that Johnstone, despite his voracious appetite, often struggled to finish. After a fruit dessert they would sit in the cabin, chatting, for a 'digestive half hour', before going out on deck to share a cigarette, or try their luck with the harpoon gun. *Puffin* was on a more southerly course than the Paras, following the main shipping route between Europe and North America, and this gave Johnstone and Hoare confidence that there would be further opportunities to resupply before the food ran out.

With the benefit of retiring to a relatively dry cabin at night and during bad weather, plenty of food and enough time off the oars every day to recover, Johnstone and Hoare were in much better physical condition than Ridgway and Blyth. But in terms of morale, the situation on board *Puffin* and *Rosie* was reversed. Despite their deteriorating mental and physical state, the Paras remained confident in their ability to complete the challenge they had set themselves. By contrast, Johnstone watched the days pass on board *Puffin* with a resigned acceptance of failure. On 20 July he wrote in his diary, *We are absolutely complacent about position, and the interesting time will be when we decide the whistle must be blown – I hope we are still in the shipping lane then.*

Although Johnstone's moods weighed on Hoare, the younger man remained optimistic and tried hard to lighten the mood on the boat. A more self-confident character than Johnstone, he was also an experienced coastal rower and, with his experience in the Territorial Army, shared some of Ridgway and Blyth's determined attitude. Despite all this, there was never any doubt who was in charge on *Puffin*; Johnstone was the skipper and would make all of the important decisions.

Blyth was a keen swimmer and on hot days would gaze longingly at the cool water, weighing his desire for a refreshing swim against his fear of sharks. On one particularly stifling afternoon, he convinced Ridgway that the waters were safe to bathe in. As Ridgway went to dive in, Blyth spotted something moving in *Rosie*'s shadow. He took a stroke on the oar, which knocked Ridgway back into the boat, and they both watched, rapt, as a huge shark rose through the water and rubbed up against the side of the boat. Ridgway was shaken by the near miss and it took a pint of Blyth's hot cocoa for him to regain his composure. Over the course of the day they saw that the area they were rowing through was infested with sharks.

On 26 July, *Rosie* was seen by the cargo ship *Madaket*, who pulled alongside and asked if they needed any food or water. Ridgway turned down the offer. He and Blyth had decided at the outset to complete the crossing without any external help and, even as they starved, they remained determined to continue on these terms.

They soon regretted this decision. Hunger was becoming an incessant pain and as the 'mental plonk' grew worse, they spent their days on the oars in a constant daydream, watching imaginary figures in the sea and sky. Malnutrition accelerated their physical decline and their bodies became covered in boils, such that lying down to sleep was agony. In the evenings they sat by the cooker to share their daily meal and they would inspect every spoonful that was eaten, mentally weighing out each man's share. Despite the pressure of starvation they disagreed over food only once. Although neither had a strong faith when they set out, both men began to pray for a ship to come.

On 12 August their prayers were answered by the tanker *Haustellum*. With their last flare they managed to attract the tanker's attention and, drawing up alongside, Captain Mitchell invited them on board to a meal of scrambled eggs, bread and marmalade, served with fresh coffee in china cups. Ridgway savoured a can of condensed milk. Neither could remember a moment in their lives when they had been happier. They caught up on the news from home and learnt that England had won the World Cup, and that Johnstone and Hoare were still at sea. While they sat at the captain's table, the crew of the *Haustellum* loaded another two weeks of tinned food onto their boat.

With their minds now free from the fear of starvation, Ridgway and Blyth cast off in high spirits. But their bodies responded badly to the rich food. Their stomachs ached worse now than when they had been starving and Ridgway spent the night sweating out a fever and being sick over the side of the boat. By morning they both felt a little better, but for much of the next week they lay about the boat, completely drained, able to row only periodically. They had to pay for the moment of relaxation that they had allowed themselves on board *Haustellum*. The mind had released its grip on the body and now faced a battle to regain it.

As August drew to an end the weather deteriorated. The winds seemed to blow from every direction except west and Ridgway and Blyth spent long periods at sea anchor, or rowing hard into the wind to reduce their backward drift. Their iron will, which had driven them this far in the face of starvation, was now deserting them. Seawater had rotted their clothes and salt sores covered Ridgway's body from head to toe. Early on the morning of 24 August *Rosie* was hit by another storm, the worst since Hurricane Alma. Through the dark early hours Ridgway and Blyth threw everything they had left into bailing out their little boat, Ridgway noting: 'I wondered why we went on. Why did we not just sit down and call it a day. Death would be peace, all peace, from this agony.'[7]

By daybreak the storm had settled to a gale and the pair retired to the bow of the boat, where they huddled together for warmth under the tattered remnants of their foil survival blanket.

As weeks became months the mood on board *Puffin* gradually improved. Unlike the Paras, Johnstone and Hoare were not struggling with starvation. Far from it: the plan to resupply from passing ships paid off and, twice in late July and once more in early August, they took on further provisions. A sense of optimism crept into their conversations and, now accepting that they might still be at sea as autumn passed into winter, they spoke of taking a more southerly route to Portugal. Johnstone's earlier feelings, that failure was inevitable, evaporated and, by 30 August, after 102 days at sea, he wrote in his diary that to give up now was 'unthinkable'.

Puffin had always been tippy and awkward to row in rough seas, but as she got lighter, the pair noticed that she became increasingly prone to whip violently from side to side, often without warning. Johnstone considered flooding the bilge to make her more stable, which was something that Mudie had recommended.

I am concerned about weight, but – if we don't fill the bilges and a really naughty one catches us abeam we could go over . . . A perplexing conundrum, with my own opinion in favour of leaving her light, so that as much as possible sticks up into the wind![8]

Johnstone and Hoare would pay dearly for this decision.

Admiring the changing seascapes, the different types of fish and seabirds, and enjoying wide-ranging conversations, Johnstone and

Hoare were rarely bored. They discussed books, the restaurants they would visit on their return, or the holiday home in France that Johnstone would buy with money from their story. At times Johnstone also pondered on the distant but comforting thought of finally finding a girl and settling down. Hoare took great interest in the shoal that followed *Puffin*, recognizing and naming the small fish by their markings. But their good spirits were frustrated by *Puffin*'s slow progress; after almost a hundred days at sea they were still only halfway across the Atlantic.

Johnstone's log showed that over the last six weeks their daily distance had fallen from over fifty miles to less than fifteen. This confounded the pair, whose charts showed only favourable currents. The reality is that, unlike the chart's illustrations, the currents of the Gulf Stream are far from uniform and, especially at the fringes, often move in the opposite direction to the stream as a whole. This fact had somehow escaped Johnstone during his research, but he rightly began to suspect the existence of powerful, unmarked currents, pushing them back the way they had come.

On the morning of 3 September, Johnstone spotted a passenger liner, but the rain was too heavy to imagine that they might be seen. As the wind grew from the north-west it became impossible to row and he spent the afternoon drinking coffee and watching the birds flying around the boat, noting their description and style of flight in his diary. High overhead he saw planes flying. *Puffin* had been at sea for 106 days and, now quite at home in this environment, it was hard to remember living any other way. Johnstone was enjoying a peace of mind at sea that had long evaded him on dry land. Perhaps rowing across the Atlantic would finally prove Johnstone's mettle to the world. Perhaps he would prove it to himself. As day passed to night the wind became a gale, and then a hurricane.

That same morning, now 1,200 miles north-east of *Puffin*, Ridgway and Blyth spotted land. After ninety-one days at sea they had arrived off the coast of Ireland. Ridgway knew that landfall was likely to be the most dangerous part of their journey and a premonition the previous week had convinced him that they would face a cliff landing. He believed that their chances of survival were slim, and shared this openly with Blyth. Blyth couldn't understand how Ridgway could have already accepted that they were unlikely to survive the landing but, to avoid a morbid discussion, helped him to add buoyancy to their film and log books so that these items might still be found even if the boat was dashed to pieces on the rocks.

For the rest of the day, Ridgway and Blyth rowed into worsening weather. By early afternoon they could make out the coastline in detail and saw only sheer cliff face. It seemed as if Ridgway's premonition would come true and, with the wind now approaching gale force, they started making ready for a cliff landing. But as the light failed and they neared the cliffs, *Rosie* was spotted by the lighthouse keeper, who called the Aran Coast Guard. Soon a lifeboat had pulled alongside them, but by now *Rosie* was out of the wind in the lee of the island and Ridgway and Blyth were determined to make landfall without assistance.

'Ignore them and keep rowing,' Blyth instructed, and for a while the pair pressed on, while the lifeboat circled them.

Having been completely consumed by their single goal, Ridgway and Blyth found it hard to accept that the crossing was finally over. They stared at the floor while they rowed, trying to avoid the lifeboat crew's anxious gaze. Eventually Ridgway convinced Blyth that they had accomplished what they had set out to do. The Atlantic had been crossed. Breaking the stand-off, they accepted a rope, thanked the lifeboat crew for their help and, with *Rosie* in tow, made landfall at Kilronan, before an assembled crowd of locals. Their first words on stepping ashore were to ask after Johnstone and Hoare. *Puffin*, they were told, was still at sea.

Two weeks later, *Puffin*'s upturned hull was found in the mid-Atlantic. There was no sign of the crew. When the vessel was later recovered, Johnstone's diaries were found on board. The last entry in them was dated 3 September, the same night that Ridgway and Blyth had landed. *Puffin* had been hit by Hurricane Faith, which overwhelmed the little rowing boat, sending David Johnstone and his friend John Hoare to the bottom of the sea.

4.

Frustration

Date: 18 November 2009
Location: San Sebastián de la Gomera, Canary Islands

'Hi, I'm Peter.'

We knew his name already. The film of Peter van Kets and Bill Godfrey's victory in the 2007 Atlantic Rowing Race had been on the big screen the previous night in the Blue Marlin. Pete was back to try for the solo trophy and, as the only competitor with a successful crossing under his belt, most people in the race camp fancied his chances. A professional adventurer, Pete was South Africa's grizzled answer to James Cracknell.

Shaking our hands, he fixed us with a stare and a wide grin.

'So, you guys married? Family men?'

'No.'

'Well, I tell you what, guys, it's been difficult leaving Kim and my baby Hannah behind . . .'

It wasn't the opening line that I had expected. There was silence for a moment as we sized up the wiry, weathered character standing in front of us. He continued to nod and grin in a way that seemed slightly involuntary.

'So, how you guys feeling about the race?' he asked.

'It's so exciting just to be here,' I said. 'We just can't wait to have scrutineering out the way and finally get out on the water.'

This raised a quiet chuckle. 'Oh, you'll get plenty of time on the water. Don't worry about that.'

Pete spoke distractedly. While the rest of us enjoyed the Canarian sunshine with only a vague, glorified idea of what our lives were about to become, Pete knew exactly what he had signed up for. Part of him was already out there, suffering on the ocean.

'What's it like out there, Peter?' Jimmy asked, nodding out beyond the marina.

'You know what?' Pete was still staring, nodding and grinning at us. 'It's terrifying. It's bloody terrifying out there.'

With this he gave a short laugh, slapped Jimmy on the back, and walked off towards the Woodvale office.

'That was reassuring . . .' I offered as we watched Pete walk away.

Pete was a commanding figure in the camp. His super-lightweight carbon-fibre vessel, *Nyamezela*, incorporated the lessons that he had learnt in the last race and some of the key fittings, including the sliding seat, were custom made. Pete had also pared down his equipment to a minimum, in contrast to many competitors, Jimmy and myself included, who took a couple of spares of everything, 'just in case'.

Pete's main rival amongst the seven solo competitors was Charlie Pitcher, rowing in *Insure & Go*. Charlie wouldn't be drawn to say that he was rowing to win, but with a yacht racing background and a big-budget campaign to match Pete's, everyone saw him as a serious contender. Charlie had a cool, urbane air about him and in the evenings could often be found on the deck of one of the yachts in the marina, sharing a sailing story over a drink. Like *Nyamezela*, *Insure & Go* was immaculately fitted out; everything had been thought of, right down to pencil holders and a well moulded into the deck for a life-raft canister. By contrast, I had threatened to cut a section out of *Spirit of Montanaro*'s gunwale to make a space for our life-raft bag. The rules stipulated that this had to be kept on deck, and in despair at ever finding room for it, I had gone to find the hacksaw. Fortunately, Jimmy had talked me down.

Discussion about the solo competition always came back to *Insure & Go*'s unusual design. Charlie had approached Phil Morrison, whose original design had been the standard for ocean rowing boats since the first 1997 race, and given him a free hand to come up with something completely different. The result looked back-to-front, top-heavy and comically short, with a draught of around eight inches, which was shallow even for an ocean rowing boat. One result of this design was that *Insure & Go* was the lightest vessel in the fleet by a significant margin; while most needed four men to push them down to the harbour for launching, I watched Charlie casually tip his trailer with one hand and stroll down the road, pulling the little boat behind him. The main talking point was the size and shape of the bow cabin, which looked like the nose cone of a jumbo jet and, given a decent tailwind, would act like a sail. Ocean rowing boats had typically been designed to minimize the effect of the wind, but a few rough calculations suggested that, in reasonable conditions, *Insure & Go*'s bow cabin would generate the thrust of a second rower. Of course, in bad conditions Charlie had a good chance of washing up on a beach in West Africa. Whatever the outcome, *Insure & Go* was generating a lot of debate.

After years of planning it was a relief to be in the Canary Islands, and to feel that our adventure was finally about to start. On our last weekend in London, our girlfriends had thrown a surprise farewell party at the Strongrooms in Shoreditch, where everyone took turns in the recording studio above the bar to put together messages and accompanying playlists for our iPods. There were sixty days' worth of recordings in all and, confident of a fast crossing, we joked that we'd have plenty of them left for the flight home.

We had flown from Gatwick to Tenerife and then hopped on the ferry to the island of La Gomera, from where the race would start. On the ferry we met Rob Casserley and Stu Burbridge, GPs working in Devon, who were rowing *Ocean Summit*. Both had spent time as expedition doctors; Rob most recently on Sir Ranulph Fiennes's Everest ascent. It had been Sir Ranulph's first successful ascent of the mountain and Rob's fifth. Stu was the stockier, quieter and more intense of the pair, his head closely shaved, in contrast to Rob's blond mane. The name *Ocean Summit* came from their plan to follow up the ocean row with an Everest summit.

Stepping off the ferry, the muggy November night was filled with anticipation and just outside of the terminal gates we came upon the Woodvale camp; a car park in which the thirty-strong 2009/10 fleet was lined up. Jimmy and I ran amongst the boats in excitement, examining how the other competitors had constructed their sliding seat and steering mechanisms, and solved the other technical problems that we had spent weeks agonizing over. Afterwards we sat alone in a café on the square eating tapas. We couldn't quite believe we had arrived. The town was quiet that night, but it would not be for much longer.

The following morning we descended into the camp, which was alive with the excited chatter of introductions being made over the buzz of power tools. Jimmy and I sized up the other crews; we had trained hard and were confident of our rowing abilities, but we were a light crew and we knew that *Spirit of Montanaro* was a heavy boat. We set about working out what the hell to do with our life raft, and fitting the other remaining bits of mandatory equipment to the boat. We had a pair of diving knives for dealing with shark attacks, and a pair of axes in case one of us became trapped inside the cabin during a capsize. We popped round to the other boats through the day to borrow tools and ask for advice; the atmosphere in the camp was fantastic – we were all in this together.

At the end of the day the rowers moved to the corner of the town square occupied by the Blue Marlin, where beer carried the day's spirited discussions on into the night. As the crowd thinned out I moved to the end of the bar to speak to Simon Chalk, whom I had spotted earlier in the evening, fag hanging from the corner of his mouth, performing his party trick of balancing a pint of beer on his large belly. Although we had never met, when I introduced myself it was clear that he already knew a little about Jimmy and me, and he gently teased us about our heavy boat. I liked him.

Simon had his first taste of adventure in 1994 when he took part in the BT Global Challenge, a round-the-world yacht race organized by Chay Blyth. Forty-six days spent crossing the Southern Ocean left Simon with a hunger for more and in 1997 he entered the first ever Atlantic Rowing Race, a biennial event set up by Chay in which competitors raced from the Canary Islands to the West Indies. Simon went on to make four further crossings, including a solo row across the Indian Ocean. In 2004, he bought the rights to the Atlantic Rowing Race, which he now ran under the name Woodvale.

With the race due to start on 6 December, we had two weeks of final checks and sea trials. Every team had to go through pre-race scrutineering, in which the organizers ensured that all the required equipment was fitted, working and of the right specification. Although we still had a few things to finish off, we decided that the best way to highlight anything we'd missed was to take our scrutineering as soon as possible. The process started badly and got worse. The key issue was that most of our electronic equipment, which had come with the boat, was not up to race specification and would need to be replaced. None of the kit we needed was available on the island; we would have to get it shipped over from Tenerife or the UK. Jimmy carefully noted each point and our to-do list covered two sheets of paper. Two weeks had seemed like a lot of time to get ready, but now we really had our work cut out.

At the end of the first week we pushed *Spirit of Montanaro* from the Woodvale camp across the road to the quayside, where we waited for a giant forklift truck to lower her into the marina. Just ahead of us in the queue were Phil Pring, a divemaster, and Skippy Cummings, a boat builder, both from Penzance. The pair had built *Vision of Cornwall* from a plywood kit, which had taken the best part of two years. Both were regular competitors in the World Pilot Gig Championships, and Skippy had spent a number of years sailing tall ships. They were one of the most experienced crews in the race, but also modest and unassuming.

The first we heard of a delay to the race start was a rumour about safety flares. Along with the other crews, we had given our flares to the race organizers when we had dropped our boat off at Tilbury Docks in October. Around the Blue Marlin there was now talk that these flares had been lost in transit. A week before the race was due to start, Simon Chalk held a meeting at the race office to explain the situation. Confusion over paperwork meant that the flares had not been cleared for unloading in Tenerife and as a result the start would be delayed by three days, while we waited for replacements to arrive.

On the afternoon the race was due to have started, Simon organized the La Gomera Cup, a short sprint out of the harbour and around a few markers. It was a chance to let off steam and give the boats and equipment a good thrashing on the sea. It had been organized as a way to keep spirits up, but the race also brought to light improvements that needed to be made. Some crews had the gearing on their foot-steering systems set badly and found it almost impossible to change direction. One of our oar gates fell off, twice. The stars of the afternoon were Phil and Skippy, who appeared on the start line flying the Jolly Roger, with underpants taped to their heads, one rowing while the other launched water bombs. Despite their efforts not to be competitive, they crossed the line in fifth place. Jimmy and I got off to a slow start, but battled hard and were pleased to finish in second.

The La Gomera Cup had fired us up for the crossing, but as the new departure date approached, we remained stranded; conditions in the Atlantic had started to turn. The weather charts that we now obsessed over showed that the semi-permanent area of high pressure over the Azores was weakening, allowing stormy low-pressure systems that were moving eastward across the North Atlantic to track further to the south. The unusual weather pattern that now drove south-westerly winds across our route was also bringing an exceptionally cold winter to north-west Europe.

At times during that December we sat in the town square, looking out to sea, drinking café con leche and enjoying the clear skies and gentle breeze. It was hard to imagine that, further off in the ocean, storms were raging. At other times the lashing rain and rising swell would keep us stuck in the marina for days on end, unable to train. On these days Jimmy would sometimes run up the hill to the statue of Christ on the edge of town. I would find a quiet spot to read, or walk down to the small internet café to email updates to our supporters and have long chats with Alice and my parents.

We tried to stay focused, to structure our day around training, eating and working on the boat. Occasionally we would join the group that congregated nightly at the Blue Marlin, but as the weeks drew on most people were running out of money to spend on beer.

After the initial rush to get things finished on the boat, the weeks of delay left Jimmy and me looking for things to do. At least that's how I felt. We tweaked this and modified that. We adjusted the steering lines and replaced nickel-plated screws with stainless-steel ones. We went through our toolkit and our boxes of spares. We went through them again, and again. We took things off the boat to save weight and added other things that we thought might come in handy. We changed the blade heights and shifted ballast around the compartments to perfect our balance. Jimmy threw himself into these small jobs as methodically as we had tackled the large ones.

We had worked closely together for three years while we prepared for the crossing, but it was only now that we were living in each other's pockets that important differences became apparent. While Jimmy was always thorough and meticulous, I lived by the 80/20 rule; the principle that 80 per cent of the result is achieved through the first 20 per cent of the work. Painfully susceptible to boredom, I was always looking for shortcuts.

One morning Jimmy took the wooden slats out of the footwell and started replacing the screws that held them together. These slats allowed us to stand in the footwell but avoid the sludge that built up on the bottom. Without an electric screwdriver, replacing the old screws was slow work. When I had finished the job I was working on, I sat for a moment watching Jimmy's quiet persistence.

'What are you doing Jim?'

'Replacing these old screws with new stainless-steel ones.'

'I don't think that's really necessary.'

'I want to make sure everything's right.'

'Sure, but I don't think it's really necessary to replace those screws. It's not going to make any difference. It's just a bit of *wood* in the *footwell*.'

Focused on the slats, Jimmy replied without responding to the frustration in my voice. 'Yes, but I just want to make sure everything's right.'

It was trivial, but threw our perspectives into relief. Jimmy's approach was to identify things that might go wrong and put solutions in place to prevent them from happening. I felt that many of the things that might go wrong probably never would, and although Jimmy's attitude was clearly the prudent one, the diminishing returns on the time we now put into the boat frustrated me. I found these small jobs tedious and as the delay lengthened I became increasingly irritated and bored, and felt trapped on the island.

I was keen to get going. We all were.

One morning Jimmy and I caught a bus to the resort where his parents were staying. Winding round the cliffside roads we chatted about his employers, who were increasingly anxious at the extent of our delay. If it lasted much longer, Jimmy might not have a job to go back to. I didn't talk too much about my own position. The previous week, while we were working on the boat, Charles Montanaro had rung. He apologized for interrupting our preparations and cut to it quickly – a position had become available, the opportunity to manage a flagship fund – would I accept a new role when I got back?

Just being out of the camp made us both feel more relaxed and I took the chance to explain to Jimmy that I was considering going back to London for a few days. My growing frustration with our indeterminate stay meant that I no longer felt mentally prepared for the crossing. I wanted to see Alice and I needed to clear my head. Jimmy listened, and although he didn't feel the same way as I did, he seemed to understand. At the resort we chatted with Jimmy's parents over lunch and spent the afternoon enjoying the pool and the gardens. It was great to spend a day away from the tension of the race camp.

For the most part we were on forty-eight hours' notice to leave, but as a longer period of low pressure developed out in the Atlantic, so too did the opportunity to take some time away from La Gomera. This was my chance. At an evening 'crisis' meeting in the race office we came together as a fleet to discuss how we should deal with the delay. Simon Chalk suggested rescheduling the race start for the beginning of the New Year, which would allow us all to return home for Christmas. Some were strongly opposed to this. They wanted to know that we could all be ready at a moment's notice should the weather start to clear. Anyone who left the island would jeopardize this. Simon kept himself out of the discussion, but between the rowers, the debate went round in circles, with each side getting more frustrated. Jimmy said a few words; I remained silent. The crisis meeting ended without conclusion, but before it did a poll was called. Of the fifty-nine people in the room, how many actually wanted to leave the island? I raised my hand, along with six others. It felt quite uncomfortable in the room as the crowd picked the seven of us out.

As we left the meeting Jimmy made it clear that he wasn't happy with my decision. He felt that the weather over the following week could get bad enough to ground flights leaving the UK, which would prevent me from getting back in time for the race start. If the race began and I was still in the UK, he was prepared to go solo. I would take the risk. I was suffocating. I had to get off the island.

I left two days later on the same ferry as Jimmy's parents. As the trimaran pulled off the pontoon and into the channel I stood in the stern, looking back at the marina, the apartments, the shop and the town square that had been my world for the last month. The familiar features receded into an indistinct blur. I felt like a deserter and suddenly wished I wasn't leaving. Jimmy's dad appeared beside me and put his hand on my shoulder. 'Don't worry. You'll see it all again soon enough.'

I spent my few stolen days back in London in a listless limbo. I was with my friends and loved ones but also separated from them by dues of time and pain that I was still to pay. An ocean that I had not yet crossed stood between me and my life, and I would not have that life back until we finished what we had set out to do.

In the end almost all of the competitors left the island. Some were gone for only a few days, others went back to work for a week, most stayed at home for Christmas and returned on New Year's Eve. Of those who had left, Jimmy and I were the first to return to La Gomera. Together with the eight rowers who had stayed on the island, we spent a subdued Christmas Day in the Blue Marlin, eating paella and the mince pies that Jimmy and I had brought back.

At the morning meeting a couple of days later there was a wave of relief when the race start was finally confirmed for 4 January 2010. But it was also strange to think that this extended 'holiday' was now coming to an end. We were getting used to our new home and friendly with the locals. The town's women's group had even sewn Jimmy a Marseilles flag, which we tied to the radio antenna in hon-our of his mother's roots in Pytheas's home town.

The following day was New Year's Eve and we decided to hire a car and drive up into the mountains with Phil and Skippy. Here in the ancient laurel forest, a mixture of alpine and tropical flora, the air was cool and heavy with moisture. It was a world away from the arid landscape along the coast. Jimmy revved the little car up and down the switchbacks which wound around the mountainside, taking us down to the coast on the north side of the island through vineyards that ran seamlessly into banana plantations.

Before heading back to La Gomera we stopped in Vallehermoso. After parking the car, we walked along the footpath up to the ghostly, deserted Castillo del Mar. Unlike San Sebastián's sheltered bay, this stretch of coastline was exposed to the naked force of the Atlantic. To the right of the path, breakers crashed against the coastal defences. As we approached the castle, we came across the remains of a fishing boat and its engine block beside the path, a tangle of shattered wood and twisted metal. We wondered how it had come to rest in this unlikely spot. Then a shower of spray rained down over the path and I realized that the boat had been thrown over the concrete defences during a storm. I tried to imagine what the sea must have been like. I pictured a stormy night and a pair of fishermen unable to keep their boat off the shore.

In the evening we joined the rest of the camp in the Blue Marlin to see in the New Year. As the clock struck twelve, flares erupted into the night sky. In shorts and flip-flops, intoxicated on cheap beer and the knowledge that our time on dry land was coming to an end, rowers cavorted around the town square and clambered onto the stage with the band, generally making a nuisance of ourselves. As our ragged group waned, the locals, formally dressed, started arriving in packed cars from all over the island. Pop music gave way to punchy Latin rhythms and the party proper began. Even as the sun's painful light rose through the curtains above my bed, dancing continued in the square below.

On our last night Phil and Skippy joined us for dinner in the small steak house which had become our favourite haunt, before we turned in for an early night. Although we knew this would be our last night in a warm, dry bed for some time, we buzzed with excitement and found it hard to sleep; the strain of the last six weeks had fallen away.

In the morning, after having breakfast and stocking up on fresh fruit, Jimmy and I walked along the pontoons, wishing each crew good luck.

We stopped at *Nyamezela* and Jimmy called over.

'Peter. As World Champion, what advice would you give two novices like us?'

Pete pulled his head out of the cabin and grinned at us. 'World Champion. Ha! Ha!'

'Really. What advice would you give us?'

Pete nodded at us in silence for a moment. 'Just enjoy it guys, eh. Just enjoy it.'

I stepped off the pontoon and onto our boat, wondering when we would next enjoy dry land underfoot. We stowed the last of our belongings and synchronized our watches. I ate a baguette, trying to preserve its texture and flavour in my memory. Jimmy wasn't hungry; his mind was already focused on the start line.

One by one the boats did their radio checks and cast off for the last time. We bunched up in the sheltered water outside the marina, waiting for the start. We all knew it was ridiculous to jostle for a few metres of advantage on the start line of a 3,000-mile race from the Canary Islands to Antigua, but we couldn't help it. At 13:30, with a horn blast from the support yacht, we were off.

5

The Pirate and the Paratrooper, 1969

May we of Apollo 11 add our sincere congratulations to the many you have undoubtedly already received for your bold and courageous feat of rowing alone across the Atlantic. We who sail what President Kennedy once called *the new ocean of space* are pleased to pay our respects to the man who, single handedly, has conquered the still formidable ocean of water . . . Yours was the accomplishment of one resourceful individual, while ours depended upon the help of thousands of dedicated workers . . . As fellow explorers, we salute you on this great occasion.

Neil Armstrong and the astronauts of *Apollo 11*
19 July 1969[1]

Date: 12 July 2012
Location: Morar, Scotland

'Have more biscuits. Just, just . . .' Tom McClean waves encouragingly at the plate in front of me, '. . . just eat them all.'

I look at the plate and Tom looks at me. His wife, Jill, sits by the bay window, sewing.

Tom loses interest in the fate of the cookies, shifts in his chair and jumps back into the story.

'In the orphanage you didn't have a name, you had a number. My number was 81. We were on parade ten times a day and then there would be "jankers", which is to say work, if you just sort of looked the wrong way. Not quick enough and you'd be on report.'

Tom left Fegan's Home for Boys at fifteen, fell in with a bad crowd and had a brush with the law before bumping into an old friend who was wearing an army uniform.

'A mate of mine had joined the Paras and it's all a bit rough and tough. Life in the orphanage prepared me well for training in the Paras, and you get paid. Beer money. I thought, "I'll have some of that." I enjoyed it. I was in 3 Para, in the same platoon as Ridgway and Blyth. Ridgway was my officer. Anti-tank platoon.'

After six years in the Parachute Regiment, Tom went on selection for the Special Air Service and was one of a handful admitted from over a hundred hopefuls. Through his training in the SAS, Tom came to believe that he could deal with anything.

In the spring of 1966 he was fighting Indonesian communists in the jungles of Borneo.

'We'd have a landing zone, landing by helicopter. Two and a half weeks on patrol. We were in four-man patrols, sleeping in trees and eating monkeys, creeping around in twenty grid squares. So anyone in there is, sort of, dead. I enjoyed that.'

Meanwhile, back in Britain, Ridgway's plans to row across the Atlantic were coming together; Blyth was now on the crew and Bradford Boat Services had delivered their boat. Tom had no idea of the pair's plans until he found a copy of *The Times* amongst the supplies that had been parachuted into his team's drop-zone in the middle of the jungle. He opened it to a picture of his old platoon commander and sergeant. Poring over the article, the nature of what they were about to attempt gradually dawned on him.

'I thought, "Bloody hell, that sounds good, I wouldn't mind doing that."'

Tom was back from operations in time to help the pair put the finishing touches to *English Rose III*, and while Ridgway and Blyth were at sea he immersed himself in every update on their progress. After their return he started to think seriously about a solo attempt; it had never been done before but Tom knew he was up to it. He mentioned the idea to a couple of friends at the barracks in Hereford, who told him that he was crazy. Undeterred, he quietly started gathering information.

But his enquiries about charts and boats soon started to arouse suspicion and Major Dodds, his squadron commander at Hereford, summoned Tom to his office.

'Now then, McClean, what's all this business with charts?'

At that moment Tom made his decision.

'I want to row the Atlantic, sir.'

Major Dodds arranged for him to have an interview with the commanding officer, who in turn wrote to ask for approval from the Ministry of Defence.

In the meantime, Tom travelled up to Ridgway's newly established Adventure School in Ardmore to speak to his old platoon commander. Ridgway was full of useful information on preparation, seamanship and the conditions he could expect to find in the North Atlantic, but he didn't fancy Tom's chances.

'Quite honestly, Tom, I don't think one man could do it.'

Undeterred he went on to see Blyth in Portsmouth. The former platoon sergeant was more upbeat, giving him an 80 per cent chance of survival. Chay told Tom to tie a twenty-foot length of rope around his leg and attach it to the boat, so that when the boat returned he would come back with it. Back in Hereford, as he waited for permission to come through, he started to draw up a detailed plan and equipment list. Eventually a reply came from the MOD: the request had been approved.

As well as giving Tom time off, the army gave him free run of the carpenters' workshop at Hereford and a hundred twenty-four-hour ration packs. His savings went on a dory, similar to Ridgway and Blyth's, and delivered with a disclaimer from its builder, who thought Tom was crazy. He named her *Super Silver*. A local businessman paid for a number of items of bespoke equipment to be made, and Tesco supplied boxes of 'goodies' to supplement the army rations. At Blyth's suggestion Tom contacted a PR agent, who found companies willing to help with the rest of the equipment.

With preparations in full swing Tom received some unexpected news; he was not the only person planning a solo row across the Atlantic.

When John Fairfax learnt of Ridgway and Blyth's success, he knew that his time was running out. As a child he had read about Harbo and Samuelson's adventure, and dreamed of being the first person to row an ocean alone. In the autumn of 1966, Fairfax left his mother's home in Buenos Aires for London to find a sponsor for his solo ocean row. Although he had never been to Britain before, he was proud to be British and determined that his rowing boat would fly the Union Jack.

Born in Rome to a Bulgarian mother and an absent British father, his first taste of adventure had been in the Italian Boy Scouts. Fairfax fondly remembered learning to build fires and trap game, but at the age of nine his career ended abruptly after an argument with another boy prompted him to steal the Scoutmaster's pistol and empty a full clip into the side of the hut where the troop was sleeping.

'It was a miracle I didn't kill someone,' he said later.

The Scoutmaster grabbed the gun and slapped him. Fairfax responded by kicking him in the groin. As he later recalled, 'That made him really mad and he proceeded to kick the shit out of me.'[2]

Soon after this he moved with his mother to Argentina, where his yearning for adventure led him into the Amazon. He would spend months at a time living off what he could catch and using what he didn't eat to barter with the locals. At twenty-two he inherited $10,000 from a relative, took a ship to New York, bought a Chevrolet and drove across the country. A couple of months in the arms of a call girl left him penniless again. It was while hitch-hiking through Panama, on his way home to Argentina, that he met 'Captain Z', the pirate and smuggler who became a father figure and mentor.

Over the next four years he smuggled guns, tobacco and alcohol, learnt to free-dive and became the skipper of one of Captain Z's ships. During one of his trips the crew was ambushed by the authorities and although Fairfax managed to escape, first hiding out in a brothel and then lying low as a fisherman in Jamaica, his past was waiting for him when he returned to Panama. After surviving a gunfight he decided that it was time to return home. Back in Argentina there followed the only blot on an otherwise impeccable CV: a year managing a mink farm to appease his mother.

Arriving in London, he quickly found that no one would sponsor his project; Johnstone and Hoare had been lost at sea only a few months earlier and most people were convinced that Fairfax's plan was suicidal. Undeterred, he decided to finance the project through evenings spent at casino craps tables. Over the course of just a few nights Fairfax gambled away first his savings, then his rent.

No stranger to being broke, or to surviving on his wits, Fairfax placed an advertisement in the personal section of *The Times* asking for help with his project. Amongst the replies was a letter from a young lady, Sylvia Cook, who offered her free time as secretary for the project. This soon extended to letting Fairfax move into the living room of her shared flat and also supporting him so that his days could be spent training on the Serpentine and in the YMCA gym.

Fairfax also won over Uffa Fox, a renowned naval architect and the inventor of a ubiquitous design of self-righting lifeboat. In March 1967, a few months after being approached by Fairfax at the Earls Court Boat Show, Uffa sent him blueprints for the twenty-four-foot ocean rowing boat that Fairfax would name *Britannia*. She looked much like one of Uffa's lifeboats. Her innovative features included a deck raised above the waterline that sloped down to a series of slots, which made her self-bailing. Uffa also replaced the traditional fixed seat with a sliding seat, allowing the rower to work more efficiently. Both these features are now common to all modern ocean rowing boats.

With Sylvia's support, Uffa's blueprints, and sponsorship from a Yorkshire businessman, things began to take shape. Archie de Jong, the nutrition expert from whom David Johnstone had sought advice, supplied Fairfax with high-calorie, lightweight rations, along with the warning that he would very soon hate the sight of them. But Fairfax was relaxed about food; one of his heroes was Alain Bombard, the French doctor who in 1952 had drifted across the Atlantic in an inflatable life raft, surviving off only what he could catch, simply to prove that it could be done. Bombard's experience made Fairfax confident of supplementing his rations with fresh fish.

Britannia was completed in December 1968, six months before the start of the summer season for crossing the North Atlantic, but Fairfax was impatient to begin his row and, rather than wait, he chose an alternative route that would allow him to put to sea immediately. His planned route from Gran Canaria to Miami would involve rowing 4,500 miles, which was 1,500 miles further than Ridgway and Blyth's route from Cape Cod to Ireland. Following the Tropic of

Cancer across the ocean and through the Caribbean, Fairfax would avoid the freezing conditions of the North Atlantic, but it was important that he made land before the summer, when the hurricane season would begin.

On 20 January 1969 Fairfax waved goodbye to his mother and Sylvia Cook at the harbour of San Agustín on Gran Canaria. Four and a half thousand miles of ocean were now all that stood in the way of his childhood dream. As Fairfax rowed out of the harbour, he resolved that his next stop would be either Miami or the bottom of the sea.

Meanwhile, in the carpenters' workshop at Hereford, Tom McClean was working all hours to get *Super Silver* ready for the crossing. Much to his chagrin, he had found himself in a race with John Fairfax and with every day that passed, Tom knew that his dream of being the first man to row the Atlantic solo was slipping away. Each small delay caused great frustration.

Before *Super Silver* was ready for the ocean, a raised deck needed to be fitted. In the space under this deck Tom would store eighty gallons of fresh water, which doubled as ballast. Tom knew that Johnston and Hoare's failure to replenish their ballast had left *Puffin* vulnerable to capsize, and he planned to refill each two-gallon water bag with seawater as it was emptied. Next, two five-foot-long plywood buoyancy compartments were constructed, fore and aft, and filled with polystyrene. If *Super Silver* did capsize, the water ballast would twist downwards and the buoyancy compartments would twist upwards, causing her to self-right. Finally, at Ridgway and Blyth's advice, Tom built a plywood shelter over the stern of the boat, three feet long and just high enough for him to crouch beneath.

The slowest part of Ridgway and Blyth's journey had been the first fortnight, spent struggling out of Cape Cod and into the Gulf Stream, and this prompted Tom to pick a different departure point. Newfoundland was 1,000 miles north-east of Cape Cod, close to the Gulf Stream and, at just 2,000 miles from Ireland, offered the most direct route across the Atlantic. But this more northerly crossing came with its own difficulties; Tom risked frostbite in the sub-zero temperatures and would have to keep a constant watch for frozen pack ice.

By mid-April 1969 the modifications to *Super Silver* were complete, but Tom had one more thing to do before she could be shipped to Newfoundland. On her bow he painted the winged dagger of the SAS along with the regimental motto, 'Who Dares Wins'. She was now ready for the North Atlantic.

It was only his second day at sea, but Fairfax was already missing female company.

> How on earth had I got myself into this mess? I kicked *Britannia* to see if she had anything to say about it but there was no response . . . Most silly this going to sea without a girl . . . I sat down to a meal (and) a steaming cup of tea generously laced with brandy, to go with one of my best cigars . . .[3]

The weather was also against him; what had started as a light breeze from the south-west when he left the harbour of San Agustín was now a steady wind. Unable to row into it, he tried instead to point *Britannia* south, but he couldn't hold her on the bearing; whatever he tried, she would eventually turn beam-on to the weather. Faced with the option of rowing south-east or north-west, Fairfax chose the latter. At least it would keep him off the African coast.

Fairfax planned to supplement his diet with fish, but by Day 9, when the fresh food ran out, he still hadn't seen a single one. It was time to open the expedition rations; one spoonful was enough to pronounce his verdict: 'Archie's food is the most horrible thing I have ever had in my life. I just cannot imagine what I am going to think about it a month from now.'[4]

A further fortnight of south-westerlies left Fairfax in a state of despair. Each night at sea anchor he would lose all the hard-won ground he had rowed during the day. Washing up on the African coast was becoming a real possibility. Overcast skies meant that he'd not been able to take a fix on the sextant for six days, and the radio direction finder was not reassuring, placing *Britannia* somewhere in the middle of the Sahara.

But eventually Fairfax's luck started to change. First he speared a sea turtle, which provided a welcome change to his diet, then a few days later he spotted a ship. The Norwegian vessel was at anchor carrying out repairs when Fairfax rowed up alongside her and asked the captain if he could offer them a tow. To roars of laughter he was welcomed aboard *Skauborg*. A shower and breakfast were followed by beer and cigars. Fairfax was in high spirits until the captain told him that he was only eighty-three miles south-west of Gran Canaria. Since leaving San Agustín he had averaged less than five miles per day.

The captain tried to persuade him to abandon the row and accept a free passage to Buenos Aires; Fairfax would be home in a couple of weeks. He was sorely tempted, and as the *Skauborg* pulled away, sounding her horn in salute, he started to cry.

Four days after his emotional farewell with the *Skauborg*, the wind finally moved round to the east. Further rendezvous with passing ships alleviated the monotony of his dried expedition rations, as did the dorado, which were now gathering in a shoal around *Britannia*. No longer reliant on Archie's rations, he threw the most offensive items overboard.

As he pushed south, the days got hotter and Fairfax began to take a siesta each afternoon. One day, woken by the shrill ring of his alarm clock, but feeling less inspired than usual at the prospect of rowing, he threw the clock overboard. This cheered him up greatly, as did the decision to smoke a pipe with his afternoon tea instead of the usual cigarette.

As he stood with the kettle in one hand and a mug of strong tea in the other, a sudden bump knocked him to the deck. Peering over the gunwale, he came eye-to-eye with a shark. Fairfax had plenty of experience of sharks in the Caribbean and felt an intense hatred for them. He fed the animal a few scraps of dorado while he devised a plan to kill it.

The shark was too large for the speargun and he risked losing his knife if he used it as a harpoon. Then Fairfax had an idea. He teased the shark with a piece of fish tied to a length of rope, pulling the bait away each time the shark snapped at it. 'The tantalizing game kept me amused for nearly fifteen minutes – by the end of which the shark had begun to show signs of nervous breakdown.'[5]

Finally, he coaxed the animal through a noose, the other end of which was tied off on a cleat. Just as Fairfax tightened the noose above its dorsal fin, the shark went berserk, dragging *Britannia* through the water behind it. Once the shark had exhausted itself, Fairfax tied it off along the gunwale and slit its belly. To his surprise two dozen baby sharks spilt out. Fairfax killed them all.

The following morning Fairfax was in the sea, scraping barnacles off *Britannia*'s hull, and enjoying being out of the stifling heat. A cloud of crustacea fragments drifted with the current down into the depths. Suddenly he became aware of something rising up from the darkness. It was a mako shark, now twenty yards away and heading straight for him. He would never make it back onto the boat in time, so instead flattened himself along the hull and prepared to strike his knife on the shark's nose. At the last moment the shark turned, and Fairfax's blade plunged into its soft underside. With a burst the animal raced away, ripping the length of its belly along the knife, and leaving the water dark with blood.

When a reporter from the *Miami Herald* later challenged this account, Fairfax responded by going out in a boat, finding a shark, diving after the beast and killing it with his knife. He left the carcass at the newspaper's door.

Under an arrangement with the ITN news organization and the *Daily Sketch*, Fairfax had agreed to provide radio updates every five days. His Marconi radio had a 5,000-mile range, but before he could use it he needed to raise a twenty-foot hydraulic radio mast and start up the petrol generator. In any kind of wind the mast would whip around violently, then collapse. Fairfax would struggle again to raise the mast, try to contact the operator and eventually get put through to London. A five-minute update often wasted an afternoon and the whole operation became a source of dread. The relief of finishing one call was always tinged with anxiety about making the next.

By 11 March Fairfax had been at sea for fifty days. He was approaching Cape Verde, 1,000 miles south-west of Gran Canaria, but he had hoped to be already halfway across the Atlantic by now. Miami was still over 3,500 miles away and there was no longer any chance of making it there before the hurricane season. He started to think about giving up. To tackle the Caribbean during hurricane season would be suicide. The best course of action now would be to row due south to Cape Verde and attempt the crossing again the following year. During the days that followed, Fairfax mulled over his options. Eventually he turned to his old mentor.

What would Captain Z do?

'Never give up' had been the Captain's motto.

Fairfax had his answer.

It was another breathless day and, with noon approaching, Fairfax put on his mask and knife, ready to go overboard for his daily cooler. Just as his toes left the gunwale he spotted a large shape moving near the sea anchor. Fairfax leapt back on board and stared intently in the direction of the sea anchor. The large shape was a shark. He tugged on the sea anchor line, which stirred the animal's interest. Fairfax tugged the line again and to his surprise the shark swallowed the sea anchor whole, before spitting it out.

The shark was a large hammerhead, and it occurred to Fairfax that the beast's head would make a fine trophy. He began baiting the water with chunks of dried fish, but to his amusement the hammerhead was no match for the dorado which raced around it, snapping the morsels from its open jaws. The shark chased its tormentors around the boat, but was outmanoeuvred every time. Fairfax enjoyed the show, but was still no closer to claiming his souvenir. To coax the shark back he speared a dorado through the gills; the blood in the water immediately attracted the predator's attention. As he had done before, Fairfax caught the beast in a lasso and let it struggle to exhaustion before dragging it on board. He cut the hammerhead into chunks for the dorado, saving the head as his trophy.

The exertion of rowing for ten hours every day was taking its toll on Fairfax; *Britannia* was becoming harder to pull through the water. He needed to find a way to lighten her. A couple of days of strong easterlies prompted him to take a gamble. *Britannia* was 800 miles from the next shipping lane, where he could reasonably expect to resupply, and if the weather held up he would be there in a month. Saving a few weeks of expedition rations, he threw the rest overboard.

Throwing things overboard felt good and Fairfax looked around for anything else that might be superfluous. His eyes settled on the Marconi radio. Without the radio there would be no need for the heavy electric battery, or the petrol generator. There would be no more wasted afternoons trying to contact London. How much time *and* weight he would save! The temptation was strong, but a pang of conscience got the better of him.

From the moment he threw the rations overboard, conditions turned in Fairfax's favour and the wind from the east grew stronger. But soon he was in a full-blown storm. For three days it was impossible to row, waves crashed across the deck and anything that was not tied down was washed away. *Britannia's* self-draining slots worked exactly as Uffa had intended and Fairfax never had to bail. He lashed himself to the tiny bow shelter and waited for the weather to pass. He slept fitfully, dreaming that he was drowning.

With the wind on her stern, *Britannia's* rate of progress increased to forty miles per day and within three weeks he was in the shipping lanes. But Fairfax's mental and physical condition was fast deteriorating; he'd even managed to fall overboard while trying to land a dorado. He was also out of food, having failed to attract the attention of a single vessel since entering the shipping lane. Fairfax was now completely dependent on fishing for survival and to compound matters he was running out of pipe tobacco.

On 23 April, after ninety-three days at sea, Fairfax heard on the BBC World Service that Robin Knox-Johnston had won the Golden Globe Race by completing the first non-stop solo circumnavigation of the world in a sailing boat. Amongst the other eight competitors were Ridgway and Blyth, who had both retired early on due to equipment failure.

Despite his blue mood, the sun-sights taken on the sextant confirmed that he was making good progress. *Britannia* was now halfway to Miami.

On 9 May 1969, Tom McClean boarded an RAF Comet bound for the Royal Canadian Air Force base at Goose Bay, Newfoundland. Flying past the tip of Greenland and over the Labrador Sea, ice filled the horizon in every direction. Tom thought about what he was about to attempt and about his rival, John Fairfax. From the reports that Tom had read, Fairfax was making relatively leisurely progress across the Atlantic, and after three months *Britannia* was still only halfway to Florida. There was still just enough time to beat him to the prize.

After landing in Goose Bay, he was transferred to his departure point in St John's and reunited with *Super Silver*. News travelled quickly around the small community and the people there helped him in any way they could. A local family, the Squires, 'adopted' Tom, giving him a place to stay, feeding him and, despite his reticence, taking him to church to pray.

Tom's days were spent down at the harbour, loading *Super Silver* with his kit and provisions, while the local dorymen offered advice about her trim and asked about his clothing and equipment.

'What about your hands?' one of them asked.

Tom showed the gloves that he had brought. The fisherman shook his head. Those would be no use in the freezing Labrador Sea, once they got wet Tom would be just as well without them. What Tom needed were the oiled wool mittens used by the Portuguese dorymen who came to St John's every year to fish off the Grand Banks. When the mittens got wet they simply wrung them out and they didn't lose their warmth. The fisherman returned later in the day; he had been to see the skipper of a Portuguese boat and bought Tom a pair.

On Friday evening Tom sat down to dinner with the Squires family. He had chosen the following day, Saturday 17 May, as his departure date. According to the weather forecast the ice pack was stationary, about 120 miles north of St John's, it was expected to be a clear day and the wind would be light. In the morning, after breakfast, his new family drove him down to the harbour, where a crowd had already gathered around *Super Silver*.

Tom said his goodbyes and climbed on board, with the sack of sandwiches and Thermos of tea that Mrs Squires had given him. He sat down and tried to settle his nerves by eating a banana. He looked at his watch and then at the faces of all the people lined up along the quayside. All that was left was to ask for someone to release the mooring lines. As he rowed out of the harbour he looked back at the faces. How many of them doubted that he would ever see land again?

Sixteen hundred miles south of St John's, Fairfax was coming to the end of his fourth month at sea. For Tom to cross the North Atlantic before *Britannia* reached Miami, he would need to make up over 1,000 miles. It was the kind of challenge that suited him.

On 21 May Fairfax celebrated his thirty-second birthday with a tin of raspberries and his last half-pipe of tobacco. He opened the tin to find that the raspberries were spoilt, and the tobacco was wet and wouldn't light. At least he still had the brandy.

Standing on deck with the bottle in his hand, Fairfax was composing an appropriate toast when a large breaker suddenly appeared on *Britannia*'s beam. He didn't have time to dive for safety and the wall of water carried him clean overboard. Spluttering to the surface, he swam back to the boat and clambered on board. Throughout all of this, Fairfax had kept his thumb pressed hard into the mouth of the bottle. Now he raised it cautiously to his lips. But the sea had found its way in and the brandy was undrinkable.

Fairfax struggled for a few days with a nasty gash where he had caught his foot when he was knocked off the boat. Being constantly damp meant that his injury healed slowly. He was now living entirely off fish and was so sick of it that he even wished he still had some of Archie's rations. On 30 May he finally attracted the attention of a ship.

The captain was not pleased to see Fairfax and stared in consternation at the list that he sent up.

'Shampoo? What in the name of God do you want shampoo for?'

'Why, Captain, to wash my hair of course.'

'Do you know, young fellow, that this ship is on charter and that every hour I lose will cost my company a thousand dollars?'

'How about some water?'

'To drink? Or to wash your hair with?'

Despite the captain's belligerent mood, he sent down everything that Fairfax asked for.

Amongst the supplies was a large quantity of cheese, butter, eggs and other perishables which Fairfax greedily feasted on. After surviving on a simple diet of fish and rice, his body reacted badly to the rich food. For days he lay in the boat, vomiting and feverish, too weak to row:

> As I was vomiting over the side, a shark came by and started swimming around *Britannia* in lazy circles. A tiger shark, looking very mean, and as I stared at it, an overpowering hate slowly began to boil up inside me and suddenly, screaming like a madman, I pulled out my knife and dived at it.[6]

Fortunately the shark took no interest in Fairfax and swam leisurely away, while he thrashed after it. The animal soon disappeared back into the depths, and when Fairfax had returned to his senses he had no idea where the boat was. Panic followed until, as he rose to the top of the swell, he spotted *Britannia* a couple of hundred yards away. If there had been a breath of wind she would simply have drifted away without him.

Back in St John's, Tom was doing his best to look confident, while a small flotilla of well-wishers looked on. Once he was through the breakwater, *Super Silver* was caught by the swell and became difficult to control. It was his first experience of rowing in the open sea and the onlookers exchanged alarmed glances. One by one the boats turned back until Tom was alone. He stopped rowing for a moment to watch the last of them disappear on the horizon. In the afternoon a naval frigate heading north on ice patrol gave *Super Silver* three blasts of its horn.

At 4 PM, Tom set down his oars for the day. He ate Mrs Squires's sandwiches and drank the Thermos of tea before throwing out the sea anchor and settling down for the night. As darkness fell a bitter northerly wind began to pick up.

The freezing Labrador Current flows south out of the Arctic, past St John's, and on to the Grand Banks where it meets the warmth of the Gulf Stream. The confluence of these warm and cold currents produces thick fog and some of the world's richest fishing grounds. Tom knew that while he was in the Labrador Current, the temperature would rarely rise above freezing and he would need to look out for icebergs. He hoped that by rowing due east in a current that was pulling him south, he would arrive at the Gulf Stream in the shortest possible time. But it was the same combination of extreme cold and unpredictable weather in this part of the Atlantic that had sent Howard Blackburn's dorymate, Tom Welch, to his frozen fate in 1883.

The temperature fell steadily through Tom's first few days at sea and the nights brought a thick frost. The wind was also picking up from the north, and by his third night *Super Silver* was being thrown around like flotsam. To clear the breakers that were emptying into the boat, Tom manned the bilge pump. As the night went on, the sea grew more ferocious. Crouched over the pumps, under the small shelter in the stern, in waves that seemed hell-bent on sinking him, he wondered what he would do if the icy water filled the boat more quickly than the pumps could shift it.

Dawn was a mixed blessing, for now he could watch the forty-foot waves as they rolled towards *Super Silver*. He felt utterly helpless. What could he do, except wedge himself into the bottom of the boat and wait for it to all be over? But Tom refused to accept his fate without a fight and took up the oars. After an hour of ineffective thrashing he accepted that it was a waste of energy, and more dangerous than simply hoping for the best. He curled up under the shelter for a meal of biscuits and curry paste and pondered over the picture of Sir Ernest Shackleton that was pinned to the ceiling: 'The Boss had been in the Antarctic for eighteen months, so my stint was nothing more than a weekend by comparison.'[7]

For two days and nights Tom sat, wrapped in his poncho, working the pumps. The sturdiness of the boat impressed him. If his fate lay at the bottom of the ocean, it would not be *Super Silver* that failed him. By the afternoon of his sixth day at sea, the winds had dropped enough for Tom to get back on the oars. He rowed on late into the night, happy that he had survived his first test.

The following morning, sat under the shelter, Tom breakfasted on tea and tinned sardines and watched the snow falling. The wind had now swung around to the east – it was pushing him straight back to Newfoundland. There was nothing he could do but throw out the sea anchor and hope that the westerly winds shown on his chart would appear.

The freezing temperatures were taking their toll. Tom had been trying to ignore the pain in his feet, but eventually he would have to take off his boots and find out what damage had been caused by the wet and the cold. His face was tender from exposure and the skin around his nose was cracked and peeling. Above all, he just felt bitterly *cold*. Sitting in his wet sleeping bag didn't help and there was only enough gas and water for so many warm drinks.

Tom woke on the morning of his tenth day at sea to very different conditions from those of the night before. The temperature had risen to 10°C and the wind was now from the north-west. He peeled the boots from his swollen feet to find a soggy mess of greyish, peeling skin. There was no feeling below the ankle and above it only an intense burning pain. He needed to restore the circulation and keep his feet warm and dry. Tom pulled on three pairs of oiled wool socks. The boots wouldn't fit again anytime soon, so instead he wrapped his feet in thick plastic food bags. The arrangement would work for now, but he needed to get out of the Labrador Current before he lost his feet.

Listening in to broadcasts between nearby fishing vessels and the Coast Guard allowed Tom to estimate that *Super Silver* was now 200 miles south of St John's. To escape the Labrador Current he would have to row another 200 miles east, to the confluence with the Gulf Stream.

Tom had now been at sea for three weeks and the weather was taking another turn for the worse. The wind had been picking up through the day and by sunset it was accompanied by heavy rain and the crack of thunder and lightning. Tom lashed everything firmly to the deck and wedged himself under the shelter, clutching the pump handles. He could feel *Super Silver*, now seeming smaller and more vulnerable than ever, being tossed into the air by the charging breakers. In his shelter Tom spent the night kneeling over the pumps, desperately trying to bail fast enough to keep the boat from sinking entirely.

Throughout the night there was a constant level of water in Silver which, I am sure, I never managed to get below a foot deep. I just had to lie in it and fight for survival in a world that had gone stark, staring crazy.[8]

Although he had only ever been a reluctant churchgoer, Tom found himself praying, desperately hoping that he was not alone, that something or someone was watching out for him.

He had expected that the storm would last for days, but by morning it had blown over. He emerged from the shelter, exhausted, bruised and happy to be alive. With a cup of hot tea in his hands, Tom started singing; it was little more than a tuneless, rasping mumble, but that didn't matter, he just needed to show that there was still fight left in him. After breakfast he set about tidying up the boat. The sleeping bag went out to dry and the last six inches of water was pumped out of the footwell. He stopped for a moment and cast his eye out across the horizon. There, in the distance, was a ship. Suddenly his head was full of thoughts of fresh food, a hot shower and a dry bed. He had always planned to complete this crossing without any assistance. Even Ridgway and Blyth had not managed that; they had accepted food from the *Haustellum* during their tenth week at sea. But, Tom wondered, what if this ship were to stop and the skipper invite him on board. Would he have the willpower to say no? He had his doubts, and was relieved when the ship disappeared from view over the horizon.

Tom didn't have to wait long to be tested. He was preparing lunch later that day when the sound of a ship's bell rang out clearly from over his shoulder. He spun round to see a Portuguese fishing boat off his port side, twenty-five yards away. The trawler chugged slowly past, raising her net, and once the operation was complete she turned and pulled back alongside *Super Silver*.

The skipper imagined that Tom must be a shipwreck survivor, or perhaps a dory fisherman separated from his ship. But Tom explained that he was fine, and didn't need any food or water, only his position. The skipper called it out and Tom called back to confirm; 46°54'N, 47°24'W. After Tom assured him again that he didn't need any food or water, the *Rio Alfusqueiro* pulled away, with the crew lining the deck, giving him victory salutes. In response, Tom grabbed a bottle of rum from his shelter, gestured with it towards the crew, and took a swig, to cheers of approval.

It was a strange little ceremony, but what a difference it made to me. My weariness had vanished. I was once again as full of battle as a fighting cock. And now it was over I realized I had passed the test without even thinking about it.[9]

Alone again, the first thing Tom did was plot his position. Running a finger along the chart, he held his breath. It had been a week since his last plot. Had all his efforts gained him anything? Was he any closer to crossing the Atlantic? The truth was better than he had hoped. Not only had he recovered all the ground lost during the bad weather in his first week at sea, but Tom was now 350 miles east of St John's. He was in the Gulf Stream.

Fairfax was still unwell from his over-indulgence, and had been managing only a few hours of rowing each day. The previous afternoon a pod of dolphins had rounded up and eaten his shoal of fish. Only three of the hundred-odd dorado had survived the dolphin attack, and Fairfax had eaten one of the survivors for dinner. His supplies thus depleted, it was a relief to be spotted by the *Bay Ross*. The skipper of the Norwegian ship invited Fairfax on board and gave him tobacco and tinned food. Fairfax was disappointed when he learnt his position, but not surprised given what little rowing he had managed: during the last week he had covered less than a hundred miles. During the same period, Tom had rowed 350 miles, and was clawing back *Britannia*'s four-month lead. Although neither rower had any idea of the other's progress, it was becoming a close race.

It was another hot afternoon and Fairfax was dozing when the boom of a ship's horn brought him scrambling out on deck. He was greeted by a wall of steel, blocking out the horizon. It was an aircraft carrier, the USS *Saratoga*, en route to the Mediterranean. The huge ship glided slowly past, as the captain brought her to a halt. A Rib was lowered and came out to *Britannia* to see if he needed help. The Rib's skipper radioed a message back to the *Saratoga* and a helicopter was scrambled. It hovered low over *Britannia* and dropped a food package, which landed a few feet away. Fairfax was impressed by the extravagance of sending a helicopter out to resupply him. There was more food than he could find space for.

The final and most dangerous part of Fairfax's journey was about to begin and it was making him nervous. After more than five months at sea, Miami was only 600 miles away and *Britannia* was now passing through the arc of islands that mark the eastern edge of the Great Bahama Bank. Here, the shallow sea is littered with reefs, and Fairfax needed to keep his wits about him. It was also coming into hurricane season. On 25 June, his 156th day at sea, Fairfax noted in his log: 'Feeling a bit wary about the Hogsty Reefs. Got a sixth sense about this sort of thing, and now something tells me I'm heading straight for them.'[10]

The following day a large squall arrived soon after dawn, blacking out the horizon. For two hours the rain came in from all angles, and the air was thick with thunder and lightning. Invigorated by the raw fury all around him, Fairfax's first instinct was to throw everything he had into rowing through it. He itched to grab the oars, but instinct held him back. Something was telling him to sit this one out. As the squall cleared, Fairfax shot a sight through the cloud and checked *Britannia's* position on the chart. The Hogsty Reefs were dead ahead of him only a few miles away. If he had rowed through the storm he would have run straight onto them.

Fairfax's instinct had served him well, but it would be another month, perhaps more, of navigating these shallow seas, before he reached Miami.

Tom had been expecting the fog and today it had arrived. Visibility was down to fifteen yards. Condensation formed on *Super Silver* and on Tom's clothes, the drops running into one another and collecting in puddles on the canvas cover, and in the folds of his sailing suit. The sea was a flat calm. Only the sound of his oars slipping into the water disturbed the silence. If a boat were to emerge through the fog, the skipper would never see *Super Silver* in time. The thought of being smashed to pieces against the hull of a passing ship prompted Tom to raise the radar reflector. He studied the little piece of foil and hoped that it worked.

After his violent introduction to the North Atlantic over the last few weeks, Tom was unfamiliar with these new conditions, but the fog was far preferable to the intense cold of the Labrador Current, and the warmer weather was helping to bring his feet back to life.

Although they were still very swollen, the numbness had gone, replaced by more burning pain. Tom took this as good news, a sign that the circulation was returning.

Light westerly winds provided perfect rowing conditions and Tom made the most of them. Occasionally the sun would break through the fog and he would begin to quite enjoy himself. There were sixty cans of beer stored under the deck and on one sunny afternoon he treated himself to a drink. He planned to save the rest for the sweltering hot days that were to come. But Tom was to be disappointed, for the few days that he had just enjoyed would turn out to be the only good weather of the crossing. Soon enough he would be fighting for his life again.

On 17 June, Tom had been at sea for exactly one month. As he rowed into the late evening, the conditions became more difficult. The wind still blew from the west, but it was picking up. A storm was approaching. Tom had already skippered *Super Silver* through four North Atlantic storms, and he knew the drill. Wedging himself under the shelter, with his hands on the pumps, he prepared for a night of bailing. As the wind continued to build it became clear to Tom that these were the worst conditions he had faced so far.

Silver was being thrown around so much that it was absolutely no use trying to kneel at the pumps or even lie down between them. I had to jam myself in there with the aid of my folded life-raft and the stores and then pump, pump and bloody well pump again . . . I didn't kid myself that night. I was literally fighting for my life and I knew it.[11]

For two days *Super Silver* was caught in the chaos of the storm, and Tom was glued firmly to the pumps. Whenever he managed to clear the deck of water, a series of breakers would roll in and flood the boat again. At times it seemed that only the polystyrene-packed compartments in the bow and stern were keeping *Super Silver* from sinking completely. The skin on his hands became soft and tore, and the joints in his fingers stiffened up around the pump handles. For the second time that crossing, Tom prayed that he would live.

When the storm finally subsided the fog returned. It seemed a long time since he had felt the warmth of the sun on his face, and without a sun-sight he couldn't calculate *Super Silver*'s position. Tom was beginning to wonder exactly where he was; what if the Gulf Stream pushed him too far north, right past the coast of Ireland and Scotland, and into the Norwegian Sea?

Facing an easterly wind, Tom threw out the sea anchor, and he was resting in the shelter when the boom of a ship's foghorn rang out through the mist. For half an hour he peered into the fog, while the horn grew gradually louder, but there was no way of telling how far away the vessel was, or even which direction the sound was coming from. Suddenly the freighter loomed into view, 300 yards away. Tom's heart jumped, first at the welcome thought of having some human contact, and then with the realization that the vessel was coming directly at him. With *Super Silver* on sea anchor there was no way he could row out of the way. There was only one thing for it. He would have to abandon ship.

The thought of leaving *Silver* made me miserable as sin. It was like planning to leave a friend to the enemy. I dragged out my inflatable life-raft and stood ready to snap the seal which would automatically blow it into shape.[12]

At that moment the ship changed course, passing within 150 yards before disappearing again into the mist, leaving Tom shaking with nerves. A few minutes passed before the foghorn rang out again. This time Tom sprang into action, grabbing the flares and diving out of the shelter. The *Regina Oldendorff* had turned and was now 200 yards away and edging slowly towards him. At twenty yards the freighter came to a stop and in a thick German accent someone shouted down if he needed any help.

'Just my position, please.'

The man standing at the rail didn't understand, so Tom grabbed his chart from the shelter and waved it above his head.

The sailor told Tom he was at 49°45'N, 26°05'W.

Now the captain appeared on deck and Tom explained again that he was fine. After wishing him good luck, the captain returned to the ship's bridge and within a few moments the *Regina Oldendorff* was underway again, sliding back into the mist just as suddenly as she had appeared. Tom watched the riveted steel plates slip past with relief. When she was gone, he checked his position on the map. Not quite halfway, but *Super Silver* was on the right course.

While Fairfax had taken the first opportunity to throw his expedition food overboard, Tom kept everything that was left from his daily ration pack; carefully wrapped in polythene were spare sugar sachets, packets of biscuits and tubes of cheese. Tom checked his supplies regularly and rebalanced the weight around the compartments to keep *Super Silver* sitting trim in the water, refilling empty freshwater containers with seawater and re-stowing them to maintain the boat's ballast as he had planned.

Tom remembers the weeks that followed his meeting with the *Regina Oldendorff* as the hardest of the crossing. Battling with loneliness and exhaustion, he often thought of Ridgway and Blyth: 'I had Ridgway's book with me and I compare myself with him. I used to look at the book quite often and it helped an awful lot.'

As time passed, Tom felt his reactions slowing down and his thought processes becoming dull. With the 'mental plonk' came a feeling of apathy. He was becoming indifferent to what was happening around him. Tom knew that with this attitude he would never make it across the Atlantic and his solution was to put together a rigid routine. He would rise at 6 AM, take twenty minutes for breakfast, then row until 5 PM with a short break for lunch. At the beginning and end of each day he listened to the news bulletin on the radio. These broadcasts were the highlight of Tom's routine. If only for a short time each day, he needed this contact with the outside world to take his mind off the boredom and the loneliness.

Setting a routine was one thing, but overcoming the temptation to linger over lunch or reward a good day's rowing with an early finish required great self-discipline. Gradually, though, Tom gained the upper hand, and it seemed to him that he was becoming mentally sharper as a result.

John Fairfax was also a source of motivation. Tom wondered what Fairfax was up to, whether he was still somewhere out there on the ocean, or if he had made land and was now enjoying warm baths, cold beer and the company of pretty girls.

'My turn is coming,' Tom told himself.

By mid-July Tom had been enjoying a week of strong westerlies. Day and night the wind was blowing *Super Silver* towards home and he started to imagine what it would be like when he reached land. His feet had now recovered enough to pull the rubber boots back on. The feeling of being fully dressed seemed, in itself, a cause for celebration and helped to take Tom's mind off the salt-sores, blisters and boils that covered the rest of his body.

It was a perfect day for rowing and Tom took full advantage of it, stopping only for a quick lunch before getting back on the oars. Late in the afternoon he spotted a ship in the distance on his port side, heading east. He tried to attract her attention with a hand flare, without success. Next he fired off a radar flare, which exploded a shower of fine metallic dust high in the sky. This time the ship changed course and soon she was alongside *Super Silver*.

The *Hansa* was on its way to Deptford with a cargo of newsprint for Express Newspapers. Tom turned down the offer of food, water and a bath and, after noting his position, gave the skipper some film to pass on to his sponsor, the *Sunday Express*. Tom was told to keep clear of the ship's propellers as they started up again, and soon he was watching the *Hansa* disappear eastward over the horizon, in the direction of home.

From the co-ordinates the skipper had given him, Tom calculated that, after fifty-nine days at sea, he was now only 700 miles from Ireland. As happy as he was with *Super Silver*'s progress, the rendezvous left Tom feeling quite alone. He wanted to share his thoughts and feelings with someone. He wished that he'd asked the skipper whether Fairfax had landed yet, and he was interested in news of the *Apollo 11* moon mission. When *Hansa* had come up alongside, Tom had been only too eager for her to be underway again, but now that she was gone, he wished that the ship had stayed with him a little longer.

That evening Tom was settled in the shelter, tuning into the news, when the radio suddenly cut out. He tried changing the batteries and moving the aerial, then he retuned the set. Finally, he gave the set a thump, but it remained silent. The loss of his link to the outside world was another blow.

But it was difficult for Tom to feel down for too long; the westerly wind was still on his tail, and helping him, steadily, towards the finish. The vapour trails of jet aircraft in the sky overhead were a reminder that land was near. He wondered where the passengers were headed. Off to a sunny beach for their holidays, no doubt. Tom spent the day singing to himself, and humming when he ran out of words.

Tom was still singing on the evening of 17 July when the wind started to pick up. He could see that it would be another night on the pumps, but that didn't dampen his mood. By now, the odd North Atlantic storm was all part of the job, he thought.

In the early hours of the following morning, while the storm was at its most violent, *Super Silver* capsized. Tom felt the water rushing over him, filling his ears and nose, running into his clothes, and then he was submerged and tumbling from roof to floor, spinning around and around as if he was in a giant washing machine. He lost any sense of how long he was submerged for or how many times the boat turned. With his lungs burning, he tried to claw his way to the surface; he reached out and his hand struck the canvas shelter cover, but he couldn't shift it. The cover felt like it was weighed down with lead. Tom was fast running out of air and starting to panic. He felt around and grabbed the inflatable life raft, which was pinning down the edge of the canvas. Wrestling it aside, he pushed himself out on the deck. But Tom was still underwater. With a desperate lunge, he pushed his head up to the surface, and gulped in a lungful of air.

Tom gathered his bearings. He was standing on *Super Silver's* deck, but up to his waist in water. The boat was completely submerged, but still afloat, thanks to the polystyrene-packed compartments in the bow and stern.

The situation seemed hopeless. *Super Silver* was as good as sunk. Tom's battle with the North Atlantic was over. He started screaming into the storm in anger and disbelief. Why had fate dealt him this hand? Why had he been so stupid as to try to row the Atlantic *alone*? After a few minutes of venting his fury into the night's sky, he felt a little better, and resolved that he wasn't going to give up without a fight.

Tom put all of his weight on one gunwale, then the other, and slowly started to rock *Super Silver* from side to side. With each rock a gunwale broke the surface and while he rocked, Tom bailed furiously with the five-gallon bucket. For a long time it seemed that nothing was happening, but very gradually both gunwales rose to the water level. Now Tom knew that he was winning the battle. He sat down in the rowing seat and continued to work away with the five-gallon bucket. By dawn, there were only a few inches of water left in the bottom of the boat.

The sight of the first rays of sunlight prompted Tom to take stock of the situation. He had lived to see the new day.

'I still had food and water for a couple of weeks. *Silver* was still all in one piece, me too. What more did I need? What more could I ask?'[13]

For ten frustrating days Fairfax had gone absolutely nowhere. More infuriating still was that Miami was less than 200 miles away. What a stupid situation; he should have been there a week ago. He wrestled with the idea of throwing in the towel and asking for a tow. After rowing over 4,000 miles, had the last 200 defeated him?

The problems started on 5 July when he had confirmed with his sponsors, ITN and the *Daily Sketch,* that he would give an interview while at sea, so that they would have an exclusive before he landed in Miami. In principle, Fairfax had no problem with this arrangement, but he wanted to get it over with as soon as possible.

First, the reporter's boat broke down, then the pilot of their seaplane refused to land because of the conditions. This exasperated Fairfax because the sea had been like a mill-pond. Finally, on the afternoon of 10 July, the journalists arrived aboard the *Costa Grande,* and Fairfax spent the evening drinking wine, eating steak, enjoying good company and forgetting that he was still 200 miles from land. When the time came for the *Costa Grande* to leave, and for Fairfax to return to *Britannia,* he felt suddenly depressed. His defences were down. He was also drunk. He tried to row, but after falling off the boat, he gave up and crawled into the shelter to sleep it off.

In the morning, with a clearer head, Fairfax decided that the best thing would be to row due west. Miami was actually NNW of his position, but with the currents sweeping due north from the edge of the Great Bahama Bank, he needed to take care not to be carried right past Miami and up the Florida coast. But at the end of the day he made an alarming discovery. *Britannia* was now a few miles *south* of where she had been anchored. So much for the currents; Miami was still 200 miles away. Fairfax resolved that in the morning he would row due north. If he could find the currents, he would be in Miami in less than two days.

For the next four days Fairfax was pushed around in circles. Each day he took a sight, only to find, with growing disbelief, that he was no more than a couple of miles from his last position. And so it was on 15 July, ten days after he had dropped anchor on the edge of the bank to await the British media, that *Britannia* was back in exactly the same spot.

Fairfax was so close to his goal, but the events of the last ten days had broken his confidence. Success now seemed further away than ever, while, on the other side of the Atlantic, Tom McClean, doggedly pulling fifty-mile days, was fast approaching Ireland.

But the following day Fairfax woke to find that his luck had changed. Overnight a south-easterly wind had nudged him into the current and he was now within sight of the lighthouse at Elbow Cay, only 120 miles from Miami. During the day a small plane flew past and dropped half a dozen packages. He retrieved two of them, and inside one he found a note from Sylvia Cook saying that she hoped he enjoyed the bananas. Everything inside was smothered in a mess of exploded banana, but he didn't care, it was just wonderful to know that his loved ones were so near. On the night of 18 July, Fairfax saw a light haze on the horizon. It was the glow of a large city. Tomorrow he would land in Miami.

Early the following morning, fast asleep in the shelter, Fairfax was woken by a thick American accent.

'John! Hey, John, where are you?'

To hear someone calling his name seemed so strange that it took a moment to be sure he wasn't dreaming. Fairfax stuck his head out into the daylight to be greeted by two men on a small fishing boat.

One of them reached out to shake his hand.

'You crazy bastard! You rowed this thing across the Atlantic? You gotta be nuts. Six months? I gotta give it to you. You Limeys are nuts!'

There, less than three miles away, Miami lay stretched out before him. After 180 days at sea it was a wonderful sight. Throughout the morning, a flotilla of boats came out to join him, including the *Dragon Lady*, with Sylvia and his sponsors on board. Half a mile from the beach he pulled alongside and asked for a tow, but they refused. He would have to beach *Britannia* himself.

'Bloody stupid!' was Fairfax's reply.

'Eventually, I did row myself ashore, and that was the hardest, longest, most irritating half mile I had rowed in my life.'[14]

On 19 July 1969, at 1.45 PM local time, John Fairfax became the first man to row alone across an ocean.

The next morning, amongst the letters of congratulations from around the world, he picked out one in particular. 'As fellow explorers, we salute you on this great occasion.' It was signed by the astronauts of *Apollo 11*. That day, Neil Armstrong became the first person to walk on the moon.

One week later, Tom McClean arrived in Blacksod Bay, Co. Mayo. The landing was eventful, with a storm throwing *Super Silver* onto the rocks and Tom leaping out to safety. He was knocked off his feet, but managed to scramble to higher ground. Looking back, he saw the boat that had served him so loyally being pounded on the rocks. At any moment she would be smashed to pieces. He couldn't let that happen. Tom climbed back down into the churning water and put his shoulder to *Super Silver*'s hull. For an hour he braced himself between the boat and the rocks, while the breakers rolled over him. The storm began to blow itself out, and he seized his moment to climb back on board and pull on the oars with all his might. Dawn was breaking as he rowed around the headland to bring *Super Silver* ashore on the sandy sweep of a deserted Irish cove and complete the fastest single-handed Atlantic row.

Our conversation is interrupted by the whistle of the *Jacobite* as the steam locomotive makes its way up the West Highland Line from Fort William to Mallaig.

'Want to see the train? Want to see the train! Quick!'

I scramble to keep up as Tom sprints through the house and out into the back garden. He leaps onto the patio table and points towards a trail of steam that's disappearing behind the crest of the hill.

While we're outside, Tom suggests taking a look at the boat.

Super Silver is in the shed at the end of the garden. She's in perfect condition, but looks quite different from the photos I've seen. Tom explains the modifications that he made to her for his second ocean row in 1987, when he retook the record for the quickest solo Atlantic row by crossing in fifty-five days. Leaning against the wall is a piece of *Super Silver*'s original turtle-deck, painted with the SAS Regiment's winged dagger and motto.

Back in the house, where Jill is still sewing, our conversation moves on. We talk about the time in 1982 when he sailed across the North Atlantic in the shortest boat and how, on hearing that his record had been broken, he walked down to the beach with a chainsaw and cut another two feet off *Giltspur* to retake his record. He talks about the forty days that he spent living on an isolated pillar of rock in the North Atlantic called Rockall to claim it for the UK and, later, his plan to sled across the Antarctic.

'I was going to hire planes and parachute out, but the British Antarctic Survey Team did everything they could to stop me. I had all sorts of ideas. An *edible* sled. You can compress pemmican hard as wood, edible glue . . .'

Tom goes on. From anybody else a story about an edible sled would sound like a bizarre fantasy, but not Tom McClean.

'Why not!'

Tom has lived his life proving that anything is possible. Eventually we come back to ocean rowing.

'I'm seventy in February. I reckon I could be the oldest!'

Jill shoots a glance at Tom and cuts in. 'I don't think so!'

I laugh but Jill doesn't.

'Why not! Why not, Jilly! I could be the *slowest* and the oldest!'

I look at Jill, and then through the bay window behind her to the white crescent of Morar Bay. Beyond that, in the distance, is the island of Rum's mountainous silhouette.

'Did you ever meet John Fairfax?'

'I met him once at the Boat Show. He's not so open as me. He's careful with what he says. Not like me, I just say what's in my head.'

'I would like to have met him,' I say.

A few months earlier, while researching Tom McClean and John Fairfax, I'd received a phone call. After putting down the phone I had leant back in my chair and looked up through the row of small, square panes along the top of my study window. Above the rooftops and chimney stacks of the opposite terrace I could see a thin sliver of hazy blue sky, mottled with high cloud. Time passed. Beside me sat a notepad with a list of people I wanted to interview. I picked up a pencil and scored through one of them. Another fragile fragment of history had passed out of living memory.

6.

Excitement

Day 1
Date: 4 January 2010
Position: 28°06'N 17°08'W
2,548 nautical miles to Antigua

All around us, backs bent to the oars, are the fifty-seven people with whom we have shared the last six intense weeks of our lives. The fleet is charging out of the bay, every crew straining to be the first to taste the open sea. Spectators cheer and blast horns from gathered yachts. Simon Chalk darts around the fleet in a small RIB, shouting final words of encouragement to each crew.

Suddenly Peter van Kets appears on our port side and he's heading straight for us.

'HOLD IT UP! HOLD IT UP!'

There's a clash of oars, Jimmy reaches across and fends off *Nyamezela*, and in a moment we are back into our rhythm. Jimmy adjusts course and Pete quickly disappears. It never occurs to us that we might see him again before we reach dry land.

I'm in the stroke seat, setting the rhythm, and Jimmy is behind me in the bow seat, looking after the steering. After three years of preparation and training, and six weeks of waiting on La Gomera for the weather to clear, we are finally off and we can hardly believe it. We are rowing across the Atlantic Ocean, and there is nowhere else in the world that we would rather be.

'This is probably a good time to say thank you for inviting me to join you on this adventure.'

I turn round to Jimmy. 'I wouldn't want to do this with anybody else.'

Out in the channel the swell picks up, rolling and knocking the boat, occasionally sending a wave over the gunwale, leaving us soaking wet and happy.

The crews strike out on their chosen bearings and, more quickly than I had expected, there are no other boats to be seen. In their place are dolphins, which swim alongside us, their slick backs breaking the water to starboard, just beyond the tips of our blades. I watch a dolphin skip playfully underneath us and emerge on our port side and I try to imagine myself amongst them, in their world, that endless expanse beneath our slender hull. My thoughts are drawn into the thrilling and terrifying vastness of the ocean; there's a feeling of vertigo in the pit of my stomach. As the fat, red sun begins to dip below the horizon, our inquisitive escorts disappear and suddenly we are on our own in the dying light, on the open sea.

Jimmy takes a short break and emerges for the night shift with luminous yellow duct tape strapped round his ankles. Salt water has soaked into his trainers, softening up his feet and taking the skin off his heels. We are only six hours into the crossing.

At some point during our second day at sea we lose sight of land. I had often imagined this moment, watching the summit of Teide on the horizon, 3,700 metres high, reappearing smaller each time as we rise to the top of the swell, until it is swept completely from view. But in the event the loss of this visual anchor barely registers. Our emotional separation from land has been taking place for weeks already. From now on, the horizon will be a shifting panorama of sea, clouds, sun and stars; a source of wonder but also, at times, of terrible, crushing frustration.

We settle into our 'turbo' shift pattern of fifteen hours each per day, giving us six overlapping hours in which we row two-up. During the day we each row for three hours on and one hour off, with an early night shift of two-on/two-off, and a late-night shift of four-on/four-off to allow for a decent block of sleep. Simon Chalk has suggested that it should be possible to keep this level of momentum up for five days, after which we plan to settle down into the more common two-on/two-off shift pattern. In the excitement of the race start we have both been rowing for much of the last twenty-four hours and adrenalin has now given way to exhaustion. It has also become clear that Jimmy's feet cannot heal in these wet conditions and every time he takes to the oars the wounds, which are now opening on other parts of his feet, reopen and get a little worse. He has also lost his appetite.

As night falls on our second evening at sea the swell grows and moves round to the west. Clouds hide the stars and the night is black. Now and then a breaker can be heard in the distance. Then again a little closer. There is a moment of silence before the wave crashes over the gunwale and I wrestle to keep control of the oars. At 10 PM Jimmy emerges from the main cabin hatch for his next shift just in time to see me get washed off my seat by a breaker that swamps the deck. My hip cracks against the gunwale and I get wedged in the gap beneath it. Jimmy escapes the worst of it behind the hatch door and now re-emerges, looking a little hesitant.

'Has it been like this all shift?' he asks.

'Yeah, plenty of breakers, but that was the worst one. They're all coming on the beam.'

I prise myself off the deck and grab the handle of the stroke-side oar, which hangs unnaturally in the air. I imagine for a moment that the impact of the wave has broken the oar, or the gate, or both. To our relief, the sturdy Braca blades, with their carbon/glass composite shafts, are fine and the gate is just a little twisted. I retire to the cabin for a few hours of damp, restless sleep.

All too soon the alarm drags me back into our dark, wet, uncomfortable world. This is the worst bit – lying awake, watching the next shift tick closer, feeling the rock of the boat being hit by a breaker, seeing the water lash against the cabin hatch, and knowing that in a few minutes I will be out there. I pull on my cold, wet cycling shorts, zip up my Musto jacket and swing open the hatch. Jimmy is fighting to hold a southerly course against weather that wants to push us east. The steering is locked off, to turn the nose of the boat hard to starboard, and Jimmy drives on the oars with slow, steady strokes.

'How have conditions been?'

'Wind and swell from the west. Wind's really gusting. A couple of big breakers.'

'What's the bearing?' I ask.

'Holding it between 180 and 200.'

A breaker slams the side of the aft cabin and the boat jolts to port.

'Ready to change?'

'I'll spin her round.'

Jimmy pulls the steering line out of the cam cleat, and with a couple of strokes on the starboard oar we are running east with the weather, making the boat a lot more stable and putting us in a safer position for the changeover. He ships the oars and passes me his seat pad and water bottle, which I drop inside the cabin hatch, before passing him out mine.

'Ready?'

'Let's do it . . .'

Jimmy leans out of the rowing position and edges round one side of the boat while I move round the other, both of us balancing precariously with one foot on the gunwale, one on the deck. I grip Jimmy's shoulder as he passes. Changeover is the most dangerous part of the shift.

Before picking up the oars I strap a surfing leash around my ankle, connecting me to a fixed line that runs along the deck. Holding a southerly course means attacking the swell at forty-five degrees – the boat rocks violently and every now and then the oars are torn from my grip by the waves. It is impossible to get into a rhythm. This is the price we pay for fighting the conditions. We later learn that crews who ran with the weather were blown far enough east to see the lights of North Africa.

The physical shock of our new routine is taking its toll, as is the prospect of another two months of these relentless conditions. Our speed increases by a third when we row two-up but the lack of rest means we're gradually slowing down and on the afternoon of Day 4 we decide to switch to two-on/two-off. Seasickness means that Jimmy is only keeping down a few hundred calories a day, but this doesn't stop him coming out and attacking the oars at every shift. I'm worried about how much of this his body can take, and also about his heels, which scab and ooze while he rests and reopen during his shifts. I know that Jimmy will make no concessions; he will drive himself on through this punishment. For him it cannot be any other way.

Our Henderson hatches are taking on water. Six of these circular hatches provide access to the compartments under the deck which contain our freshwater ballast and most of our food. The volume of water is relatively small and the boat is not at risk, but soggy chocolate bars are bad for morale. I think that the leaking is due to the weather and the fact that these hatches weren't entirely watertight in the first place. But Jimmy thinks that the leaking is because I'm misthreading the hatches when I screw them back down and he calls me out on deck periodically to remind me of this.

A rich band of early morning sunshine caresses my face, cutting through the chill. The gentle trickle of water brings a feeling of peace and I savour the moment. I have no idea where I am, but I am quite happy. There is tightness in my hands and I stretch out my fingers, which brings a deep sensation of relief through the joints and along the tendons in my fingers. Now the feel of a wooden oar handle in my curled fingers rises from my memory and brings me suddenly back to reality. I am on a rowing boat, six days into crossing the Atlantic Ocean.

I sit up, reach forward into the netting by the main hatch where I keep a few items of personal kit, and pull out a foil pouch containing cold porridge, rehydrated the night before with not quite enough water. I barely notice the temperature or consistency, or even the taste; my attention is focused on the pleasure of having food in my mouth. With a large plastic spoon I devour breakfast in a few scoops, scraping around the corners of the pouch for every last scrap. I lick the spoon clean and put it back in the netting. My attention turns away from food and it dawns on me that things are unusually still this morning. There are no waves crashing against the cabin or tumbling over the deck, no rush of white water under the hull; in their place is the rhythmic tug of acceleration as Jimmy drives on the oars. I watch him through the perspex hatch door, pulling slow, powerful strokes. The headphone cable disappears into the neck of his Musto jacket. He is wearing Lycra shorts and trainers with the backs cut off, a modification which is giving his infected heels a chance to recover. Completing the outfit is a pair of shin-pads – the strapping on them helps to stop his feet slipping out of the back of the trainers.

I flick the handle and swing the main cabin hatch open. The air is cool and still.

'Morning, Jim.'

'Morning.'

'The sea – it's so flat, it's . . . it's like glass.'

In every direction for as far as the eye can see barely a ripple disturbs the surface, and suddenly it feels like the sea has accepted us. Our initiation is over.

'Could you pass me the camera?'

I lie back in the cabin and pull the red waterproof video camera out of the netting.

Jimmy does a short video clip before we change over. It's a clear, cloudless sky and in the cool of the morning it's a joy to be on the oars, filling my lungs with sea air. I've stopped trying to keep my clothes clean and dry and have taken to rowing naked instead. There is the challenge of ensuring my tackle is comfortably tucked away when moving up and down the slide, but otherwise I find it a significant improvement on wearing wet, dirty Lycra shorts, in terms of both comfort and hygiene. I've experimented with Sudocrem, an antiseptic lubricant, which Jimmy applies to his bum before each shift, but I don't like the greasy residue it leaves on my woollen seat cover, so instead I simply rub a little surgical spirits on my bum and crotch with a cotton pad once a day to keep them clean, and otherwise air them as much as possible.

The sun's only been up a few hours when Jimmy takes over from me, but already it's hot. We're a couple of hundred miles closer to the equator than we were a week ago. I lie in the cabin and avoid the sun glaring though the perspex hatch. The rear hatch is open and occasionally there is the slightest hint of a breeze. I'm dozing off when Jimmy shouts from deck.

'A whale! Adam, get the camera! Quick, quick, get the camera, it's a whale!' Jimmy's voice is crackling with excitement.

I grab the camera and pop my head up through the rear hatch.

'I saw a whale! An explosion in the distance, a big puff of vapour, over there.'

I scan the horizon with the camera and do my best Captain Ahab impression.

'There she blows! There she blows . . .' But the animal is gone.
'Was it a sperm whale?'

'It was *probably* Moby Dick.'

'I'll get the harpoon gun!'

The whale has made Jimmy's day and I am sorry to have missed
it. One day, all that will be left of our adventure will be a collection
of moments like this.

As we settle into the routine our time horizon shortens. Sitting in
the midst of an endless, changing seascape, the world reduces into
this present moment. Dry land and all the things I took for granted
in my life there have started slipping away, like the moments after
waking from a dream. *This* reality is lived shift by shift, through the
daily rituals of eating, sleeping and maintaining our bodies. And in
this simple, necessary pattern of existence a sense of freedom
begins to emerge.

A few moments on the oars shakes off the chill. There are no clouds
tonight and it feels like a cover has been peeled back from the sky.
The darkness is pierced by a million points of light that recede end-
lessly in a magnificent panorama. A shooting star announces itself
in a moment of brilliant incandescence and then is suddenly gone.
There's no swell or hint of a breeze and the boat feels perfectly balanced in the water. These are ideal conditions and we also seem to
have the benefit of a following current, all of which makes this
evening's rowing a pleasure. We pass through an area of luminous
algae and the effect is spectacular; the oars leave fluorescent green
puddles where they strike the water. I watch the luminous swirls
recede into the blackness and feel that the ocean is putting on her
best show for us tonight.

To pass the time, I do a short sprint every twenty minutes and try
to beat my previous speed. Driving harder on the legs and flicking
my shoulders at backstops, it's satisfying to watch the distance
between each fluorescent puddle lengthen. I'm in the habit of saving my chocolate rations for a pick-me-up during the night shifts
and after an hour I put down the oars to eat a Snickers bar and take
a pee in the 'shit bucket'.

I'm on the oars, getting back into my rhythm, when suddenly I hear something in the darkness, just beyond the tip of my starboard oar, which sends a shiver through me. It sounds like breathing. Then there's a trickle of water and I hear the breathing again, but now I realize what it is. It's a dolphin. Actually it's a pod of dolphins. In the darkness I can only just make out an occasional break in the water, but I can hear a dozen or more of them, blowing all around the boat, just beyond the tips of my oars. I put down the oars and reach my hand out into the water. I want to let them know that I'm here on the boat and that I know they're there and that I'm grateful for their company. But they stay just out of reach, so I pick up the oars again and continue to row, with the dolphins swimming alongside, blowing every now and then to remind me that they're still there.

The good weather continues into our second week at sea, and with Jimmy's appetite now returning it feels like we've found our rhythm. Our daily audio message has become the highlight of my day, taking me back to that evening with our friends and family in the Strongrooms. Like my chocolate ration, the audio message is something that keeps me going through the night, it breaks up the shift and gives me focus.

My favourite time of day is sunrise; the feeling of being warmed by the first rays of the sun, the breeze across my face, the gentle lull of the ocean swell and in every direction the sea and the sky stretching to an endless horizon. I roll the word 'endless' around my head until it dissolves into the fresh morning air.

My calm is broken by a problem with our batteries. The batteries trickle charge through the day from solar panels mounted on the fore and aft cabin roof. Most of the electricity is used to power the Katadyn PowerSurvivor 40E desalinator, which I've been running for three hours every afternoon to produce eight litres of fresh water for drinking and cooking. This power usage is not sustainable. The battery voltage has fallen by almost 20 per cent since the start of the race and Jimmy reminds me of the warning from Woodvale's electrician – if the voltage falls too far the batteries will not charge effectively.

Jimmy brings a sense of urgency to the situation, and when he insists that we stop running the watermaker, I feel responsible for not highlighting the falling battery voltage earlier. We live off our freshwater ballast for a few days while we study the battery monitor's lethargic rise. We can drink thirty litres of our 150-litre ballast without incurring a time penalty, but after that we lose six hours for the first five litres, plus twelve hours for the next five and so on, at an increasing rate. The race penalties are in place to prevent crews increasing their speed by ditching weight and in doing so compromising their boat's self-righting design. The organizers will be checking the seals on all of our bottles of freshwater ballast at the finish line. I am keen to restart the Katadyn for an hour per day and to supplement this with our ballast. I have low expectations of the back-up hand-held watermaker, which seems more like a survival option. But Jimmy will not entertain the idea of taking a time penalty and, until the batteries have fully recovered, the Katadyn stays off. This means our only option is the hand-held.

We have this conversation during the afternoon while we are rowing two-up, with Jimmy sitting behind me in the bow seat. It's hard to argue with Jimmy's point that, if the batteries do fail completely, it will be the end of our crossing. Right now though, more important to me than the battery problem itself is the feeling that Jimmy has made a decision which is not open to discussion. The layers of our characters have started to peel away, and with them the idea that we are on an equal footing.

At the end of his shift Jimmy retrieves the polystyrene box containing the hand-held watermaker from the forecabin and disappears into the rear cabin with it. He emerges an hour later, and to my great surprise he's clutching a full bottle of fresh water. Before we change over, he reminds me how to use the hand-held – a device with a large lever which drives seawater through a filter to remove the salt.

'One pump every few seconds. Don't pump it too hard or it won't work.'

I immediately ignore this advice and the system depressurizes, which means I have to pump the seawater out of the machine again before fresh water starts to drip from the end of the clear plastic pipe into my water bottle. It is, literally, a drip, but many drips soon add up and after twenty minutes I have almost a pint of fresh water.

In fact the output from the hand-held is about two-thirds that of the electric. This is great news; the hand-held will keep us in the race.

The heat is oppressive and has been getting worse as we have pushed further south. A short, choppy swell means the rear hatch must be kept shut, turning the cabin into a stifling, airless oven. My red towel hangs over the main hatch, blocking out the worst of the sun. The hand-held is resting across my chest and I pump its handle like a metronome. I sit up to check the sports bottle that is wedged behind the redundant Katadyn. Another ten minutes should do it. I shift position so that I can switch the pumping over to my right arm. I do this for two hours every day. Three litres of fresh water is just enough for drinking and rehydrating my meals, but there is nothing left to wash my sheepskin seat cover. Things will get easier when we start running the Katadyn again. I think back to my old life. A hundred litres of water to run the washing machine; fifteen litres to flush the toilet; forty litres of sweet, precious water down the drain every morning in the shower.

Before I go out for my next shift I open my diary and write 'Day 16'. I stare at the page. The days have become more or less indistinguishable. I knew it would happen but this is sooner than I had expected. I write *Starting to get bored of the routine*, then close the book and tuck it back into the netting.

I'm back on deck for the 12 till 2 shift. Although there's no shade, the breeze makes it feel cooler out here. As I settle into the shift, the main cabin hatch opens. Jimmy is sitting just inside, recording a video update. He turns the camera towards me, '. . . and there's Adam, serene as a Hindu cow, putting no effort in whatsoever.'

Jimmy has been watching me row, day by day, as my stroke has shortened and I've stopped driving with my legs. I hadn't noticed this change. For me, it has been lost in the process of adapting to our new environment. But I have become aware that Jimmy is watching me. He sits inside the hatch before changeover, studying my rowing technique. It makes me feel uncomfortable, and when Jimmy comments on my shortened stroke I become defensive. Yet another example, I tell myself, of Jimmy trying to order me around.

At changeover, while Jimmy is settling into the rowing position, I get the shampoo and shower gel out of one of the hatches, pull a bucket of water on board and scrub myself down. With my hair lathered up, I step up onto the gunwale and dive down into the beckoning blue. I've been looking forward to this all shift. The water is wonderfully refreshing. Jimmy passes me the snorkelling mask and I inspect below the waterline. The Coppercoat is doing a great job; there is very little growth on the hull. Five small black-and-white striped fish chase each other around the keel. I wonder if they will follow us all the way to Antigua. I peer into the endless deep and wonder what's living down there in the darkness. Back on deck I stand in the footwell with the sun on my back and I'm dry in a few moments. I towel the salt crystals off my skin and retire to the cabin to savour the simple pleasure of being clean and dry.

A flying fish hit Jimmy in the face last night. He holds it up: a good specimen, almost nine inches long and double that across the wingspan. I've had a couple of near misses – they are attracted to the navigation light, which is mounted just behind the rower's head. I sometimes hear them thud into the side of the boat at night. This one becomes dorado bait. Large dorado have been circling the boat for several days and we have hooked a couple but have yet to land one. Today the bait is ripped off the line almost immediately. The jar of wasabi powder will have to wait.

It's Day 18 and the time has come to change course. Rather than taking the direct route between La Gomera and Antigua, our passage plan follows two sides of the triangle, rowing south and then west. Today we hit twenty degrees north, the line of latitude at which the trade winds should start to fill in from the east. The trades have been helping mariners across the Atlantic since Columbus and now, turning west, we hope that they will do the same for us. It's an uplifting moment and from today I will keep a daily record of the remaining mileage to Antigua, an exercise which had seemed too depressing to consider until now.

After three weeks at sea the solar panels are generating enough electricity to run the Katadyn for eighty minutes every day, which is enough for a couple of litres each. A further hour on the hand-held keeps me topped up for the day and Jimmy often gets by without using the hand-held at all. Our system has been working well, but this afternoon when I come off my shift and turn on the Katadyn I am confronted by a very fine spray of water from the pressure release valve on the side of the machine. I turn it off and hope that the problem will fix itself, but when the machine grunts back into life so does the leak. I sit for a moment in frustration and disbelief, before I explain the situation to Jimmy.

'How much water is leaking?'

'Too much.'

'Then we need to call Jim Macdonald.'

Jim is the Katadyn dealer who came out to La Gomera eight weeks earlier to run a workshop for the crews. He listens to the problem and then assures me that it is easily solved – there is a replacement valve in our spares kit. But I need to be *very* careful when screwing the spare valve in. The thread is plastic and easily damaged. He repeats this piece of advice several times. I have only one chance at this.

The boat rocks from side to side and I hit my head on the bulkhead. I start to feel seasick and the nausea gets worse as I wrestle the bulky machine from its bracket. I stare with absolute concentration at the old valve and then at its replacement. Removing the broken part is easy and now I repeat Jim's warning about the plastic thread to myself, while gingerly spinning the spare in the empty gap. For an hour I sit in the footwell of the hot, airless cabin, trying to get the thread on the new valve to catch, applying more silicone lubricant, stopping periodically to stick my head out of the hatch for a gulp of fresh air and trying not to be sick. In growing frustration I apply more pressure. There is a popping sound. The seal slips into the gap and the thread catches. A few turns of the spanner, a flick of the switch and the watermaker springs back to life. It is the end of my break and I stagger back onto the deck, relieved to be out of the cabin.

After the shift I pull the bottle of surgical spirits and the cotton pads out of the netting and carry out my usual personal admin routine. Soon the cotton pads are satisfyingly black with dirt and sweat, and my disinfected skin feels fresh and dry. With the day's grooming done I pull my diary out of the netting and after recounting my struggle with the watermaker, I add: *Really bored of this monotony. I think days 20–30 will be the hardest. After that it should feel more like we're rowing back to our loved ones.*

We have rowed almost 900 miles and there is consolation in the fact that at our present speed we will be halfway across the Atlantic in a week's time.

This prediction proves to be a vain hope with news of bad weather approaching. A text from Simon Chalk to our satellite phone warns of thirty-knot westerlies, lasting for four or five days. So much for the easterly trade winds. Jimmy and I agree that until the storm hits we will row three hours on, one hour off. There will be ample recovery time once the storm hits and we're confined to sea anchor.

The prospect of five days at sea anchor worries me. Trapped together in that tiny cabin, as the days pass and we are blown, mile by mile, away from our destination. The terrible, airless heat during the day, the two of us squashed together, unable to stretch our cramping limbs, drifting in and out of consciousness but never really able to sleep. It seems to me that it's worth trying anything to avoid time at sea anchor.

Jimmy has just come off for his one-hour break and is standing inside the main cabin hatch facing me. The afternoon sun reflects off his sunglasses.

'So I reckon we should try to get as far south as possible,' I say.

'South?' Jimmy pauses for a moment. 'No, we don't want to row any further south.'

'Listen, if we push south we will be closer to the edge of the storm when it hits and it should blow over us more quickly –' I try to gauge his reaction '– and that way we'll end up spending less time at sea anchor.'

'No,' he repeats. 'We don't want to row any further south. We're at twenty degrees already. We don't want to be any further south than that.'

'So what bearing do you think we should take?'

'West! Let's row west into the storm until we can't row any further, then throw out the sea anchor.'

I smile and nod. 'Rowing two-up into the eye of the storm!'

Yes, that would be more like the adventure that we expected

when we stepped off the pontoon in La Gomera. Fighting the wind and the waves, battling the sea right into English Harbour.

'I like the idea, Jim. But seriously, I think the best option is to put ourselves in position to get off sea anchor as quickly as possible and get on our way.'

The sunglasses hide any change in Jimmy's eyes, but his tone is different.

'Adam, the storm system is huge. Rowing fifty miles south isn't going to get us out of its path.'

'I know, but it might shorten the time we spend at sea anchor . . . anyway what's wrong with rowing down below twenty degrees?'

'As we get closer to Antigua the winds are going to push us south. The storm will probably push us south too. If we row south now we'll end up too far south and it will be a fight to get back up to seventeen degrees. We could miss Antigua completely.'

Jimmy's getting louder and he's talking more quickly. The situation is becoming tense, but I feel strongly about this.

'So, the winds are *meant* to become north-easterly, but there's no way we can *know* what the winds are actually going to be like in two weeks' time. We've got 200 miles to play with until we're south of Antigua and if we row south now there's a good chance we'll spend less time at sea anchor.'

Looking at Jimmy, I can see that we're on the verge of a full-blown argument, so before he has a chance to respond I try to defuse the situation.

'OK, listen, let's row south-west, then.'

'No! We are NOT rowing below twenty degrees! If we row south now we're going to spend the rest of the race fighting a beam sea. You remember what that was like when we left La Gomera. The waves were breaking over the deck, everything was soaking wet. It was *dangerous*. No, we're NOT doing that again.'

We stare at each other for a moment in silence. One of us is going to give way and we both know who it will be.

'Fine! Fine. OK. We row west.'

Without another word Jimmy sits down and closes the hatch behind him. I'm alone on deck and I can feel myself deflating like a let-down balloon.

I'm angry. Angry with myself, angry with Jimmy, with the coming storm, the sea, angry with Simon Chalk. Everything makes me angry. Everything that has conspired to put me in this position.

How could I have handled things differently? What could I have done which would have resulted in me rowing south now, away from the storm, rather than towards it? I analyse the conversation, the day, the crossing and the last three years of preparation over and over in my head.

From inside the cabin, Jimmy breaks into my spiral of anger and self-pity.

'Adam, what direction are you rowing in?'

I clench my jaw to stop myself swearing at him. 'I'm rowing WEST Jimmy.'

'No, you're not.'

I look up at the compass and see that Jimmy's right, we're heading south-west. I turn the footplate to put us back on the right bearing. I'm even angrier with myself now for giving Jimmy the opportunity to undermine me.

'Why are you asking me what direction we're rowing in?' I spit.

'You weren't rowing west.'

'What, are you checking up on me now or something?'

'I'm not checking up on you, Adam. You're paranoid.'

I'm livid, but there's not much else I can say. Jimmy was right, I wasn't rowing west. I stew on this for the rest of the hour and I bring it up when Jimmy comes back on deck for his next shift.

'Look, Jimmy. I've agreed to row west, so I'm rowing west, that's the end of it. I don't like the feeling that you're checking up on me.'

'Your problem, Adam, is that you lack concentration.'

'Come on, we both daydream a bit when we're rowing. I'm sure your mind wanders too.'

'No, it doesn't. I'm worried that you're not concentrating when you're rowing, you're not rowing on the right bearing and you're not concentrating on the AIS screen when you're rowing at night. If you don't see a tanker coming at night we'll both end up dead. You need to sort it out.'

We have an hour rowing two-up until my break. We row hard and in silence. I'm steering from the bow seat and I focus intently on the compass, making sure our heading doesn't deviate from due west.

Towards the end of the shift Jimmy spots a small whale, breaking the water about twenty metres from the boat. Neither of us has seen a whale close up like this before and we are mesmerized. Then another charcoal back kisses the surface in front of the boat and soon there are dozens of them, swimming alongside us. We're rowing in the midst of a pod of minke whales. The animals slow down, they seem inquisitive, and in that moment, while the sun fades into twilight, Jimmy and I are not alone on the ocean, we are one of the pod.

Over the last three weeks we have thrown everything we have into rowing 900 hard-earned miles. I wonder how many of those miles we will lose in the storm, and how Jimmy and I will cope with being trapped for a week in that tiny cabin. For now, though, the whales give us something positive to share, a welcome distraction from our own sullen thoughts.

7.

The Loneliest Row, 1974–1996

Date: 7 January 2012
Location: Christchurch, Dorset

At Rossiter's yard in Christchurch an ocean rowing boat lies forgotten, sat on a grass verge between the fence and the toilet block, slowly rotting away. The boat is large, with a long hull and egg-shaped cross-section, which makes the cabins broad and spacious. She seems designed for stability and for spending long periods at sea, an expedition boat rather than a racing boat. Most people probably walk past her without looking twice, but to someone with an interest in these things, *Sector Two* is more than just an 'ordinary' ocean rowing boat.

Alice finds it hard to share my enthusiasm for the old wreck, but then she notices something poking out of the netting that's mounted on the cabin wall.

I lean forward and pull out a brown glass coffee jar. The metal lid is stiff – the thread has been sealed with tar. Inside is a box of matches. 'ENGLAND'S GLORY, SJ Moreland, Gloucester' is written around a monochrome image of HMS *Devastation*, a Victorian battleship.

I carefully slide the box open and see that it's full: four dozen tiny pink heads, waiting to be struck. For a moment I imagine sitting on this boat in the middle of an ocean, going through the daily routine of preparing a meal. I can almost feel the gentle rhythm of the swell and the sun beaming down through the high cirrus. A feeling of lightness and of peace comes back to me. I put the matches back in the jar and screw down the lid.

The boat is a sorry sight. The bow and stern cabin bulkheads, into which the hatches were once fitted, are missing, leaving the

eorge Harbo (*right*) and Frank Samuelson (*left*) had emigrated from Norway to the nited States in search of a better life, but saw a chance to find fame and fortune by owing back the other way. Their rowing boat, *Fox*, was named after their sponsor, ichard Fox, a New York publisher and boxing promoter. [1896]

ter crossing the Atlantic, Harbo (*left*) and Samuelson (*right*) rowed on to Le Havre and en up the Seine to Paris where they put *Fox* on display. It was now dawning on them at fame and fortune would not come as easily as they had hoped. [1896]

'Will five fortitudinous oarsmen over twenty-eight join me and engage in the second-ever transatlantic rowing voyage?' David Johnstone (*left*) and John Hoare (*right*) met when Hoare replied to an advertisement that Johnstone had placed in *The Times*. [1966]

James Johnstone

Johnstone (*left*) and Hoare (*right*) looking fit and well on day eighty-three of their crossing. This photograph was taken by a crewman on board the American coast guard vessel *Duane*. It was the last sighting of the rowers. [11 August 1966]

James Johnstone

The final entry in Johnstone's diary is dated Saturday 3 September 1966. That night a hurricane swept across the North Atlantic, and Johnstone and Hoare were lost at sea. *Puffin*'s upturned hull was spotted six weeks later by the crew of the Canadian naval vessel *Chaudiere*. [1966]

The Penance Way

Chay: the youngest of a family of six children, he had had to fend for himself since leaving school at sixteen . . . [Here was] someone to whom winning meant progress, who wanted and, indeed, was used to progress.' Captain John Ridgway describes Sergeant Chay Blyth (*pictured*). Ridgway had been Blyth's platoon commander in the Parachute Regiment. [1958–67]

Chay Blyth

Captain Ridgway originally tried to join Johnstone's expedition, but Johnstone felt uncomfortable around the steely young Parachute officer and turned him down, prompting Ridgway to set up a rival expedition. Here Ridgway is pictured on board *English Rose III*, mid-Atlantic. Ridgway and Blyth pushed themselves to the limit and at one point faced starvation in their bid to beat Johnstone and Hoare across the Atlantic. [1966]

John Ridgway

Ridgway (*right*) and Blyth (*left*) depart from Cape Cod. Ridgway had served as a merchant seaman but Blyth had never been to sea, and until their departure the pair had spent only a few hours rowing together. [4 June 1966]

Ridgway Blyth

John Fairfax posing with *Britannia* before his crossing. Among the loyal supporters who helped Fairfax to the start line was Uffa Fox, renowned naval architect and designer of the ubiquitous self-righting life-boat, on which *Britannia* was based. [1968]

Tiffany Fairfax

Fairfax had missed the season for crossing the North Atlantic, but he was impatient to set out to sea. His solution was to take the much longer mid-Atlantic route, departing here from Gran Canaria. [20 January 1969]

Tiffany Fairfax

From his days in the Caribbean working as a pirate and a smuggler, Fairfax had developed an intense hatred of sharks. Here he lassoes a shark and ties it to the side of his boat. [1969]

Tiffany Fairfax

When Fairfax cut open a shark to discover that it was pregnant, he felt no remorse about killing the whole brood. [1969]

Tiffany Fairfax

Fairfax killed many sharks while rowing the Atlantic. At one point, in a fit of rage, he dived into the sea with a knife between his teeth and chased after a tiger shark – losing sight of his boat in the process. Fairfax mounted the head of this large hammerhead on Britannia's bow as a trophy. [1969]

Tiffany Fairfax

Tom McClean was in a race against Fairfax to complete the first solo row across the Atlantic, and although Fairfax had a four-month head-start, McClean chose the much shorter North Atlantic route. McClean is pictured here departing from Newfoundland. [17 May 1969]

Tom McClean

Like Ridgway and Blyth, with whom he had served in the Parachute Regiment, McClean treated the row like a military operation. Rowing in the icy waters of the Labrador Current, he almost lost his feet to the intense cold. [1969]

Tom McClean

McClean was serving in the SAS, fighting Indonesian communists in the jungles of Borneo, when he discovered that Ridgway and Blyth were planning on rowing across the Atlantic. [1969]

Tom McClean

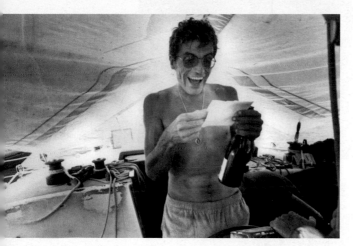

eter Bird was the first person to row solo across the Pacific.
.unning low on supplies, but not wanting to break his voyage with
stop on land, he was resupplied at sea. Here Peter is on board the
esupply vessel, opening birthday greetings after six months alone
t sea. [February 1983]

ouis Bird

ade from composite materials and equipped with a watermaker and Argos
ositioning beacon, *Hele-on-Britannia* was in many ways the first 'modern' ocean
wing boat. Peter here on *Hele-on-Britannia* during his 294-day solo Pacific row. [1983]

uis Bird

Peter Bird with his partner Polly Wickham and their son Louis. Peter was a doting father and carried Louis's picture with him everywhere, but he also had a restless nature and never really settled into family life. [1992]

Louis Bird

Peter Bird arrived in Vladivostok a couple of months after the collapse of the Soviet Union. While he waited for the right weather conditions, armed gangs fought for control of the city. Here Peter rows *Sector Two* around the Golden Horn Bay in Vladivostok. [1992]

Louis Bird

Sector Two had undergone a number of structural modifications since Peter's first attempt in 1992 and the colour scheme had also changed. Here *Sector Two* sits in a quiet corner of Rossiter's Boat Yard in Hampshire, showing the damage that brought Peter Bird's struggle to an end. [January 2012]

Adam Rackley

Thirty years after his 1966 row, Chay Blyth established the Atlantic Rowing Race, which opened up the sport to a wider audience. Here Chay (*left*) and Andrew Roberts (*right*) row the first Challenge Class Boat past the Tower of London at the race press launch. [April 1995]

Chay Blyth

A sombre statistic hung over the sixty rowers at the start line: during the last hundred years only thirty-nine people had successfully rowed an ocean and five had died trying. Here the fleet waits for the race start in the harbour at Los Gigantes, Tenerife. [October 1997]

Simon Chalk

Chay's relaxed enforcement of the race rules almost led to a mutiny at the start line, with one sponsor putting up prize money for teams who agreed to split off and form a rival race. Here Chay talks to Team Ryvita at the race start in Los Gigantes, Tenerife. [October 1997]

Simon Chalk

Graham Walters, a carpenter by trade, had constructed his kit boat in ten weeks and the *George Geary* was still an empty shell when she rolled out of the container in Tenerife. Walters now had a fortnight to complete the entire fit-out, a process that had taken other crews six months or more. [Leicester, 1997]

Graham Walters

Other crews and their support teams rallied round Graham Walters and his rowing partner, Keith Mason-Moore, to ensure that their boat was ready for the race start in Los Gigantes, Tenerife. [October 1997]

Graham Walters

The French husband and wife pair rowing *La Baleine* abandoned her after seventeen days at sea. Chay ordered that all abandoned boats which could not be towed back to land be burned so as to avoid creating a risk to shipping. [29 October 1997]

Simon Chalk

New Zealand Olympic rower Rob Hamill (*right*) and his countryman Phil Stubbs (*left*) celebrate winning the inaugural Atlantic Rowing Race in Port St Charles, Barbados. Their forty-one day crossing was a world record. [22 November 1997]

Rob Hamill

With their focus on reducing weight, *Kiwi Challenge* didn't have a satellite phone, and so could only imagine that they were in a head-to-head with British Olympic rower Peter Haining and his rowing partner David Riches. In fact Haining and Riches had dropped out on the second day of the race and Hamill (*left*) and Stubbs (*right*) were almost 600 miles ahead of the next boat. Here they approach the finish line in Barbados. [22 November 1997]

Simon Chalk

Leven Brown's decision to squeeze a four-man team into a boat designed for two meant that conditions on board *Artemis Investments* were extremely challenging, but the boat also had an exceptional power-to-weight ratio. Here *Artemis Investments* leaves New York, with (left to right) Leven Brown, Ray Carroll, Don Lennox and Livar Nysted. [June 2010]

Leven Brown

One upshot of losing his fourteen-man vessel, *La Mondiale*, the previous year was that Leven was able to crew *Artemis Investments* with his 'dream team' from previous expeditions. The two shifts comprised of Lennox (*left*) and Carroll (*right*), who were known collectively as the 'Beckhams', and Brown and Nysted, who were the 'Neanderthals'. [2010]

Leven Brown

During her first month at sea, *Artemis Investments* suffered two capsizes and had broken a number of speed records. On day thirty-seven of their crossing, the largest vessel in the North Atlantic requested a rendezvous with the smallest. Here the liner *Queen Mary II* emerges from the mist. [24 June 2010]

Leven Brown

f ever there were an epitaph for those who rowed oceans or climbed mountains or
ent to the poles . . . it is that we are much smaller . . . than we crack ourselves up to
. It's a wonderful thing to go through,' explains Leven. Here *Artemis Investments* lands
St Mary's, Scilly Isles, after 44 days at sea, breaking Harbo and Samuelson's 114-year
cord by 11 days. [31 July 2010]

ven Brown

After a summer spent rowing her on the Thames, Jimmy Arnold (*left*) and I (*right*) pack *Spirit of Montanaro* with ninety days of provisions and equipment in preparation for shipping her out to the race start. [London, October 2009]

Adam Rackley

After years of planning it was a relief to be on the Canary Islands and to feel that the adventure was finally about to begin. But relief turned to frustration as winter storm delayed the race start by a month. Jimmy and I tried to keep busy by structuring our days around training sessions. [La Gomera, December 2009]

Adam Rackley

The La Gomera Cup was held on the day that the race was due to have started. It was a chance to let off some steam and give the boats a good thrashing on the sea. Here Jimmy (*left*) is in the bow seat and I (*right*) am in the stroke seat. [6 December 2009]

Adam Rackley

'Get the wasabi ready, it's sashimi for dinner!' With a shoal of dorado never far from the boat, fishing provided a distraction and a welcome break from the regular diet of freeze-dried food. Here Jimmy shows off his catch. [February 2010]

Adam Rackley

fter 43 days at sea, Peter van Kets came up on the VHF radio and suggested a id-ocean rendezvous. It was uplifting to see another human being. Here I swim ross to shake Peter's hand. [15 February 2010]

lam Rackley

Although we had been desperate to reach Antigua for the last eleven weeks, now that we could see land, it suddenly felt like the adventure was over too soon. Here Jimmy takes his first, unsteady step on dry land after seventy-six days at sea. [22 March 2010]

Adam Rackley

'You are the only person who will ever know how tough this really was.' Jimmy (*left*) and I (*right*) enjoy our first moments on dry land. To the left stands van Kets, who had landed a few hours earlier, and to the right is Simon Chalk, the race organizer. [22 March 2010]

Adam Rackley

cabins open to the elements. The bulkheads have been ripped away along the line of the join with such precision that it's as if the cabins were split open with a giant tin-opener. Inside is a tangle of rope and equipment; the radio is still attached to the wall and a sea anchor lies on the floor, wires and string hang from the ceiling. In the stern cabin the plywood floor is delaminating and a sheet headed 'Argos code messages' is stuck to the ceiling. Back on deck, the wooden structure of the boat is visible through holes in the fibre-glass sheathing.

I sit in the simple wooden rowing seat and roll slowly up and down the slide. I imagine the feel of the oars in my hands and think about the man who rowed this boat. On the bow, beneath a picture of a small bird set against a rising sun, is his signature, 'Pete Bird'.

On the side of the boat is a plaque.

SECTOR TWO. In 1996 Peter Bird a hugely experienced ocean rower set off from Nakhodka (Russia) with the intention of rowing to San Francisco (USA) in this boat. Unfortunately on 3rd June a distress signal was received. Within four hours of the signal being received a Japanese vessel was on site but sadly only found this boat in much the same condition you see now. Peter's body has never been found. Peter Bird is still the ocean rower with most time at sea (937 days) and Sector Two remains as a tribute to Peter and reminder to others of how dangerous the world's oceans can be.

The next day I climb to the top floor of a block of flats that looks out onto Victoria Park, in east London, to meet Joan Bird, Peter's mother. Joan is ninety-four.

'How long have you lived here, Joan?'

'Since 1968.'

'Those stairs must keep you fit.'

I'm sitting at the dining table in the living room. On the shelves and walls are a lifetime of memories. Opposite me is Tony, Peter's older brother. Joan feels her way into a chair and glances at me sideways.

'My eyesight isn't so good any more, but I still have a little peripheral vision.'

Being almost blind doesn't stop her offering me a cup of tea.

When Peter was a child in the 1950s, London still was a thriving port and the family lived a stone's throw from Tower Bridge. He loved watching the bridge being raised and lowered, and the buzz of activity that surrounded the docks.

Tony remembers Peter's independent streak. 'We used to go to school over at Sloane Square and I remember one time when Mum wrote to complain that her son had come home sunburnt. The school wrote back, "Mrs Bird, if he has come home sunburnt he didn't get sunburnt at school because he hasn't been for two weeks." Of course, Peter was over in Hyde Park, lying in the sun.'

'Yes, school and Peter didn't get on very well,' adds Joan, 'and yet his reports weren't bad reports. He was always so . . . good-natured.'

Peter left school at fifteen and found a job at an advertising agency. When the firm went bust he bought a sleeping bag and went hitch-hiking with a copy of Kerouac's *On the Road* in his rucksack. Travelling became a way of life and Tony remembers Peter and a friend 'siphoning their way around Europe one summer in an old Borgward car, grape-picking'.

Photography was one of Peter's lifelong interests and he spent a couple of years as a cruise-ship photographer, travelling all over the globe. When he returned to London at the age of twenty-six, his goal was to earn enough money to build a catamaran and sail around the world.

Tony remembers, 'He got a job selling those fuzzy picture things . . . what were those things, Mum?'

Joan is chuckling, ' "Artwork", I guess you'd call them.'

It was while selling pictures door-to-door that he met Derek King, a new member of the sales team. A couple of years younger than Peter, Derek had just completed a four-month solo row around Ireland. When Peter learnt that Derek had plans for a global circumnavigation, he asked to join. Derek welcomed Peter on board, but felt certain they needed a third person, and despite Peter's concerns about having a woman on board, Carol Maystone, an acquaintance through mutual friends, was invited to join them.

Since they lacked the money to build their own boat, Derek approached John Fairfax, who agreed to lend them *Britannia II*.[1] The team had *Britannia II* completely refurbished, but when she arrived at the start of their expedition in Gibraltar, they discovered that the new fibreglass skin was not properly bonded to the wooden structure. Stripping off and reapplying the fibreglass turned what had been planned as a short stopover into three and a half demoralizing months.

After one failed start, the trio finally cleared Gibraltar in April 1974, and spent a fortnight making their way out of the Mediterranean and down the Moroccan coast to Casablanca. By now it was clear that Carol wasn't enjoying the expedition and she left the crew. On 9 May Derek and Peter rowed out of Casablanca while Carol stayed on dry land and eventually married the Frenchman they had met during their two-week stopover there.

As time passed on the ocean, Peter found that this existence suited him: 'I could sit and dream and look at the sea, never tiring of it,' he said. 'Unlike Derek, who could never sit for long without leaping up and throwing out the fishing line or coiling a rope or writing for an hour. He was too restless for this kind of life I thought.'[2]

By the time they landed in St Lucia, both men had realized that they lacked the stomach to continue, and the expedition was abandoned by mutual agreement.

Peter returned to London and, as Tony remembers, 'He was doing all sorts of things to earn a few quid. To give him his due, he'd try anything. He wasn't proud.'

But he was restless; there was something missing in his life.

Peter had been back in London for a few years when it was reported that Patrick Satterlee, a former US Marine, planned to row *Britannia II* from California across the Pacific; if he succeeded, it would be the first non-stop solo crossing of that ocean. On hearing the news, Peter was surprised by how he felt. It was as if he had missed his chance. Peter realized that he needed to find a way to get back out onto the ocean, and when Satterlee quit after only a day Peter travelled to San Francisco, where Ken Crutchlow was looking after *Britannia II*.

Ken's connection with ocean rowing had begun in 1969, when he travelled to Miami to report on John Fairfax's solo Atlantic row for the *Daily Sketch*. He went on to found the Ocean Rowing Society in

1983 and, to this day, keeps records of every ocean rowing attempt (a chronology of successful and attempted ocean rows is included at the back of this book). I visited Ken in his home in Cricklewood, north London, where he described to me the first time he met Peter.

'The boat was stored at my office in Sonoma and we had let it be known that we had a boat that was provisioned and ready to cross the Pacific.'

The result was that they attracted a lot of the wrong type of people.

'We had a mother and her young daughter who wanted to do it. I asked if she had any knowledge of the ocean. She didn't. I asked her why she wanted to do it. She said because it would make her famous. She had no concept of the risks or what was involved.'

Ken started to wonder if he would ever find a suitable candidate.

'Then Peter Bird arrived and I had no idea who he was. I asked if he had any experience of oceans or rowing and he said, "The last time I saw that boat was when me and Derek King rowed it across the Atlantic."'

From that moment Ken became closely involved in all Peter's expeditions. Ken had written the words on the *Sector Two* memorial plaque.

In October 1980, Peter rowed *Britannia II* out of San Francisco, bound for Australia, but after five months she capsized in the surf off the coast of Maui in the Hawaiian Islands. *Britannia II* was destroyed on the rocks.

Peter was determined to continue, but possessed neither a boat nor funds. Salvation arrived in the form of Foo Lim, a local yacht-builder who was so charmed by Peter that he offered to build him a new boat for free. The use of modern composite materials meant that *Hele-on-Britannia* (meaning *Carry on Britannia* in Hawaiian), which was completed six months later, was only a quarter of the weight of *Britannia II*. Rather than continuing from Hawaii, Peter decided to start again from California.

As he rowed out of San Francisco in August 1982, the press was gathered on the quayside.

'What are you going to do differently this time?'

With a wry smile he replied, 'I'm not going to wreck the boat on Maui.'

The video recordings that Peter made over the course of his 6,000-mile voyage capture the weariness and grinding routine of an ocean rower's life.

'The freedom of the seas . . . but then I think about it a little more and I realize that there is no freedom. My cell is thirty-five feet long by five feet wide and out there is the exercise yard. And that's what it comes down to. It's a small prison.'[3]

When he ran out of books, Peter's tonic for boredom was to tune in to the BBC on his short-wave radio. But he would never admit to being lonely when at sea. 'I am not lonely because I choose to be alone,' he told those who asked, perhaps to avoid talking about how the isolation really affected him. He was always uncomfortable discussing his feelings.

Peter's progress was delayed by long spells of bad weather and, after six months at sea, it became clear that his provisions would run out before he reached Australia. Although the south-west Pacific, through which he was now passing, is peppered with islands, Peter was not prepared to break his journey with a landfall. Determined to help an ocean rower in need, Ken chartered a boat in Tahiti and sailed west to meet him.

With boxes of freeze-dried food loaded into the hold, and guided by location updates from *Hele-on-Britannia*'s ARGOS beacon, Ken set off to track Peter down. After half a year spent alone on the ocean, Peter was euphoric when the rig of the trimaran appeared on the horizon. As the boat drew close, the skipper brought out his bagpipes and played 'Highland Laddie', while Ken dived into the sea and swam over to *Hele-on-Britannia* for an emotional reunion. Clutching a bottle of champagne in one hand and a fried egg sandwich in the other, Peter celebrated the mid-ocean rendezvous before loading his new supplies onto the boat. At sunset, with heavy hearts, the two went their separate ways.

Difficult conditions in the months after the resupply affected Peter's morale. At times like this he found it helped to talk about how he was feeling to the video camera.

'I've done six hundred miles in six weeks since the resupply . . . I just can't get south. Bone weary. Had enough of it. I can't escape from it. No escape from this reality. I've been out here too long and it's got me. I want to see some green. It's just blue, blue, blue and it makes me feel blue. It's Easter. I'd love to be stuck in a traffic jam.'[4]

As conditions and progress improved, so too did Peter's mood, but less than a hundred miles from Australia Peter became caught in a weather system that pushed him north. As *Hele-on-Britannia* started to drift dangerously close to the Great Barrier Reef, an Australian naval vessel, the *Bendigo*, was sent out to provide assistance. Tony remembers that Peter felt uncomfortable about being rescued.

'He just wanted to row up on the beach, that was his objective, but there was no chance in the world he was going to do that.'

With conditions worsening and the *Bendigo* itself now in danger, Peter relented and a tender was sent out to retrieve him. *Hele-on-Britannia* was taken under tow, while the captain picked his way back to safety through the Reef, but the speed of the *Bendigo* and the ferocity of the weather broke Foo Lim's boat in two on the way back to port.

After 294 days at sea Peter became the first person to row solo across the Pacific and the first person to complete the route without touching land. When Peter stepped off the *Bendigo*, Joan, Tony and Ken were there to welcome him.

In Joan's east London flat, Tony pauses thoughtfully. 'Talking to you is bringing a lot of it back now.'

Tony gets up and goes through to the kitchen to prepare lunch, leaving Joan and me in silence for a moment at the small dining table. With mottled light from the large window dancing across her kind old face, Joan sighs softly.

'He was one of those people, if he walked in the room, the room came alive. Everybody loved him. It was such a waste.'

Peter was an engaging storyteller with a dry sense of humour, but he rarely spoke about the time he'd spent on the ocean. Andrew Golland knew Peter for some time before learning about the rowing:

'He never talked about that stuff, and then when you knew that about him it just seemed to turn things upside down because he just didn't seem like the kind of guy who would want to spend three hundred days alone in a boat. He was charming. A lot of people considered Peter to be their best friend. I considered him to be my best friend. He was a tall, good-looking bloke and a lot of women fell in love with him.'[5]

Despite his gregarious nature, there was also a solitary side to Peter. Even as a young child he had wanted to become a hermit when he grew up and later, in his twenties, he saw in himself something of the Steppenwolf, Herman Hesse's solitary, tormented creation. With this feeling of detachment from the world around him, Peter was always ready to exchange laughter and companionship for another chance to be alone on the ocean and at peace with his thoughts. Few people understood this about him.

On his return from the Pacific in 1983, Peter moved back home with Joan for a while before taking a flat in Camden owned by Ken Crutchlow's father. Even as he now passed into his forties, Peter remained restless. He had no interest in a steady job and did what work he needed to get by, largely freelance photography and driving for a friend's film-production company. Andrew Golland remembers, 'He would come and sit in our offices sometimes, working on his book, but when people called up he would pretend to be Sharon, the secretary. He had this bubble of fun around him all of the time. I don't think he got very far with the book.'

Ken was in the UK that year when Peter gave a talk at the Earls Court Boat Show about his South Pacific row:

One chap in the audience shouts out, 'You must be mad', and of course Peter has heard this many, many times, so he says, 'Wait a minute, wait a minute. Where do you live?'
And the chap replies, 'Brighton.'
'And where do you work?'
'London.'
'You take the train every day?'
'Yeah, I take the 7.30 every morning.'
'How many years have you done this for?'
Of course the guy falls into his trap, 'Twenty, twenty-five years.'
And Peter says, 'And *you* call *me* mad?'

Nine years passed between Peter's South Pacific crossing and his next rowing expedition, but the ocean was never far from his thoughts. He would sketch boat designs and think of ways to fund another expedition. He met fellow ocean rower Geoff Allum for lunch once a month at the Pizza Express on Wardour Street and they would chat about Peter's plans to sail around the world.

As time passed, Peter became interested in the idea of rowing the North Pacific from Russia to North America. The French rower Gerard d'Aboville had recently rowed from Japan to North America, but Peter felt that a true crossing should be from continent to continent. Starting in Vladivostok, he planned a route which would involve crossing the Sea of Japan before reaching the open ocean. Ken got in touch with Sector, the Italian sports watch company who were already sponsoring d'Aboville, and, to his surprise, found them receptive to the idea of supporting another ocean rower. Ken remembers that the Italians were charmed by Peter.

> We went to Milan and after a good lunch we went back to the board-room to talk business. Peter went through his pitch, 'I want a boat, I want to row from Vladivostok to San Francisco, I can do it.' And one of them said, 'What is it going to cost? What's the budget?'
>
> Peter shuffled his paper and paused before saying, 'Gentlemen. The budget for this project is one million US dollars.'
>
> There was complete silence, no one said anything and everyone was just looking at Peter. He took a moment and then said, 'I've always wanted to say that! Actually the budget is one hundred thousand pounds.' And everyone started laughing, and of course the budget was approved.

With funding in place, Peter went to the Earls Court Boat Show to introduce himself to Nic Bailey, a naval architect known for his record-breaking trimarans. The boat that Peter commissioned him to design, *Sector Two*, included advanced features like solar panels, carbon-fibre oars, a watermaker and an emergency position-indicating rescue beacon (EPIRB).

'In a way,' explained Geoff Allum, 'Pete was the father of modern ocean rowing. Rowers today would recognize all the kit on board Peter's boat and understand it as a modern boat.'

Nic took inspiration from the design of Viking longships: a long, narrow hull and shallow draught for speed, and a thin keel along the length of the hull that made it easier to hold a course, particularly in cross-winds. The egg-shaped cross-section maximized the volume inside the boat, both under the deck where nine months' provisions would be stored, and in the cabin that would be Peter's home. Another modern feature was the airtight cabins which, combined with a freshwater ballast stored under the deck, meant that *Sector Two* would self-right in the event of a capsize.

Armed with Nic's plans, Peter began building *Sector Two* at a workshop on Cable Street in east London, using the skills he had learnt helping Foo Lim build *Hele-on-Britannia* in Hawaii. At this point Ken introduced Peter to Ivan Rezvoy, a Russian expedition leader. Ivan would become the team's 'fixer' in Vladivostok, and would also handle the technical and logistical aspects of supporting Peter's crossing, but in the meantime he moved in with Peter and helped him build the boat.

In an accent mellowed by many years of living under the Californian sun, Ivan takes me back to the winter of 1990/91. 'We had no money and it was bloody cold. I had just been prospecting for gold in Western Siberia, but living in Camden that winter was bloody miserable.'

The pair slept in all their warm clothes and, often short of money to buy food, Peter kept the kitchen stocked by asking suppliers for 'samples' for his forthcoming expedition. They worked long days in the Cable Street workshop, which they shared with a team of theatre-set decorators. 'We used to go down the pub with them and that's how Peter met Polly.'

It's clear that, even with the passage of time, Polly Wickham finds it difficult to share her memories of Peter, but I sense that she feels a duty to help me record Peter's life for the sake of their son, Louis. She tells me it was the boat that first caught her eye.

'There were all these bits of wood and string stuck to the floor.

Then someone explained that this guy was building a boat to row across the Pacific and we all laughed, we couldn't believe that these bits of wood and string were going to become a boat. But it was a beautiful thing when it was finished.'

Polly found Peter funny and charming, and also too 'normal' for someone who wanted to spend his life rowing alone across oceans. He rarely discussed either his past rowing adventures or his North Pacific plans with Polly; he needed to keep his life in London and his life on the ocean separate and was uncomfortable when she found some film from his time on the South Pacific. 'It's not me,' he explained of the weary, shrunken figure on the screen.

A few months into their relationship Polly became pregnant. As a lifelong bachelor who prized his independence, Peter's first reaction was to panic, but as Polly's due date drew near he came round to the idea of being a father, and he was at her side for Louis's birth in December 1991. He moved into her flat in Fulham, and it appeared that Peter was finally settling down, but Polly noticed that he never really unpacked his things. 'He was always ready to go at a moment's notice. He didn't want anything to get in the way.'

In March 1992, with Louis a few months old, Peter, Ivan and Ken travelled out to Vladivostok for his first attempt at the North Pacific. Ivan remembers that Peter was a doting father. 'He loved Louis tremendously. He would talk continuously about Louis. He carried his picture everywhere with him. But then he would be talking about Louis when he was eight thousand miles away from the kid and clearly that's not normal.'

The team arrived in Vladivostok as the former Soviet Union was falling apart, and were amongst the first foreigners in what had until then been a closed city. Ivan explains, 'Vladivostok in the nineties was absolutely wild, like Hong Kong perhaps one hundred years ago. The Soviet Union was no more and every night there was shooting in the streets between the Russian gangs who were dividing up the city.'

Starting from Vladivostok presented particular difficulties. The westerly winds that a rower would need to leave the peninsula were intermittent and usually only occurred in May, while there was also a very limited weather window for crossing the Sea of Japan.

Through the weeks that the team spent gathering the last of their supplies, making final modifications to the boat and waiting for the right weather conditions, they were treated like VIPs and put up in the dacha that had once belonged to President Brezhnev.

To the cheers of the crowds gathered on the quayside, Peter rowed out of the Golden Horn Bay, in the centre of Vladivostok, on 6 June 1992, with Ken and Ivan alongside in the launch. It was a perfect summer's day and, accompanied by a light tailwind, he set a south-easterly course out into Peter the Great Bay, which led on to the Sea of Japan. Although only 500 miles across, the Sea of Japan had never been rowed before and the conditions were expected to be challenging. Local meteorologists also warned that it was now late in the season to be attempting a crossing, increasing the likelihood of headwinds. Sure enough, the following morning the wind started to build from the south-east. With *Sector Two* now being blown straight back into land, Peter headed for an inlet near the entrance to Golden Horn Bay, where he dropped anchor alongside the freighters, oil tankers and ice breakers that were also sheltering from the storm.

Unaware that Peter had turned back, Ivan was growing increasingly frustrated with the ARGOS locator equipment, which seemed to show that Peter was still in Vladivostok. It was only when Ken pointed at *Sector Two* from the hotel window that Ivan realized the equipment was accurate.

On 10 June, with the typhoon passed, Peter took to the oars again and over the next two days made his way out into the expanse of Peter the Great Bay. But before long the weather turned and a headwind gradually pushed *Sector Two* west, across the bay and away from Japan. Monitoring Peter's progress back in Vladivostok, Ivan grew alarmed when the ARGOS update showed that *Sector Two* was being blown towards North Korea.

At one point he was twenty miles from the North Korean border. The North Korean coast is covered in barbed wire and they'll shoot anything that gets near the beach. Our major fear was that his boat would hit North Korea and he would be killed instantly. Ken Crutchlow, who is the only person in the world I know who could pull off this stunt, went into the North Korean embassy in Vladivostok, pushed his way through the guards and started shouting at the diplomats. They were all terrified of him.

Oblivious to the interventions taking place on his behalf, Peter dropped anchor and waited for the weather to pass. Despite being on the edge of no-man's land, the surroundings were idyllic: 'I had stumbled onto the perfect anchorage – deserted beaches and wooded hills sloping gently down to the clear blue water.'[6]

Three days later he raised anchor and set off again into Peter the Great Bay, but within hours *Sector Two* was halted by the capricious wind. Peter had now been at sea for nearly three weeks and was thirty miles further from San Francisco than when he had started. The weather window for crossing the Sea of Japan had closed and, determined to try again the following spring, Peter returned to Vladivostok and from there to London, while *Sector Two* spent the winter in a container on the quayside in Vladivostok.

Over the next nine months Peter slipped back into the life with Polly and Louis that he had left behind. Now that he was a father, more people asked why he wanted to go back out into the North Pacific. Peter would always say that he was doing it for Louis – perhaps this was a way for him to avoid talking about his own motivations. At sea he was often bored and frustrated, and even depressed, but there were also moments of great contentment, which kept him dreaming of the ocean when he was back on dry land. For many of those close to Peter it was only later, in coming to terms with his death, that they really understood the grip that the ocean had on him in life.

Friends noticed that during this time Peter was even more restless than usual, distracted by his unfinished business in the North Pacific. Until he had succeeded there he couldn't turn his attention to anything else.

In the spring of 1993 the team returned to Vladivostok, this time with *Sector Two*'s designer, Nic Bailey, who had come to help make modifications to the boat. Nic found Vladivostok a memorable experience.

It was the Wild West, or the Wild East I should say. There was a culture of theft and violence. You'd be robbed then offered your stuff back in the restaurant the next day. The guy at reception had a pistol stuck in the back of his trousers. One night there were two dead bodies on the steps outside the hotel. The next day the bodies were gone but no one ever cleaned up the blood.

This year the weather window opened earlier in the season allowing Peter to cast off from Vladivostok on 12 May and, a month later, to become the first person to row across the Sea of Japan. Rowing on through the Tsugaru Strait, between the Japanese islands of Honshu and Hokkaido, and from there out into the North Pacific proved challenging, with progress through the strait hampered by inshore currents and winds. This meant that Peter was only a few hundred miles from land when, on the night of 12 July, Hokkaido was struck by a massive earthquake. The tsunami that followed rose to thirty-two metres on the island of Okushiri, near the mouth of the Tsugaru Strait. Peter had passed through that area some weeks earlier.

Over the next five weeks, Peter covered hundreds of miles but made virtually no progress; instead he was pushed around the ocean in huge loops by the wind and currents. It became so frustrating that he gave up plotting his course on the chart. Towards the end of August, just as he started to make progress, *Sector Two* was hit by a tropical storm, which caused her to capsize a number of times. In all Peter would capsize twenty-six times during this 1993/4 attempt; that he was still alive to speak about them was testament to *Sector Two*'s self-righting design and to his own safety-consciousness.

Peter always put safety first; Geoff Allum remembers that his persistence had saved his cousin Don's life during his 1987 Atlantic solo crossing. 'Don had a dory with a buoyancy chamber at each end and one of the chambers was just covered with a canvas flap and Pete said, "If that goes upside down it will sink." And Don said, "Oh it'll be all right, it'll be all right." And Peter came over and helped us to make a door for it because he was absolutely insistent. Don overturned thirteen times during his final night approaching

Ireland and when he got back he said, "Pete's nagging saved my life." '

After the tropical storm had cleared, the headwinds and unfavourable currents returned and through the months of September and October Peter's eastward progress totalled less than fifty miles. On 10 November, with food running out, he managed to contact a passing bulk carrier, *Ocean Trader*, which carried out a resupply. On 5 December he was resupplied again, this time thanks to Ken Crutchlow, who had convinced the skipper of a container ship, the *Sealand Spirit*, to track Peter down and deliver boxes of food and clothing that would see him through the winter. Seeing Peter's small boat, and fully aware of the bleak conditions that he would face over the coming months in the North Pacific, the captain became quite emotional, but he could not convince Peter to accept a tow back to Japan for another attempt in the spring. After 200 days at sea, *Sector Two* had covered only one-third of the 5,500 miles to San Francisco. In a letter he sent back for his mother, Peter wrote, *This row is more frustrating than a Bosnian Peace negotiation.*

On 12 March 1994, having survived the North Pacific winter, Peter finally conceded defeat. After 304 days alone at sea he had made it just beyond halfway. At his average speed of ten miles per day it would have taken another nine months to reach San Francisco. He was picked up by the log carrier *Edelweiss* and taken back to Japan.

Polly waited patiently for Peter's return. She had hung Peter's picture above Louis's cot so that he would recognize his father. Now that Peter was back, she couldn't understand why he wanted to leave them again in order to spend more time suffering on the dangerous, unforgiving ocean. Polly found that he 'avoided emotional topics as he did a nine-to-five job', and while Louis kept them together, it became increasingly difficult for her to have any kind of relationship with Peter.

In the spring of 1995, Peter arrived in Russia for the third time. Rather than starting in Vladivostok, he moved fifty miles east to the port of Nakhodka, where he hoped to find better conditions. But the favourable May winds never materialized and it wasn't until mid-June that he was able to leave the harbour. Peter made two attempts that month, each time turning back in the face of headwinds, and perhaps also because deep down he knew that it was now too late in the year to face the North Pacific. *Sector Two* was loaded into a shipping container for another winter and, much sooner than he had hoped, Peter was back in London.

Having been committed to the North Pacific project for six years, Peter was now losing his appetite for it. But he was still not prepared to accept defeat. And besides, however his own feelings might have changed, the project had its own momentum, with Sector continuing to support him despite the expedition running many times over the original budget. In early 1996, before leaving for his fourth attempt, Peter met Geoff Allum for their monthly lunch on Wardour Street.

'He gave me his navigation watch from his South Pacific voyage. He just slid it across the table in Pizza Express and he looked a bit tired, so I asked him if he really wanted to go ahead with this and he said, "It's what I do. I don't know how to do anything else." He was tired of it by then. He was nearly fifty.'

Ivan was now living in California, from where he still worked alongside Ken as part of Peter's land-based support team. Visa problems meant he could no longer join Peter in Russia, but Peter stopped over in California on his way back out to Nakhodka. Ivan remembers, 'The last time he didn't really want to do it, but there was no way back really. To stop would be boring and, of course, back in London he had new responsibilities. I guess he was pushed as much as he went of his own free will.'

Peter was forty-nine years old and had filled into his 6'1" frame; his cheerful face was now crowned by a wave of greying hair. Alone and, this time, without the distraction of official dinners or public attention, Peter quietly set about rolling *Sector Two* out of the storage container and checking his equipment and provisions. He had done this many times and, with the boat on the water for only a couple of days the previous year, there were few preparations to make. She appeared to be in excellent condition, but what Peter didn't know was how the long periods at sea, damp storage conditions and freezing Russian winters had affected the wooden structure beneath her fibreglass sheathing.

The winter ice was only just thawing when the dock workers

helped Peter to lower *Sector Two* into the harbour. He cast off on 27 March 1996, far earlier in the season than on previous attempts, and he hoped for more favourable conditions as a result. Peter paid for his early departure with bitterly cold conditions, but after eight days on the oars he was already halfway across the Sea of Japan.

On Day 12 Peter reached Japan and despite the terrible cold and constant sleet and snow, he felt that the currents were on his side. Once he passed through the Tsugaru Strait, though, his luck started to change. For the best part of a week easterly winds kept him pinned to Japan's Pacific coast. The conditions brought back memories of his 1993 crossing and the prospect of another failed attempt:

> *Went to bed with a falling barometer. I felt a depressingly familiar pattern about to return. I really thought about the consequences of failure, more often all the time – but there it is – there's a chance I may not do the trip. I could not do another 304 days at sea.*[7]

After more bad weather and a capsize he began to notice signs of wear on *Sector Two*; the aft hatch was coming apart. The journal entry on Day 29 includes a detailed description and diagram of the problem: the aluminium frame connecting the plexiglas hatch to the hatchway in the bulkhead was starting to come away at the hinge.

> *I think that the hatch could come apart if I don't do something. The hatches are an integral part of the boat!*

Peter was only too aware that if the hatch broke off during a capsize, the cabin would be flooded, *Sector Two* would fail to self-right and he would be forced to abandon ship. The following day he made a repair using a couple of bolts and a spare piece of aluminium, but concerns remained about the seaworthiness of the boat.

That evening he finished reading *Great Expectations* and made a start on *Postcards* by Annie Proulx, listing in his journal the dates on which he started and finished each book, along with his opinion of it.

As time went on the weather wore him down. It rarely stopped raining, he was painfully cold and there were long periods at sea anchor during which the easterly winds stole his hard-won miles.

Too pissed off to write yesterday. I am too pissed off today but there's not much else to do because I am on the wrong side of a bloody great storm. It's horrible rain, seas dumping on the deck every few minutes, drifting south with small sea anchor. I've a headache from too little oxygen inside the cabin – I am opening the hatch every fifteen minutes in between waves. The barometer still dropping – I hate it so much! What makes it worse is the slow progress – oh how I want to be in Fulham.

Peter's thoughts were increasingly of home, and particularly of his four-year-old son:

I miss my family that's the main thing. I miss Louis very much. The difference is that he's growing up and I'm missing his life. He will change more than anybody. He will change as a person and I really miss him.[8]

Using his SSB radio, he repeatedly tried to call friends using a service which patched his radio into the telephone system. On his forty-seventh day at sea, Peter finally found a signal and called half a dozen friends and family, including Joan, Tony and Polly. The calls put Peter in good spirits for the rest of the day, but when he woke the next morning he felt more depressed than ever; the voices from home had reminded him of how far away he was from them.

One person Peter hadn't spoken to was Louis and he tried the SSB again a few days later in hope of getting through to him.

Yippee! Got through to Polly, spoke to Louis, says he wants a remote control car. Polly says he is terrible! Louis sounded different on the phone – I told him and he told me I sounded different too!

*

A number of people have helped me to piece together Peter's story and there's one more that I'm keen to meet. It's an early afternoon in May, the rain has just stopped and the air in the City is humid. Ranks of dark suits march purposefully past the window of the

Caffé Nero on London Wall, clutching sandwiches and coffee. I'm quietly cursing the sweetener that I've accidentally put in my macchiato.

Sitting opposite me is a twenty-year-old man with broad shoulders and a powerful build. The panini in front of him is a late breakfast.

'I just want to restore her to the state where I can row her on the river.'

I wonder if there's more to it than that.

'Well, you've certainly got the shoulders to be an ocean rower,' I say. 'You should go out to La Gomera one year and watch the start of the Atlantic Rowing Race, see what it's all about.'

I'm explaining the idea behind this book when I notice his right arm.

'How long have you had the tattoo for?'

'Oh, a couple of years.' He stretches out his forearm to show me more clearly. 'Polly drew it for me.'

The picture is of Peter rowing *Sector Two*.

'He's a hero to me.'

On his sixty-seventh day at sea, now 1,000 miles off the coast of Japan, Peter made his final journal entry. Despite all the frustration that he had suffered since entering the Pacific, he was in an optimistic mood. Another storm was approaching, but this time from the west. After seven weeks of battling against cruel headwinds, the wind was now finally on his stern, and it was picking up.

> *1st June 1996, Saturday – At last a firm SW wind. The gale arrived at last. It's good that I'm heading in the right direction for once! Long may it last! Although the gale began in the South it's passed to the West behind me, this had produced the SW winds.*

The following day, with the storm raging outside, Peter was most likely sheltering in the bow cabin. It would take a couple of days for the weather to pass, but he was happy knowing that the wind was pushing him eastward, towards the people he loved. From a distance, the wave would have probably appeared to be just like any other, but as it drew near its shape changed and soon it became clear that *Sector Two* was in the path of an enormous rogue wave. Even if Peter had seen the tower of foam and water rushing towards the boat there was nothing he could have done. As the wave crashed down on her, the pressure of hundreds of tonnes of water blew out both of the airtight cabin bulkheads.

In an instant Peter Bird was sucked out of his cabin and into the churning chaos of the storm.

Now flooded, *Sector Two* would not self-right, and after a few minutes of submersion the EPIRB automatically activated, broadcasting to the world that Peter Bird's struggle with the North Pacific was finally over.

8.

Despair

Day 24
Date: 27 January 2010
Position: 19°48'N 31°57'W
1,699 nautical miles to Antigua

We've been rowing three hours on, one hour off for twenty-six hours, and the GPS tells us we are no longer making progress against this headwind. It is time.

With a heavy heart I open the forecabin hatch and pull out the sea anchor, which is connected to fifty metres of 12mm rope. A short line comes off the bow of the boat and we attach it to the other end of the fifty-metre rope with a D-link that shuts with a screw fitting. I give the fitting a final twist with the pliers to make sure it is tight – if that comes loose we will lose both the rope and the sea anchor.

The sea anchor is a twelve-foot parachute which opens in the water and reduces the speed at which we get blown backwards in bad weather. A thin orange floating line tied to the top of the parachute is used to collapse it and pull it back in. We throw the sea anchor overboard and, keeping tension on the main rope, it quickly opens, a giant red and white shape, hovering eerily beneath the boat. As the wind pushes us away from the sea anchor, Jimmy pays out the main rope, while I do the same with the floating line, careful to avoid creating any knots. At fifty metres the line goes taut and our bow swings into the wind. I tie the floating line off on a small cleat.

We set about tidying up the deck. The oars are stowed and lashed together; the freshwater jerry cans come into the aft cabin, as do a few days of ration packs; rubbish is cleared away, zip-tied in thick polythene bags and stowed in the forecabin. With preparations complete we retire to the aft cabin, where we top and tail, Jimmy lying with his head beneath the stern hatch and my feet wedged under his shoulder. There isn't enough room for us to both lie flat.

It's mid-afternoon and the heat is terrible. The waves jolt us into each other and the sweat that runs off us puddles on the mattress cover. It feels like we're suffocating in a tiny airless coffin. I think about the wind stealing our hard-earned miles and a horrible, powerless frustration bubbles up inside me. I take some deep breaths and try to relax like Jim, who's dozing off and listening to music, but whenever I look at my watch, each minute seems to take hours to pass.

I pull our satellite phone out of the netting, unwrap it from various waterproof bags, and send a text message to Alice and my parents explaining that we are on sea anchor. 'Now having to face my biggest fear. Boredom.'

I get a message back from my dad, saying that the thirty miles we've covered rowing two-up into the storm is the fleet record for the last twenty-four hours. I also get a message from Alice – she's been waiting for me to mention the 'B-word' and has hidden a harmonica in our 'treat bag'.

After the big shift we've pulled I know I should be savouring the rest, but I simply can't lie still. I pull my feet out from where they're wedged under Jim's shoulder and spin around on my back so that I can sit up with my feet in the footwell and look out through the perspex door of the main hatch. I pull my diary out of the netting but can't find the words.

Day 24 – Sea Anchor @ 2 PM Despair.

I light the Jetboil and heat half a pint of water. I throw in a peppermint tea bag and pop down the plastic lid. I stare out through the main hatch. Waves break along the gunwales from different angles and spray across the hatch. The sun is glaring in. I need to get out of this cabin.

'I'm going out.'

Jimmy glances up and nods.

I put on my sunglasses and Crocs and wait for a lull in the waves to open the hatch. I crawl up to the bow rowing position and sit with my back against the hatch, gripping the Jetboil mug in one hand and a small plastic bag in the other. I wedge my feet beneath the gunwales to steady myself against the jolt and shudder of the waves. Inside the plastic bag is a Marks & Spencer luxury mini Christmas pudding from the stocking that Jimmy's girlfriend, Hanna, packed for us, and the harmonica. I roll each spoonful of pudding around my mouth until its thick richness has melted away, then burst the raisins between my teeth. My taste buds are dulled by three weeks of freeze-dried rations and the flavours are so intense. A delicious whisky aftertaste lingers in my mouth. When the pudding is gone I blow mournfully and tunelessly into the harmonica.

Over my right shoulder the sun stands alone in a cloudless sky. Every now and then a wave breaks on the bow and I get soaked, but sitting out here is much better than lying in the cabin with my feet wedged under Jim's shoulder. I ponder the horizon and think about the phone call from my boss when I was back in La Gomera, offering me a promotion. It's career-making – the future is set. Or is it? Deep down I know that something's not right.

As I sip the last of the peppermint tea I weigh up my hopes and ambitions. All those things I imagined I might do with my life. But perhaps I am just being naïve, perhaps the time has come to finally pack my dreams away and to focus on *normal* ambitions, like building a career and a reputation. Perhaps that is the way to a decent and fulfilling life. I can see it all laid out before me, each milestone along a clear and well-mapped path. The alternative is hazy and uncertain – there is no map, only a yearning for adventure, a hunger for *more* of whatever life has to offer.

I try to clear my mind and immerse myself in the surroundings. I look up at the flawless sky and savour the quality of wind in my ears, the warmth of the sun and the cold spray on my skin. For a perfect moment I am only these sensations. I *am* nothing, nowhere, endless. Will moments like this mean anything months and years from now? Or will this communion with the ocean and the sky fade and die, like the glistening rainbow on a dorado's back?

The stern hatch swings open and Jimmy's head appears; he's doing a recording for the video diary. I catch snippets of his commentary in the wind.

'The wind's blowing up to about thirty knots today . . . this is what I can see out of the stern hatch, nasty waves taking us the wrong way . . . I don't know how long we're going to be here for looking at this view but it might be a few days and there's not a lot to do . . . Listen to some music. Eat food. And get hot. It's *really* hot'

Jim disappears back inside before he can get caught by a wave. Out on deck the time passes quickly and before long the sun is low in the sky and the air is starting to cool. I crawl back along the deck and into the cabin. Jim is listening to his iPod and reading the palm-sized Gideon Bible he was given in La Gomera. Time off the oars has stiffened our hands into claws, with fingers that won't open. We spend the night tossing and turning through a thin and hazy sleep, bumping and kicking each other as we try to get comfortable. For endless hours I stare blankly into the darkness, trying not to look at my watch.

Restless night passes into listless day. Unaccustomed to the inactivity, our lower backs throb and ache. I lie by the main hatch, listening to *The Old Man and the Sea*, drifting in and out of consciousness. With the weather deteriorating further the hatches now stay firmly closed. The vents that we installed to let air in while keeping water out are no match for a decent wave and after a faceful of seawater we reluctantly decide to screw the vents shut. As the sun rises higher in the sky I find myself longing for the cool of night again.

In my diary I note, *24 interminable hours at sea anchor. A deep, throbbing sense of powerlessness, with occasional and overwhelming pangs of claustrophobia.* I dare not imagine another four days of this.

In the early afternoon I head out on deck to stretch my aching muscles and to escape the oppressive heat of the cabin, leaving Jimmy with our tiny oven all to himself. A few moments later I pop my head back in.

'Fancy a row Jim?'

Jimmy looks up and pulls out his earphones.

'What?'

'From the angle on the line it looks like the sea anchor is kind of just hanging down below the boat, doesn't look like we're actually being blown back much. I wonder if it's worth giving it another go on the oars. See if we can make any headway.'

Jimmy doesn't need convincing. In a few moments I'm retrieving the sea anchor with the orange floating line and he's coiling the fifty-metre rope back into the bucket. I take the pliers out to free the rope from the D-link. We adopt our usual positions with Jim in bow and me at stroke and before long we're bracing our backs against the wind and the swell. It feels great to be on the oars and as we warm up the stiffness in our backs softens, as do our 'crunchy' finger tendons.

It's soon clear that we're not making much headway, but we agree to finish the shift anyway. I check the GPS after the two hours is up. We've only covered a few hundred metres, but feel much better for the exercise. Before heading back to the cabin I throw out the sea anchor, while Jim pays out the floating line. Tonight we will sleep a little easier.

It's the afternoon of our third day at sea anchor. Jimmy is out on deck and I am enjoying having the cabin to myself.

'Adam. Can you come out here, please?'

I can see him through the perspex, kneeling at the bow of the boat. 'What is it?'

'Just come out, please.'

When I get on deck Jimmy has a piece of rope in his hand.

'What's meant to be attached to this, Adam?'

I'm confused. I have no idea what he's talking about. But then it dawns on me. Jimmy is holding the line that comes off the bow of the boat. I last saw that line when I was attaching it to the fifty-metre rope with the sea anchor on the other end of it. I attached the two with the D-link. But there is no D-link and no fifty-metre rope and, now the penny drops, *there is no sea anchor*.

I feel sick. Jimmy is looking at me, expressionless.

'Shit! Shit! Shit!'

We are no longer on sea anchor. We no longer *have* a sea anchor.

I think desperately about what to do. 'The drogue. We've got a drogue. There's a four-foot drogue in the forecabin. And we've got a fifty-metre towing line, we can use that.'

I make a move to get the drogue, a miniature version of the sea anchor, out of the forecabin. But as I do, Jimmy's hand moves towards the end of the thin orange retrieval line which is cleated-off by the forecabin hatch. I see that the retrieval line is under tension and realize, as Jimmy has, that if we're lucky, the sea anchor may still be attached to the other end. Jimmy starts pulling on the orange line. It's a relief to see that there's definitely something on the end. We pull in the retrieval line and lift the sea anchor onto the deck, in silence. Then we pull in the fifty metres of rope attached to the other end of it.

When everything is coiled back on deck I look at Jimmy and apologize for my mistake. I didn't screw the fitting on the D-link tight enough and at some point in the last twenty-four hours it worked loose and fell off. Jimmy's expression softens. We reattach the bow line and the fifty-metre rope with a climbing karabiner as a temporary measure. The karabiner isn't stainless steel and will eventually rust, but it will do the job for the next couple of days. My confidence has been shaken and I don't quite feel up to trying out the Zeppelin knot I've been practising.

The following day is our fourth at sea anchor. Jimmy's feet are looking a lot better – I should know, because for most of this week they have been sitting a few inches from my face. The skin is starting to heal beneath the scabs and they are less swollen. The other benefit of being at sea anchor is that I've pumped almost ten litres of fresh water. I proudly show Jimmy the half-full jerry can. I'm feeling generally more optimistic. To make the cabin bearable during the hottest part of the day we each spend a couple of hours on deck, giving the person in the cabin some space to relax.

In the early afternoon, it's my turn on deck, and I recline in the bow seat, sipping mint tea. Out of the corner of my eye a slick back breaks the water. It disappears, but soon there's another. I kneel up on the gunwale and suddenly I can see half a dozen whales in the water. They seem to be playing in the surf around the boat and I imagine that it is the same pod of minke that swam alongside us as we rowed into the storm.

Today is the roughest day yet. A breaker crashes over the bow and sprays across my back. Another wave comes in on our beam and I grab the gunwale to steady myself as we rock violently from side to side. Whales glide past, twenty to thirty feet long and charcoal grey on top, with white bellies and flippers. They ride the surf past the boat, skimming just below the surface of the wave, as it curls and breaks. Then they turn and swim back past the boat, looking for another ride. They seem curious and playful; it is impossible to tell exactly how many there are.

One whale surfs in a wave coming in off our starboard bow. It speeds towards the boat and as we dip into the trough of the wave, the animal's huge body is suspended in the wall of water above us. The whale is now approaching with only thirty feet between us and its eye is level with mine. My chest pounds and my body tenses, but just as it looks like we are going to be wrecked under its huge bulk, the whale flips onto its back to show its white belly and dives down into the depths beneath us. The animal is gone and we bob up the crest of the empty wave and back down into the trough on the other side.

In my diary I note, *From the weather reports it sounds as if we have two to three more days of this, but the claustrophobic panic has gone and I feel at ease riding out the storm with Jim in our hot, uncomfortable little cabin.*

9.

The Challenge, 1997

Date: 27 February 2011
Location: Near Hawick, Scottish Borders

'I'm round the back. I'm round the back with the chooks.'

The gentle Scottish lilt is coming from the other side of the wooden outhouse and, as I walk towards it from the hire car, the crunch of the gravel under my feet rings out in the crisp spring air. It's a cloudless morning in the Scottish Borders and the voice belongs to Sir Chay Blyth. I've spent so much time reading about Chay and his 1966 North Atlantic row with John Ridgway that I feel I know him already, which makes me a little nervous about our meeting. Chay does not suffer fools, gladly or otherwise.

Chay is clearing out the chicken pen. I introduce myself and offer some small talk. He nods and mutters something about the chooks before turning his attention back to them. He throws a cup of petrol onto a smouldering pile of hay and feed bags, and it explodes into flame. He chuckles to himself and now, as we walk round the chicken pen and towards the front of the house, I have his full attention.

Chay has a full head of white hair and the same stocky build of his youth. Inside, the house is modern and orderly. He offers me a cup of tea and shows me to the sitting room.

'By the way it's *Chay*, with a hard *Ch . . . Chay*. Not *Shay*.'

'Of course. Sorry.'

When Chay brings in the tea I'm standing by the sliding glass door, looking out into the garden. He glances past me at a rooster scratching in the flower bed.

'Trying to destroy all the *bloody* plants . . . yeah, he's quite a boy all right.'

He offers me a seat and settles back into the sofa. Chay knows that I've come to talk about the 1997 Atlantic Rowing Race.

'You know I get more questions about rowing the Atlantic than I do about sailing. Amazing . . . So what's this book of yours about, then?'

'It starts in 1896 with Harbo and Samuelson . . .'

Chay nods thoughtfully and looks away, out of the glass door. 'Samuelson and Harbo. You know there wasn't a day out there when we didn't think about Samuelson and Harbo.'

I allow for a respectful pause before I continue.

'. . . and I'd like to talk about the '97 race, because in the history of the sport it was a pivotal point in terms of opening up –'

Chay interrupts. 'It is *the* point. There is no other point after that.'

And with that he takes a breath, leans back and begins his story.

At the same time as Chay and John were rowing the Atlantic, Francis Chichester was circumnavigating the world, single-handed, in his fifty-four-foot ketch *Gypsy Moth IV*. It was not the first time a lone yachtsman had completed a circumnavigation; that accomplishment had gone to Joshua Slocum in 1898. But Slocum had taken a 'leisurely' three years and had avoided the dangers of Cape Horn by rounding South America via the Magellan Straits. What made Chichester's project audacious was his plan to take a single stop in Sydney and also to be the first single-hander to successfully round South America via Cape Horn. Almost every small boat that had attempted this route had been knocked down, pitch-poled (flipped end-over-end) or sunk. The voyage so captured the public's imagination that, when he returned to Plymouth in May 1967 after eight months at sea, a quarter of a million people gathered to welcome him ashore. Chichester was knighted and became a national hero.

Ridgway was a keen sailor who had spent time in the merchant navy and, soon after Chichester's return, he confided in Chay that he planned to attempt the first *non-stop*, single-handed, global circumnavigation the following year. Unlike Chichester, he would not land until he had circled the globe. But Ridgway was not the only person with eyes on this prize and by the end of 1967 several people had announced their plans for a non-stop solo circumnavigation, including the eccentric Bernard Moitessier, an adventurer who had spent most of his life at sea, and Robin Knox-Johnston, an experienced merchant navy officer. Not long after that, the *Sunday Times* proposed a race, the Golden Globe. Although Chay didn't know how to sail, he was determined to take part. 'If John could do it, there was no reason why I couldn't.'

Chay set sail from Southampton on 8 June 1968, but not only was *Dytiscus III*, the thirty-foot family cruiser that he had borrowed for the race, completely ill-suited to this kind of expedition, he had also arrived at the start line with less than a week's sailing experience. It was perhaps no surprise, then, that his attempts to round the Cape of Good Hope almost met with disaster.

'Chichester talks about capsizing once during his circumnavigation. Well I had no bloody clue. I capsized eleven times in a day.'

With his boat badly damaged, and now realizing that he lacked the experience to round the Cape of Good Hope, Chay retired from the race. In April 1969, after 313 days at sea, Knox-Johnston landed in Falmouth to win the Golden Globe. In fact, of the nine competitors who started the race, he was the only one to finish.

Most of the others were forced to retire due to equipment failure, including Nigel Tetley, who completed the circumnavigation only to sink off the Azores, less than a week from the finish line. Moitessier was the race favourite and although he left Plymouth two months after Knox-Johnston, he rapidly made ground on him. When Moitessier rounded Cape Horn, the two looked to be head-to-head in a race up the Atlantic into Falmouth. Moitessier didn't carry a radio and so it was only when a message landed on the deck of a ship moored in Cape Town Harbour that the world learnt he had decided against returning to Plymouth and claiming the prize. Instead he would continue on around the world for a second time. The message that Moitessier had fired by slingshot as he sailed past the harbour read, 'I am continuing non-stop towards the Pacific Islands because I am happy at sea and perhaps also to save my soul.' He eventually landed in Tahiti after one and a half circumnavigations.

The saddest tale was that of Donald Crowhurst, a businessman whose appetite for practical jokes had cost him **first** his RAF commission and then an army commission. Crow**hurst had** planned to turn around his failing electronics business by demonstrating a number of experimental technologies that he had added to his trimaran, *Teignmouth Electron*. Crowhurst had no ocean sailing experience and, knowing that many of his innovations would never work, he wintered in a small harbour in Argentina rather than risk death in the Southern Ocean. He kept a fake log and radioed fictitious updates of his passage around the world back to his supporters. As he sailed home up the Atlantic the subterfuge eventually became too much for him and the journals that were found on board *Teignmouth Electron*, which was found abandoned after Crowhurst had jumped overboard, follow his descent into insanity.

Back safely in England, Chay resolved not to be beaten by the ocean. As far as he was concerned, nearly meeting his death off the Cape of Good Hope was simply a setback and so, with characteristic bloody-mindedness, he returned in 1970 with *British Steel*, a fifty-nine-foot ketch named after his new sponsor. With the Golden Globe taken, Chay's new goal was to complete what Chichester himself had once described as 'the impossible voyage', the first solo, non-stop circumnavigation of the world *against the prevailing winds and currents*. Knox-Johnston had claimed his place in history by sailing eastward around the world non-stop, so Chay would sail westward. Ten months later, he was welcomed ashore and into the record books.

Chay was now established as a yachtsman but still needed to find a way to earn a living. Given how sailing for sport and for adventure was now enjoying a golden age, he imagined that amateurs might pay to take part in an ocean yacht race as a member of the crew. In keeping with his own approach to adventure, no prior sailing experience would be required to join his crew.

'Now there's a thing called UNCL in France, the equivalent of the Royal Ocean Racing Club. They were running the Atlantic Triangle Race – Saint Malo to Cape Town to Rio and back to Saint Malo. So I called the organizers up to ask if I could charge the crew to pay towards expenses. And they said, "Yeah, no problem at all." They couldn't give a stuff – French, of course. So I toyed with the idea and did my sums and I was very nervous about the whole thing because it had never been done before and would it make a profit?'

While he was trying to decide whether it would be possible to turn this idea into a business, Chay was interviewed by the *Daily Mirror* newspaper.

'The journalist asked me if I had any other adventures up my sleeve, so in that given second in time I made my decision and I told him that I want to enter this boat in the Atlantic Triangle and I'm going to try and get people to pay. "Well that's *terrific*," he said. "How much is it?" Well I'd worked out the cost so I doubled it and figured this would be a good way of working out if we'd have some interest or no interest.'

The article generated enough interest for Chay to fill his boat, and this idea of ocean racing as a business eventually grew into Challenge Business, an organization set up by Chay in 1989 to run the British Steel Global Challenge, which later became the BT Global Challenge.

Chay and the other directors of Challenge Business were always looking at ways to expand and rowing appeared, to Chay at least, to be an obvious option. 'I'd rowed the North Atlantic, so what was to stop us having a race?'

In April 1995, ninety-nine years after Harbo and Samuelson's first crossing, Chay and Andrew Roberts (another Challenge Business director) rowed under Tower Bridge and gave a press conference on a boat on the Thames to launch the inaugural Atlantic Rowing Race. It would start in October 1997 and would be a single-class race, open to pairs. True to Chay's philosophy, no prior rowing or ocean experience would be required; competitors simply needed to raise £10,500, for which they would receive a twenty-three-piece, plywood, flat-packed boat kit and a place in the race.

Challenge had commissioned Phil Morrison, an experienced naval architect, to design the kit. The boat needed to be streamlined enough to race but stable enough to withstand an ocean storm. To ensure it would be self-righting, ballast compartments that could be filled with fresh water were fitted under the deck which, along with watertight front and rear cabins, made the boat highly unstable when upturned; the same concept as was used in *Rosie*, the boat that Chay had rowed with Ridgway.

Chay expected less than a dozen entries, but forty-two teams put down a deposit, of which thirty made it to the start line at Los Gigantes on Tenerife. Alongside the British entries were boats from the US, South Africa, New Zealand, Ireland, Germany, Norway and two from France.

Crews arrived at Los Gigantes a fortnight before the race start to carry out final sea trials, tweak equipment and set their boat's trim by shifting ballast and supplies between the deck compartments. The exception was Graham Walters, whose boat, the *George Geary*, was rolled out of its container in Los Gigantes as an empty shell. Graham, a carpenter by trade, had spent the last ten weeks putting the kit together in his back garden and now had two weeks to complete the fit-out, a process that had taken most crews six months or more. It seemed an impossible task but it was clear that Walters knew what he was doing. I later spoke to Teresa Page, who worked for Challenge Business at the time. She explained that 'unlike many teams we had no concerns about [Walters] as we could see quite quickly that he was very capable. There were other teams who appeared completely ready because they had theirs kitted out by a boat builder, but didn't necessarily know how everything worked on board.'

Faced with the enormity of just getting to the start line, Walters never seemed to lose his good humour. A modest and likeable character, other crews and their support teams rallied to help him and by the time Walters's team mate, Keith Mason-Moore, arrived, two days before the race start and laden with 250 kilos of excess baggage containing the last of the fittings and equipment, there was a team of five working round the clock to get the *George Geary* on the water.

Joseph Le Guen, on board *Atlantik Challenge* was the only competitor to have rowed an ocean, with a successful Atlantic solo crossing in 1995. Le Guen was forthright in character and also in appearance, with a bushy moustache and barrel chest, his thick neck merged into broad shoulders. A furrowed brow and weather-worn complexion gave him an air of authority and experience. His rowing partner, Pascal Blond, was a bull of a man with a close-shaved head who rarely spoke. 'Ex French Foreign Legion,' recalls Chay. 'A very nice guy – very quiet.' Even so, news quickly spread around the race camp that Blond was a convicted double-murderer and Le Guen his parole officer.

Blond had arrived in Tenerife from the high-security prison in Moulins. Now aged thirty-four, he had spent most of his adult life behind bars, with a seven-year sentence for a gang killing when he was eighteen and another seven years for beating a man to death in a bar fight two years into his parole. The words 'Little Bear' tattooed in fading blue ink around his wrist hinted at the temperament of his youth.

Moulins prison was notorious for its insanitary conditions and for the riots in 1992, during which the French special forces had to be called in to retake the jail. But despite their sometimes fraught relationship with the inmates, the authorities at Moulins were so enthusiastic about the idea of the race as part of Blond's rehabilitation that they financed Le Guen's project and had a group of inmates construct the kit in the prison workshops. It took two months to complete and, when they were finished, the inmates toasted *Atlantik Challenge* with cups of orange juice.

Despite Le Guen's love of the open ocean and his spirit of adventure, the competitive aspect was not lost on him. 'We will be rowing like hell to beat the English,' he told reporters.

Their quiet confidence and physical presence and Le Guen's experience made *Atlantik Challenge* one of the race favourites, but Chay had his eye on another of the international boats. *Kiwi Challenge*, rowed by Phil Stubbs and Rob Hamill. As Chay recalls, 'Rob Hamill was an Olympic rower going all-out to win and he approached things in an incredibly professional way.'

Hamill learnt about the Atlantic Rowing Race while training for the Atlanta Olympics. His team mate, Phil Stubbs, was a New Zealand national surf and dragon-boat racer, as well as being a yachtsman, triathlete and adventure racer. While many boats were sheathed in fibreglass and had a steel or timber core built into their plywood keel, *Kiwi Challenge* was a product of Hamill and Stubbs's obsession with weight. Batteries were essential for powering the watermaker and GPS equipment, but they were also heavy, so the Kiwis dispensed with a back-up. The pair settled on bringing one

T-shirt each and five tapes for the Walkman and even argued over the weight of a fishing line and lures.

Later, when I call Rob Hamill, he explains that he was shocked by some of the other competitors' attitude to weight.

'We went round one apartment and there was this stack of batteries, AA batteries. And I remember thinking "Are these guys serious?" There were about ten kilos of batteries. I mean that's one thing, but what else? What about food? What does that say about their psychology? It's the tip of the iceberg. Phil and I were crossing people off – of the thirty crews, we wrote off twenty-seven as non-starters in the competitive sense. Most people were there for the adventure. Except for Peter Haining!'

The Kiwis saw that the competition would come from Peter Haining, the other Olympian in the race, and his rowing partner, David Riches, in *Walter Scott Partners*. In everything they did these two teams measured themselves against each other – as Haining told a reporter after a training row around Los Gigantes, 'David and I now hold the record for the course from the Old Port to the New Harbour. It took one hour thirty-four minutes, which was twenty-six minutes better than the Kiwi crew. We kicked ass.'

As a result of their obsession with weight, *Kiwi Challenge* carried no satellite phone or long-range radio communications and the mandatory VHF radio only worked within line of sight. Not knowing their race position piled on the psychological pressure.

'It was terrible,' explains Rob, 'it really enhanced the tension. Phil and I almost had a knuckle-up at one point because we didn't have that communication with the outside world.'

But the uncertainty was also a powerful motivator for the Kiwis, as Hamill later recorded: 'What [if] say someone else was also closing on [the finish]? They'd be rowing their hearts out and we knew that we must do the same. We gave it heaps and reeled in ninety-three nautical miles in twenty-four hours. Go on Peter Haining, beat that! As always through the voyage, the thought of beating [Haining] – or being beaten by him – drove me on.'[1]

Chay felt that the race should be an opportunity to develop the ocean rowing boat design and wanted teams to be innovative with Morrison's basic kit. 'We drew up rules but we wanted to let them adapt the boat however they wanted with sliding seats, different types of oars and so forth. Well! You would not *believe* the controversy over that.'

The crews jealously eyed features like the fins on *Atlantik Challenge*, the modified keel on *Wabun*, and the large hooped safety rail on *Mount Gay Rum Runner*, which some believed could be fitted with a sail. Many of the competitors felt that Chay was too lax in enforcing the rules and this caused friction in the race camp.

Chay's eyes widen as he recalls his frustration. 'Christ, it went on *and on* and you've got a controversy that this boat and that boat have some massive advantage. Ah Christ, it was *incredible*. The rowers were without doubt the most *difficult* people to deal with.'

The feeling that they were embarking into the unknown also contributed to the tension in the camp. Only thirty-nine people in history had successfully rowed an ocean, with five ocean rowers lost at sea.

'The statistic was hanging over our heads,' recalls Rob on the phone. 'It was like going to war. And I have to say the camaraderie was just extraordinary, with that feeling of, "Will we see each other again?"'

Chay tried to draw a line under the competitors' complaints about the rules by making it clear that *all* boats would remain as they were. Those with modifications would keep them and those without would not be permitted to make any. This decision galvanized some crews against Chay and a few days later David Mossman from *Key Challenger* and Simon Chalk from *Cellnet Atlantic Challenger* invited twenty crews to a private meeting. Mossman explained that these crews had been chosen because their boats remained true to the original race specifications. Mossman and Chalk wanted to boycott the start, which was in a few days' time, and to hold a breakaway race, which Mossman's sponsor, Key Choice Insurance, had agreed to put up prize money for.

Chalk and Mossman's audacious bid gained little support.

'We felt huge amounts of loyalty towards Chay,' explains Rob.

And there was also the security of knowing that the Challenge Business support yacht would be shadowing the race. Of course, if Chay had his way there would not have been a support yacht. He leans back in the sofa and a mischievous grin spreads across his face.

'So we're drawing up the rules and Andrew Roberts said, "We'll have to send one or two of the boats as safety boats."

'I said, "What do you mean *safety boats*?"

'He said, "We've got to send a boat."

'I said, *"Bugger-off!* If they want to be heroes let them get out there."

'Anyway, Andrew was adamant and he was quite right of course – the first night proved that.'

The race started on the morning of 12 October 1997 and within forty-eight hours, three crews had withdrawn: *This Way Up*, *Walter Scott Partners* rowed by Haining and Riches, and the first all-woman ocean rowing attempt, *American Pearl*.

'That first night they went off and we'd told them about the acceleration zone (an area of strong winds in the channel between Tenerife and La Gomera). We told them to keep away from land and of course some of them ignored it and that first night we had three rescues. It was only a force five. It was neither here nor there really. Christ! One of the rowers calls up on the sat phone and says they're in a gale and I say to Teresa [Page], "Where the hell's the gale?"'

Food poisoning put *Walter Scott Partners* on the back foot from the start and, although they left Los Gigantes shoulder to shoulder with Hamill and Stubbs, a twenty-minute battle out into the channel saw the Kiwis gradually edge ahead. Despite having 3,000 miles ahead of them, neither crew was able to treat the race as anything other than a sprint and Haining and Riches rowed two-up through the night in an attempt to make ground on Hamill and Stubbs. After eighteen hours on the oars, Riches, who had not been able to keep down any food or water since leaving Los Gigantes, succumbed to exhaustion and Haining was left to battle against the deteriorating weather on his own. Now struggling to keep the boat off La Gomera's rocky coastline and concerned for his partner's condition, Haining called for help on the sat phone. *Walter Scott Partners* was out of the race.

While the weather was a significant factor on the first night of the race, equipment failure forced the hand of those crews that dropped out during the later stages. The German boat, *Wabun*, withdrew on Day 10, followed by the French husband-and-wife pair rowing *La Baleine* after seventeen days at sea. The boats were now too far out in the Atlantic to be towed back to shore and, because of the risk to shipping, maritime law required that all abandoned vessels be sunk. Chay recalls the support yacht crew burning *La Baleine*. 'So we doused the thing with petrol and we fired a flare at it, real Viking stuff – all we needed was a body inside.'

The sixth and final boat to withdraw was *Spirit of Spelthorne*, crewed by the Boreham brothers, Matt and Ed.

'Oh Christ, yes,' recalls Chay. 'God, the *trouble* we had with them bloody pair.'

The Borehams' problems started twelve days into the crossing when their battery system failed. Unable to run the watermaker, they started drinking the emergency water ballast but remained determined to continue rowing. By Day 26, knowing that they would run out of water long before they reached Barbados, the decision was made to call for help on the VHF radio. Then, when they failed to get a response, something snapped in Ed, who had been taking antidepressants.

It was late in the afternoon and Matt was preparing dinner, mixing water and freeze-dried beef stroganoff on the gimbal stove. The mood had been subdued since earlier in the day when a cruise liner passed by without responding to their emergency message.

Suddenly Ed stood up on the gunwale and dived into the sea. He had decided to swim for the nearest land – which was the Azores, 700 miles away.

Matt sprang to the edge of the boat and caught his brother just as he surfaced.

'What the fuck are you doing?' he screamed as he dragged Ed back on board.

But Ed was in shock and couldn't bring himself to say anything to Matt, let alone look him in the eye. He simply threw his soaking clothes onto the deck and climbed into the cabin, where he spent the next three days curled up in his sleeping bag. Eventually, there was no option but for Matt to activate the EPIRB, which would send a signal, relayed by satellite around the world, requesting immediate rescue.

'What they did is set off the beacon . . .' Chay pauses, he's laughing and shaking his head, '. . . and what the beacon says is "activated by salt water", so what they did is get the beacon in the water and tie it on with a bit of string then have a sleep and wait for rescue to come. And sure enough the beacon breaks the string and drifts away, so suddenly we've got a beacon and no bloody boat. Christ, what's going on here? I remember getting the phone call from *3Com* (the support boat). "We've got the beacon, we're here! There's no boat!" And we thought, "Christ, they've sunk, what's going on?" If it was me I'd have strapped the bloody thing to my chest.'

With rescuers now fearing the worst, a Portuguese air-sea rescue plane was scrambled from the Azores and the *Spirit of Spelthorne* was spotted, twenty-one miles from her EPIRB signal. *3Com* was alongside within a few hours and once the brothers had abandoned ship, the *Spirit of Spelthorne* was doused with petrol and set alight. The brothers watched, in sad silence, as three years of their lives, and more money than they could afford, slowly succumbed to the flames and the sea.

The rooster is outside the glass door, peering in at us. Chay stares back at the rooster and is thoughtful for a moment.

'He's quite a boy all right . . .'

I interrupt his reverie. 'And how about the route? How did you decide on a mid-Atlantic crossing?'

A grin dances across Chay's eyes and he is animated again.

'Well the North Atlantic is nothing like the *middle-of-the-bloody-Atlantic*. It's like chalk and cheese. I laughed my bloody head off when Fogel and Cracknell were crying their bloody eyes out (Ben Fogel and James Cracknell took part in the 2005 Atlantic Rowing Race, and made a documentary called *Through Hell and High Water*). I thought *Jesus Christ*. It's lovely weather, the sea's warm, *what the hell's the problem*? You could drift across, for God's sake. You could sit there and just eat and drink. Which is what that woman (Jan Meek) did . . . she did it with her son as well (Dan Byles) . . . she decided she was going to take a hundred days – what a *sodding nightmare*!'

Chay chuckles to himself and shakes his head. 'Oh deary me! *Deary-my-ass!*'

Jan Meek and Dan Byles, in *Carpe Diem* were, at fifty-two and twenty-one, respectively the oldest and youngest competitors in the race. Byles's original team mate, a fellow army officer, had pulled out, prompting his mother to step in. Being recently widowed, the training, planning and fundraising gave her a welcome focus. She looked and felt rather out of place amongst the Olympians, marines and adventure racers, but no one could fault her energy and determination.

Meek and Byles shared an apartment with the Kiwis in Los Gigantes but the attitudes of the two crews to the race and their approach once out at sea could not have been more different. Preparing for every eventuality, *Carpe Diem* sat on the start line weighing almost 1.5 tonnes, twice the weight of *Kiwi Challenge*. While the Kiwis had a man on the oars every moment of the day, mother and son would share a two-hour break in the late afternoon to enjoy a gin and tonic and exchange anecdotes over dinner. Two weeks into the race *Carpe Diem* was only 200 miles from the start line, while Hamill and Stubbs had covered over three times that distance.

The race had almost ended for *Kiwi Challenge* only a few hours out of Los Gigantes when their watermaker broke. The seas were too rough in the acceleration zone to carry out repairs, so they made for El Hierro, the last island before the open ocean. After a couple of hours sitting alongside the fishing boats in a small harbour they had repaired the loose contact on the watermaker motor and were underway again. Hamill and Stubbs were relieved to learn over the VHF radio that they had only slipped to fourth place. By Day 4 of the race, happy with the progress they were making, *Kiwi Challenge* threw ten days' rations overboard to reduce weight: an exercise they repeated as the race progressed.

Both strong characters, Hamill and Stubbs hadn't felt the need to nominate a 'skipper' before they set off, but as the weeks passed it became clear that Stubbs was the more forceful of the two. At one point, Stubbs leapt from his seat to challenge Hamill to a fist fight and Hamill responded by threatening to set off the EPIRB to call a rescue and end their race. But they were both determined to row as hard as they could each day, and despite the mood on board, they were putting the miles behind them.

After forty days at sea, the mast of *3Com* appeared on the horizon. Stubbs was immediately on the VHF to ask their race position.

'*Kiwi Challenge*, you are number one.'

The Kiwis were ecstatic to discover that not only were they in first place, but they were also *560 miles* ahead of the next boat in the fleet. After a two-minute celebration they were back on the oars, completing the last seventy miles into Barbados in eighteen hours and setting a new record by rowing the Atlantic in forty-one days.

Chay clears his throat and sits forward a little. We've been in his front room for a little over an hour and I suddenly get the feeling that this interview is being drawn to a close. 'So we came up with the idea that we'd set them off from the Canaries and get them into the Gulf Stream. We decided to land in Barbados because it was the easterly-most island and if they missed that they'd have a choice of other islands.'

Eight days after the Kiwis landed in Barbados, Blond and Le Guen arrived, while the first British crew to cross the finish line, the husband-and-wife team David and Nadia Rice on the *Hannah Snell*, took third place after fifty-five days. Searson on *Commodore Shipping* and Immelman rowing *Key Challenger* both crossed the line solo, their partners, Clinton and Mossman, having been taken off by the support boat due to a back injury and food poisoning respectively, during the first week of the crossing. In all, twenty-four boats arrived at the finish line.

Carpe Diem was the last boat to arrive in Barbados, with the mother and son having spent 101 days at sea.

'What surprised us most is that the finishers all ended up in Barbados. I was astounded. They did bloody well to get there.'

Many of those who took part in that first Atlantic Rowing Race had their lives shaped by it. Withdrawing from the race affected Matt Boreham deeply, and he came back to Tenerife the following year to attempt a solo crossing. It ended in failure, as did his third attempt in 1999, but in 2004 he successfully rowed across the Atlantic in eighty-four days in the *Alison May*, a sixteen-foot boat that he designed and built himself. The crossing put Boreham in the record books for rowing the shortest boat across an ocean. After that, he returned to the Atlantic in 2008 with Alan Lock, a former naval officer. They commissioned Rossiter Yachts to build *Gemini* and had a successful crossing from La Gomera to Barbados in eighty-five days. (The following year, *Gemini* would be back on the Atlantic, renamed the *Spirit of Montanaro*.)

Boreham held his shortest-boat record until 2007, when the title was taken by Graham Walters. Graham had completed two further successful ocean rows since the 1997 race, and made a fourth crossing in May 2007, taking ninety-nine days in a fifteen-foot vessel. As well as taking Boreham's obscure record, Walters set another – for rowing the oldest boat across an ocean.

'It's old and it weighs 2.5 tonnes, so it's a bit like trying to row a skip filled with concrete,' Walters had explained matter-of-factly before setting off. Built in 1966 by Colin Mudie, *Puffin* had last been crewed by Johnstone and Hoare. Walters took a copy of their journals with him as a reminder of those who had gone before.

Jim Shekhdar on *Boatcom Waverider* went on to complete a solo Pacific crossing in 2001 and Jock Wishart on *Mount Gay Rum Runner* returned to the ocean to highlight the impact of global warming by rowing to the magnetic North Pole in 2011. Rob Hamill trained the Kiwi crews who won the next two Atlantic Rowing Races in 2001 and 2003. Joseph Le Guen went on to attempt a solo Pacific row in 2000 while his crewmate and ward, Pascal Blond, justified the Moulins prison authorities' enthusiasm for the race by coaching a youth rowing club.

All these characters found something on the ocean that changed their lives, but none more so than Simon Chalk. It was Chalk and Mossman who had led the 'mutiny' against the race organizers at Los Gigantes. Simon went on to make his name synonymous with ocean rowing by completing a further four successful ocean rows across the Indian and Atlantic oceans. In 2004 he bought the Atlantic Rowing Race business from Chay.

When I mention Simon I am pleased to see Chay relax back into his chair. He has time to tell one more story.

We ran the race three times and by the third one Andrew said, 'I'm finished with the bloody rowing races.' He didn't want to know. Matthew (another of the race organizers) and I were stood on the harbour wall (in Los Gigantes), looking down onto all the boats on the water, milling about and sorting themselves out. We were about to go out on the launch to start the third race and I said, 'What do you think, Matthew?' and he said, 'For Christ's sake, let's pack this. Done. That's it.'

What you have to understand, you see, is that the rowing was a very small part of what we did. So we had this final race and off they went and I think it was a few weeks later I got a phone call from Chalk and he wanted to get into the rowing race and would I be interested in selling the thing? So I told the Board of Challenge Business and we all burst out bloody laughing. Hell!

Christ, so we're trying to put a value on this thing and I said, right, we'll give him the rights to the boat and we'll give him the rowing machine. We met in a Happy Eater in Exeter and it was me and Andrew and Chalk said, 'So how much do you want for this?'

I said, 'You're not going to get this for nothing.'

Chalk asks, 'How much?'

So I gave him our price and he says, 'Oh. OK. Done.'

Andrew and I come out and we're in hysterics in the car. We could hardly bloody drive. And Chalk comes up with the money.

I would like to sit here all morning drinking tea and listening to Chay's stories but I'm afraid of outstaying my welcome. Before I leave there's something he wants to show me. I follow him into a more formal sitting room on the other side of the house. We walk past a small cabinet by the window in which I notice the British Empire Medal that he was awarded after the Atlantic row in 1966 and next to it the Commander of the British Empire medal that accompanied his *British Steel* circumnavigation in 1971. But Chay walks past the cabinet to a table by the fireplace on the far side of the room. On the table sits an old book. There's not much of it left, it's falling to pieces and the cover is missing, but he holds it up with reverence.

The book is an anthology of the fishing dory – the type of boat that Harbo and Samuelson, he and John Ridgway used to row across the Atlantic. He carefully turns through the pages, pointing at the sepia-toned pictures. These boats couldn't be more different from modern ocean rowing boats. The characters sitting in them are from a different world.

'An old boy gave this to me at a boat show. He came up to me and said he wanted me to have it.' Turning the pages, Chay talks about his visits to Newfoundland and his respect for the people there. I look at the pictures and think of Blackburn, who rowed his fishing dory from the Grand Banks back to Newfoundland, and Welch, who froze to death on the way. I feel there's a reason why Chay is showing me this book; I get the sense he's trying to explain something. The late-morning sun glows through his thick white hair. He stops at the last page and is silent.

'I appreciate you taking the time to see me, Chay. I've really enjoyed listening to your stories.'

As we walk back towards the door I pause to look at the medals in the cabinet.

'Well, I hope you've got enough for your book. If you need any more get in touch with Teresa Page, she did all the *organizing*, she'll have the details.'

I shake his hand and walk back out into the fresh morning air. By now, the sun has thawed its crisp edge. As I rev the little Peugeot hire car up the gravel drive I glance in the rear-view mirror. I can see Chay closing the front door behind him and in my head I hear him chuckling, 'Oh deary me! *Deary-my-ass!*'

My last glimpse is of him walking back towards the passage that leads behind the wooden outhouse. Off to check on the chooks.

10.

Expectation

Day 28
Date: 31 January 2010
Position: 20°12'N 32°24'W
1,720 nautical miles to Antigua

The distant roar is suddenly close, then there's a crash on the side of the cabin and a rush of spray and the boat is lifted and tossed like flotsam in the surf. It's our fourth night at sea anchor and the roughest. I'm awake and fidgety, unable to stretch out flat, with my feet wedged back under Jim's shoulder. But there's something comforting about lying in this cabin in the cool of the night, peering up through the hatch while the storm breaks around us. As I drift back to sleep I dream that I'm lying in bed, listening to the patter of rain on the bedroom window.

We wake to a different sea. It is calm and the westerly wind has died down to a stiff breeze. After five days at sea anchor it's a relief to un-stow the oars and lock them back in the gates. We shift enthusiastically into turbo, which means that we will row two-up for six hours out of every twenty-four. On average the boat moves a third faster when there are two of us on the oars. The following day the wind drops away completely and although the cloud cover stops it from getting too hot, the air is humid and heavy. It feels thick and so does the sea. Thick and languid, like warm syrup.

I settle on the word 'languid' and repeat it every time my oar dips into the sea, stretching the syllables across each stroke. In this moment there is nothing else.

The flat calm provides ideal rowing conditions and our daily mileage increases from thirty-seven miles to forty-seven, then fifty-six, almost as if we're gaining momentum. Rowing turbo leaves us with three two-hour breaks at night and each one is an opportunity to grab ninety minutes of precious sleep. We also have three one-hour breaks during the day to carry out the 'admin' routines that have evolved over the last month at sea.

One PM marks the end of my shift. I slide the oars across, step up onto the gunwale and dive into the sea. I've been looking forward to this for the last three hours. The water is deliciously cold and refreshing, and for a moment I escape from our tiny craft and become part of the vast ocean. I arch my spine and kick back up to the surface.

I swim to the boat and pull myself up onto the gunwale. Jimmy is looking out across the water. He can't escape into the cool of the sea because of the pain the salt water inflicts on the skin made raw by chafing. He doesn't complain, but I know he's frustrated.

When I'm back on board, Jimmy picks up his oars and starts rowing. I towel off and retire to the cabin. I check the battery monitor before turning on the watermaker. Although the overcast conditions mean that it is a little cooler for us during the day, the reduced charge through the solar panels also means that we have less fresh water. Today we will each have a couple of litres and I supplement this with fifty minutes on the hand-held. I pump slowly and rhythmically, periodically changing arms. I make a bottle and a half of fresh water before it's time to come out for the next three-hour shift.

I open the hatch, stand up in the footwell and stretch my back. Jimmy takes a few more strokes before he stops, pulls across the oars and has a drink. I arrange my sheepskin seat cover in the stroke rowing position, pull the straps tight across my red Crocs, pick up the oars and pause for a moment while Jim slides his oars back out. We move together up the slide, dip our blades and drive. I set the rhythm from the stroke seat while Jimmy, behind me, controls the steering. I focus on my rhythm and my stroke. *Focus*.

As we get into our rhythm my thoughts rise into the cumuli. I study their distinctive formations and pick out familiar shapes which gradually shift and merge into new forms. A voice from behind breaks my reflection.

'Would you lengthen your stroke, Adam.'

I grunt and roll in a deliberate manner up to front stops, then drive hard with my legs, pulling the handles to my ribs at backstops. *Focus*.

We row two-up for an hour before it's Jimmy's turn to take a break and time for me to swap over to the bow rowing position. Jimmy stands on deck, pulls the spare bucket out from under the gunnel and scoops it in the sea. He cools off by dunking his head in the bucket a couple of times, before disappearing into the cabin.

Although I can't see through the smoked perspex of the hatch door, I know Jimmy's routine. Firstly a sharp antiseptic tang pricks my nostrils as he mixes TCP with a little water and rubs it on his buttocks. It's quiet for a few moments, then there's some rummaging, followed by the sweet fragrance of talcum powder. A little powder rises through the cabin hatch, which is slightly ajar. Clean and dry, Jimmy now turns his attention to ways of reducing his chafing. He lies in the cabin with a roll of duct tape, a piece of foam padding and the scissors from the medical kit, thinking of how his shoes and seat padding might be modified. Although his feet are still blistered, red and swollen, the open wounds are gone and the skin is growing back over his heels. The most acute pain is now from the blisters on his buttocks, some of which have become infected. He doesn't mention it but I know his wrist is also giving him trouble, the result of an old football injury that never properly healed. For now, though, the wrist is the least of his worries.

Before the break is over Jimmy will go through the med kit, looking for things to help with the pain, like the burn dressings which have a layer of padding built into them; there is only one pack and he uses them sparingly. He will also select some painkillers. The 'ladder' starts with Ibuprofen and moves up through Diclofenac, Codeine and Tramadol. Everything is carefully rationed.

The final part of the routine is to apply a fresh layer of Sudocrem. Now the hatch swings open. It's been an hour and Jimmy emerges with a sock over his cock, waving his seat pad. He's sandwiched a third layer of foam between the two neoprene pads and cut out a cross-section at the front. Seeing the broad grin under his thick beard gives my spirits a boost.

'I don't want to speak too soon but I think I've cracked it!'

'Looks like you've built a booster seat! What's that hole at the front for?'

'Stop the tackle rubbing between the thighs. I can tuck it in here out of the way.'

We swap over so he can take the bow seat. It's our final hour of rowing two-up for today and we're both looking forward to the two-hour breaks that will come with the night shifts; a chance to grab some sleep.

We joke that as we approach Antigua, we'll raid the last remnants of the med kit and give ourselves a jab of adrenalin with the EpiPen, before sprinting the final fifty miles.

At the end of the hour I come in for my break and Jim passes me two ration packs out of a Henderson hatch.

'What have I got?' he asks.

I peel off the duct tape that is holding the ration pack together and know what he'll want.

'Savoury mince or veg pasta?' I offer.

'Veg pasta!'

Jim's favourite.

Back when we were putting the ration packs together our concerns were calories, convenience and weight. The thick, gloopy consistency of the meals when mixed with boiling water wasn't a concern for us then. But food now has a big effect on morale and we savour the taste and texture of every spoonful. The bland fish pie, an early favourite of mine, has fallen out of favour in comparison with packs like the vegetable tikka, which actually has some texture in the form of small dried vegetable pieces.

Cashew nuts and milk chocolate bars are a hit with us both, so it's always a disappointment to find salted peanuts or dark chocolate in the ration pack instead. I can't stomach the 'cherry' and 'choc orange' protein bars, so give mine to Jim, whose discipline in eating them can't be overstated.

Peanuts and wasabi powder add crunch and spice to my spag bol and, once the boiling water has been stirred in, I reseal the foil pouches and sit them beside the watermaker to stew.

Through the perspex hatch, I look at the sun resting on the surface of the sea. I pull the sat phone out of the netting and read our text messages. Despite the good mileages we've been doing, the race update from my dad says that over the last few days we've slipped from tenth to twelfth place. Somewhere out there, other crews have found the trade winds.

By Day 34 we've been on turbo for almost a week and our daily mileage is starting to slip. In particular, the night shifts are getting much harder.

My two-hour break is almost over when Jimmy calls out in the darkness: 'Ten minutes!'

I've been awake for a few minutes already, savouring every second as they painfully slip away.

'Yuup!'

I lie in the darkness desperately fighting the urge to fall asleep again. The next thing I'm aware of is Jimmy calling out again.

'Five minutes, Adam!'

Damn, where did those five minutes go?

'Yuup!'

To stop myself falling asleep again I reach up and turn on the cabin light. It's painful and I pause for a moment, shielding my eyes, before spinning round and sitting up in the footwell. Half a sachet of caffeinated High-5 EXTREME goes in my water bottle and with two minutes till my shift starts I swing open the hatch.

Jim is *attacking* the oars. Despite the cool of the night, he's dripping with sweat, his discarded Musto jacket and an empty chocolate wrapper lying on the deck.

'How's it going Jim? Looks like you've taken a double shot of EXTREME.'

'Check out the AIS.'

On the screen there's a little green triangle in front of us, also pointing west. I use the arrow buttons to move the cursor over the triangle and the words OCEAN SUMMIT appear.

'Rob and Stu.'

'They popped up at eight miles and I've taken us under seven. Let's shut them down.'

Jimmy is racing, he's in his element.

Knowing another boat is only a few miles away is a strong motivator. I scan over my shoulder for their nav light, but there's only darkness. Up above, the sky is blank. Nothing is getting through the clouds tonight. It's exhilarating to be racing and every twenty minutes I put in a sprint to see if I can break four knots. The shift passes quickly and by changeover I'm also dripping with sweat.

'I'm going to take a quick dip.'

'You're going to take a dip?' he asks incredulously.

I look at him in the darkness.

'Yeah, I'm going to take a dip. I'll be quick.'

There's something foreboding about diving head-first into the darkness, so I sit on the gunnel and slip over the side into the cool water. I duck my head under and wash the sweat off my face, then float on my back and look up into the black sky. My fingers are loosely curled around the boat's grab line. There is 8mm of nylon cord between me and the endless, enveloping emptiness.

That night we pass within a few miles of *Ocean Summit* and Jimmy has a short conversation with them on the VHF. By late morning they've disappeared from our AIS again. When I come in for my break I flick through the messages on the sat phone. The race updates we've been getting from my dad over the last few days have been encouraging us to take a more southerly course. This morning's message is along similar lines.

BOATS SOUTH OF 19N HAVE 0.2 TO 0.3 KNOTS FROM WIND. LIKELY TO PERSIST.

I want to talk to Jim about our decision to stay above twenty degrees north, but the disagreement which led to that decision is playing on my mind. We have good days and bad days, but it often feels like an argument is simmering just below the surface and I don't want to trigger another one. I'm mulling over all this later in the day when another update arrives.

TOP 20 BOATS ALL SOUTH OF U GAINED 10NM AVERAGE ON U IN LAST 24 HRS. NEED TO GET SOUTH!

The following morning I come out to join Jimmy for the first three-hour shift of the day. I have a few minutes before I'm due in the stroke seat and I check the GPS. We're at 19°52'N 36°30'W.

'Jim . . . have you seen my dad's text updates?'

'Yeah.'

'So, what d'you think?'

'I think it would be a shame to give up our latitude at this point in the race.'

I'm anxious about labouring my point, but Jim seems quite relaxed, so I decide to try again.

'But how about if we aim to get down to say . . . somewhere closer to nineteen? Maybe aim for forty or fifty miles south over the course of a few hundred miles, see if we can find some trades?'

'OK.'

I had braced myself for an argument, but now my shoulders relax. Perhaps the balance is returning to our relationship.

We've been at sea for five weeks and life has become a single monotonous routine. *Ocean Summit* appears again on the AIS, along with the vets on *Reason Why* and Peter van Kets on *Nyamezela*. We spend a week leap-frogging one another and it's clear that even over these short distances the conditions affect each boat very differently. For a while we get stuck in a bewildering current that pushes us north-east, *against* the direction of the wind and swell, and it seems the sea is determined to stop us getting south to the trades.

After nine punishing days on turbo we revert to the two-on, two-off shift pattern. The extra three hours of rest we now get each day feels like a great luxury, but Jimmy's extra rest time is quickly eaten up by his admin routine; the relief from alterations to his seat padding is only temporary, and it's getting tougher and tougher to maintain his body.

A headwind begins to build and our daily mileage drops from fifty-three to thirty-five. The day after that, we cover just twenty-six miles and it's clear that we'll be back on sea anchor soon. This evening my dad's update brings the frustrating news that the fleet average for the day was forty-two miles, exactly twice our daily mileage. As a result we've dropped to fourteenth place.

On Day 40, despite only light westerly winds and both of us on the oars, the boat starts to move backwards. It seems that we are in the grip of more cruel currents. Unsure of what the best course of action is, we experiment with the sea anchor. Rather than hovering below the surface in front of the boat, the sea anchor sinks straight down beneath us, dragging fifty metres of line along behind it. After that, there's not much to do but tidy the deck while we study the speed and course of the boat on the GPS. Satisfied that the sea anchor is slowing our backwards drift, we retire to the cabin.

In the evening I call Alice on the sat phone. We've been speaking about once a fortnight and although Alice is keen for me to call more often, I'd rather speak less. It's wonderful to hear her voice, but the sudden jolt back to my old life cracks open the armour that I've built up to deal with the harsh reality of this world. One piece of news comes as a surprise: despite our recent efforts to get south, we are now the most *northerly* boat in the fleet.

I share this news with Jimmy and it strengthens our resolve to push south, as does an update from my dad later that evening which simply reads:

MUST GET BELOW 18N!

By 10.30 the following morning, although the wind has picked up, we find that it is possible to make progress rowing two-up. We plot a new more southerly bearing and christen the gruelling 'super-turbo' shift pattern with three shifts of thirty minutes on, thirty minutes off, which we keep up through the night. Over the next four days we cover 186 miles and push another ninety-five miles south to 17° 42'N.

Early on the morning of Day 43 I'm getting ready to come out for the daybreak shift when the VHF radio crackles to life.

'*Spirit of Montanaro, Spirit of Montanaro*, this is *Nyamezela*. Over.'

It catches me by surprise to hear another voice in the cabin. I stare at the radio for a moment before grabbing the mic off the wall and pressing TRANSMIT.

'Peter! This is *Spirit of Montanaro*, how you doing? Over.'

'Hey, man! How you doing? Listen, man, looking at the GPS you're pretty close by, looks like our paths might cross. We should meet up, have a *cup of tea*, ha! What do you think? Over.'

'Pete, great to hear from you. We should definitely meet up. We'll plot a course to rendezvous. Over.'

'Yeah, see you soon, man.'

'We'll see you in a bit Pete.'

'*Nyamezela* out.'

I hang the mic back on the radio and pop my head out through the hatch.

'D'you hear that, Jim?'

The atmosphere on the boat lifts and Jim and I beam at each other.

I consult the GPS and see that NYAMEZELA is flashing red to indicate a collision course.

'He's south-east of us, about two miles away.'

We change over and I alter our course, paddling gently on the oars, holding a bearing. I watch van Kets catching up with us on the GPS and soon he's on the radio again; he has spotted our nav light. Jim comes back out on deck and together we scan the horizon to the south-east. As both boats rise to the crest of a wave, we catch the twinkle of a nav light and in a few minutes *Nyamezela*'s silhouette is illuminated in the breaking dawn.

As *Nyamezela* approaches, Jimmy ducks into the cabin and comes back out with the video camera. For modesty's sake he has also put on some shorts.

The camera's running.

'Hey, Adam, do you want to explain what's going on?'

'We're just popping in to see Peter van Kets. We're in the middle of the Atlantic Ocean and he's just arrived . . .'

'We're slap bang in the middle of the Atlantic . . .' Jimmy continues.

'. . . after rowing fifteen hundred miles . . .'

'. . . and there he is.'

Jimmy turns the camera to *Nyamezela*, which is now twenty metres off our port side.

A South African flag flies proudly from the stern and Pete is wearing his team T-shirt, with 'Own Your Life' written across the chest. Even from this distance, we can see that he has lost a lot of weight, he looks shrunken, hollowed-out. He's really suffering. I remember meeting him in our first week on La Gomera and finding him friendly but somehow distant, his mind already steeling itself for the ocean. Now I understand.

'How you doing, man?' I ask.

'How does it feel to see another face?' asks Jimmy.

He cracks a familiar smile.

'So weird, man! It feels so good. How you doing?'

'A few blisters but in good condition,' replies Jimmy. 'How have you found this crossing compared to the last one?'

'Ha! A lot slower. I think I enjoyed the pairs crossing more.'

From the way *Nyamezela* moves in the swell we can see that it is extremely light and as soon as Pete stops rowing, the wind blows him away from us. I paddle briefly to keep us within talking distance. Jimmy puts down the video camera and explains about his sores, which are getting worse and worse. Perhaps Pete has some advice?

'Here, let me give you some stuff . . . it's miracle cream.'

Pete ducks into his cabin and pulls out a clear plastic tub.

'What's in it?'

'It's eucalyptus and olive oil and some other stuff. Natural oils. I told these guys what I was doing and they made it up for me. It's miracle cream.'

'Are you sure you've got enough?'

'I've got loads . . . Hey wait, I'll swim over to you.'

Jim and I look at each other before Jim calls back. 'I'm not sure you should do that, Pete. I'm not sure you should leave your boat.'

Pete considers this for a moment, then decides to stay put.

It is wonderfully uplifting to have this human contact and we hope this rendezvous is also doing Pete's morale some good. He tells us a story about a small tern that he found sheltering on his deck during a storm. He brought the bird into the cabin and it kept him company for two days until the weather cleared. I'm surprised when Pete tells us that he calls his wife at least once a day on the satellite phone – I find that speaking to Alice only makes the distance between us feel more real.

Jim and I want to do something for him. We suggest swapping some rations, but he has the same Expedition Foods freeze-dried meals as we do. We offer him some biltong, but he has plenty of that too, so Jim digs around in the treats bag and finds our last fruit bar. The sea is too rough for us to pull alongside, so I dive in and swim over to his boat. While I'm clinging on to *Nyamezela*'s grab line we shake hands.

After half an hour we say farewell to Pete and go our separate ways. The wind catches *Nyamezela* and we soon lose sight of her in the swell. Jimmy and I and our little boat are alone again on the ocean. But the meeting leaves us in high spirits and over the following days laughter and thoughtful gestures come more easily, while the daily race updates show that our more southerly course is paying dividends.

It's 1.40 AM on Day 47 and I've just ducked into the cabin to grab the video camera. The GPS, which is counting down the distance to Antigua, is about to tick below 1,000 miles, an important milestone for us. I record an update on our supplies, which are beginning to run low. The stock-take yesterday afternoon confirmed that we have twenty days of food left, which means that to reach the finish we need to either increase our average distance to fifty miles per day, or we need to eat less. Given that our daily average so far is under forty miles, rationing is the only sensible option. We've been talking about this for the last week or so and Jimmy has already started cutting back; a handful of spare freeze-dried meals are stuffed in his netting.

I'm relatively relaxed about our rations, and actually more concerned that we will soon run out of toilet paper. Whatever happens, I'm confident we won't starve; we've barely touched the twenty kilos of BP-5 we're carrying. These emergency rations are a high-calorie, vitamin-enhanced biscuit, a little like an unappetizing digestive, and if needs be we could live off them, if rather joylessly, for a further thirty days. There is also the fishing line, although we've yet to have much luck with it.

I estimate we'll be spending thirty more days at sea while Jimmy reckons forty. Given Jimmy's more cautious attitude, I'm worried that we're going to have a confrontation about cutting back on our daily rations. I'm relieved when instead he suggests that we simply split the remaining food and each decide on our own approach to rationing.

I'm on the late-morning shift when the VHF crackles to life. *Ocean Planet*, the race support yacht, crewed by Tony Lovering and Peter Hogden, who himself rowed in Chay's 1997 race, is en route to us, having checked on *Nyamezela* yesterday. Jimmy comes out on deck to scan the horizon and eventually spots a mast to the east. It takes a long time for the bright yellow hull of the sixty-foot ocean racer to come into view. Jimmy pops back into the cabin to grab the video camera and put on some shorts.

It's a flat calm day, with light winds, and *Ocean Planet* is still a long way off when Tony's voice rings out across the water.

'DO YOU WANT A PINT OF BEER?'

Beer is the last thing either of us wants. But I do remember that back in La Gomera Tony had mentioned that *Ocean Planet* was provisioned largely with freeze-dried blueberry cheesecake.

'How about some BLUEBERRY CHEESECAKE?'

Peter and Tony must have eaten the cheesecake, but as the boat circles us, with Peter on the wheel, Tony disappears below deck and puts a few things in a bin bag, which he tosses to us.

'Did you hear about *Limited Intelligence* and the marlin?'

'Marlin? No, what about them?'

'A huge marlin came in, smashed through the stern of the boat, the beak's gone through the watermaker compartment and snapped off . . . the beak of the marlin . . . snapped off in the stern of the boat . . .'

'*What?* Is it still going? The boat?'

'They're still going. They've had to leave it in there and patch around it.'

'My God! That's incredible . . .'

As I'm digesting the news, Jimmy calls back to them.

'How are you doing anyway, guys? You look well.'

Peter replies, 'You know . . . we're doing all right.'

'Only problem,' continues Tony, '. . . is that I've still got a LILY WHITE ASS!'

Tony is still waving his bare bum from the bow of the boat when Peter turns the wheel onto a course for Antigua. They will be there within a week to welcome the arrival of Charlie Pitcher, who is leading the race in *Insure & Go*. As the bright yellow hull disappears from view I picture Charlie, debonair as ever, setting foot on the pontoon in English Harbour. Then, for a moment, I imagine Jimmy and myself crossing the finish line and I feel a surge of emotion. I quickly raise my guard again and block the thought from my mind.

In the bag that Tony has thrown us are a can of rice pudding, a few packets of Super Noodles and, to my relief, a roll of toilet paper.

Our meetings with *Nyamezela* and *Ocean Planet* have left us feeling more at ease with our situation and with each other, and things are made even better by the fact that Jimmy's chafing is clearing up; PvK's miracle cream is working.

Late in the afternoon of Day 51 a westerly begins to build. It offers some relief from the heat, but makes the rowing harder and overnight our speed drops to below a knot. At 3 AM we reluctantly drop the sea anchor.

The following day it's uncomfortable and rather claustrophobic in the cabin, with Jim and me squashed together like sardines, but at least it's not too hot. That evening, I lie with the main hatch slightly ajar and my feet resting on the wall of the cabin, listening to my audiobook of *The Old Man and the Sea* and pumping fresh water on the hand-held. Thinking about the Old Man wrestling with the marlin, I resolve to try my luck with the fishing line again.

Just as I start to doze off, Jimmy puts down the Gideon and looks over.

'Hey. Adam.'

'What?'

'How about a cigar?'

'Cigar? Not sure about that, but I'll definitely join you for a wee dram.'

I rummage around in my netting and pull out three miniature bottles of whisky.

'Will it be the ten-, the fifteen- or the eighteen-year-old, *sir*?'

I climb out through the hatch and sit on the port-side gunnel. Jim follows and sits in the bow rowing position. The sun is low in the cloud-mottled sky. To the west, the horizon is a palette of reds, oranges and golden yellows. We roll with the swell. Jim bites off the end of his cigar and, shielding it from the wind, strikes a match to it.

'I gotta say, with the beard and the cigar you do look the part. Fancy a nip?'

I pass him the fifteen-year-old, then crack the top off the ten and take a slug. I slurp air through the liquor, then I roll it around my tongue before finally savouring its warmth in my chest.

'Ahh. Lovely.'

'This *is* the life.'

'Oh yes. This is the life.'

I feel a glow of contentment.

'So what will you miss, Adam, when you're back on dry land?'

'I'll miss the simplicity of life out here . . . you know, away from everything you have to deal with every day in normal life. We've just got a single purpose out here and nothing else to worry about. And I'll miss those amazing nights when the sky is so clear and filled with stars – you never see *anything* like that on dry land. How about you?'

'I'm just enjoying being out here, really enjoying the sea. A shame about all the rowing! But it's great to be out here. It feels a real privilege to be doing this.'

'I know it's going to sound weird, but when I'm sat back at my desk in the City on a gloomy November afternoon, I do think I'm going to miss all the sunshine and exercise.'

'You're going to miss the heat and the rowing? Are you mad?'

Before turning in for the night, we watch an episode of *Black-adder* on Jim's iPod. I drift off to sleep wrapped in a feeling of peace: I am at peace with the ocean, with our situation and with Jimmy.

We're back on the oars at first light. The wind has died, the sky has cleared and it's already one of the hottest days we've had. During the midday shift I notice a dorado swimming just off the tip of my starboard oar and again remember the Old Man wrestling with the marlin. We've seen plenty of dorado during the trip and even hooked a few, but without managing to land them. The fish hugs persistently to the tip of my oar and I point it out to Jim when we change over.

'Look at that big fat fish. That dorado is mine. Get the wasabi ready, it's sashimi for dinner!'

I dig the hand line out of the Lewmar deck hatch and bait it up with biltong. I throw out ten metres of line, tie it off on a handle beside the main hatch and retire to the cabin. The stern hatch is open and I try to imagine that there is actually a breeze flowing through the cabin. I wait a while, and check the line a couple of times. Eventually, I stop checking the line and am just starting to doze off when there's a splash behind the boat. As I get up to peer out of the hatch, Jimmy calls.

'Adam, I think there's something on the line.'

I hurry out on deck and test the line. We've caught a fish!

As I pick up the big red hand spool the line suddenly goes slack and a dorado, about a foot and a half long, with a beautiful rainbow of colour along its back, leaps into the air. Now the fish dives and I cautiously pay out a little line. I think about the Old Man letting the marlin exhaust itself. But the dorado is now on the other side of the boat and I can feel the nylon running over the rough surface of our keel. I'm worried that the abrasion will snap the line so I continue to pay it out. The fish jumps again before diving down under the boat.

The line is getting in the way of the oars so Jimmy stops rowing and we chat excitedly as the dorado starts to swim in smaller and smaller circles around the boat. Slowly and carefully, I wind the line back onto the spool and eventually the fish is lying alongside the boat, breathing hard and exhausted to the point of indifference. Jimmy scoops it up with the spare bucket. The fish lashes wildly as I strike its bulbous forehead with the back of an axe. It takes half a dozen blows to dispatch the animal and we both feel sad to watch it die. The flash of vibrant colour on the dorado's back goes dull.

I gut and fillet the fish and even before throwing the offal overboard, the water beneath the boat is churning with the rest of the shoal, eager for a share of our dinner. We try some sashimi, which is rather chewy, but fried in the pan the fish is delicious and has a tight, meaty texture.

Fishing is fun but messy. There are fish scales and blood all over one corner of the deck and although I scrub everything down with Fairy liquid, the boat smells like a fishmonger's for the rest of the week.

*

Tonight *Ocean Summit* is on our AIS again. This time Rob and Stu are five miles ahead and on the same bearing as we are, so we set ourselves the target of catching them by morning. We soon decipher their shift pattern; every hour and a half *Ocean Summit* stops and spins round ninety degrees, while the boys change over. We row hard through the night; it's great to have a target and we both work at eating away a little of the mileage each shift. Tonight Jimmy and I are a team: this is what all those early mornings together on the river and late nights in the gym were for.

We catch sight of *Ocean Summit's* nav light in the twilight just before dawn. When Jim comes off the daybreak shift he calls Rob on the VHF and agrees a rendezvous, but *Ocean Summit* makes us work for it and closing the last 600 metres takes twenty minutes of hard rowing. We spot Rob first, kneeling out of the stern hatch, holding a video camera. As we draw closer, Stu comes into view in the bow rowing position.

Jim calls over. 'So I think this is where we say, "Fancy meeting you out here!" How have you been?'

There's a pause before Stu replies, 'We're doing all right, but we're just getting really hacked off with the weather. Any normal year we'd be there by now . . .'

Stu has lost a little weight, but they both look healthy. Rob is wearing a T-shirt and Speedos. The sun has made his mane of hair even blonder.

Rob notes my appearance, 'You're naked . . .' before turning his attention to Jimmy '. . . and that is an amazing beard.'

'Yes, it is an amazing beard. Look at you boys, both clean-shaven. It looks like you've just left.'

Stu replies, 'I tried growing a beard for a while, but it didn't look right. It just looked kind of *ratty*.'

I can relate to that. 'Yeah, tell me about it! But I didn't bring a razor.'

Stu puts down his oars, which means I can put down mine, and starts talking again about his frustration with the weather. Rob interrupts him.

'Your boat on the AIS last night was amazing, I don't know how you did it.'

Jimmy and I laugh.

'Ah, you know, it was just the guns . . .'

'Yeah, we worked pretty hard last night to close you down.'

Stu is keen to know if we've had any update on the weather or our estimated arrival date.

I give him my dad's most recent forecast, 20 March.

'But your dad originally thought the tenth,' explains Jimmy. 'Basically we've been thinking the trip would take another twenty days for the last two weeks.'

Stu nods. 'A week and a half ago I got excited because I thought, awesome, I can start counting down now, but I just seem to keep counting up.'

Rob asks, 'Can you ask your dad for a revised schedule because my fiancée's there from the twelfth to the nineteenth . . .'

I feel for Rob. The pressure of an arrival deadline, an increasingly unachievable one, must be a heavy weight to bear.

'. . . and I've got Everest as well. I'm flying to Nepal on the twenty-fourth . . .'

It takes Jimmy and me a moment to digest this.

'You're kidding. Mount Everest . . .'

'You're flying to Nepal . . . on the twenty-fourth . . .'

'Are you going too, Stu?'

'No. Time-wise and financially there's just no chance for me now.'

I turn back to Rob. 'Everest. That's amazing. So you'll have just about learnt to walk again and you'll be off to climb Everest.'

'Hats off to you.'

Stu brings the conversation back to his frustration with the weather.

'The combination of the delays beforehand and then this – it's just mental, isn't it?'

'Apparently the last boat's due to get in mid-June.'

'Sean McGowan?'

'Six months at sea. Solo.'

'Unbelievable!'

'Poor Sean!'

'You just can't imagine it.'

Jimmy senses that the boys could do with a pep talk. 'Well, you're doing really well and you both look well and in really good spirits too.'

We tell Rob and Stu about our recent fishing success and, before going our separate ways, we exchange a few rations. As the boats drift apart, the conversation stops and an air of dejection descends on *Ocean Summit*. Rob is standing on deck with his head hung low. I watch him lift his right hand and bite a nail.

Jim shouts over some final words of support.

'Listen, guys, we'll see you again in a couple of weeks. We'll get in within a couple of hours of each other and we'll hit the pub together. Keep your chin up, you're doing really well . . . and don't worry Rob, your fiancée will wait for you . . . and you'll make your flight.'

Rob looks up and gives half a laugh before his head drops again.

The Record Breakers, 2005–2010

Date: 26 February 2011
Location: Near Selkirk, Scottish Borders

'There were five tonnes of ocean rowing boat going in one direction and 37,000 tonnes of soya bean going in the other. Although she was tied onto the side of *Island Ranger*, *La Mondiale* would move out by two metres then slam back into the hull and that was disintegrating our starboard side as the guys were climbing up the ladder. Metal was being bent, fibreglass was being smashed.' Leven stops and clears his throat. 'It was one of the most nerve-wracking moments of my life.'

Leven Brown and the thirteen-man crew of *La Mondiale* had been settling into another hundred-mile day, and were on track to beat the thirty-three-day Atlantic rowing record that Leven had set with the same boat the previous year. *La Mondiale* was surfing down a wave when it happened; no one noticed an impact, but Leven immediately knew that something was wrong. The boat felt heavy, and then began to spin uncontrollably in the water. A look over the stern confirmed that she had lost her rudder. The crew speculated that it could have been knocked off by a whale – they had seen a number of them near the boat. It was mid-afternoon, the wind was starting to pick up, and Leven faced a difficult decision: to limp across the Atlantic, at the mercy of the winds and currents, and hope to arrive somewhere in the Caribbean in a few months' time; or to send out a Mayday, rescue the crew and abandon the boat. Emotions on board *La Mondiale* were running high.

'The romantic in me would love to have drawn the phoenix out of the fire and limped into Barbados, but we were two thousand miles away at the time. If you'd been out there on your own the decision would have been easy, we would have drifted across and taken the boat. But with a larger crew, fourteen people, to look after it's a different story.'

At 10.21 GMT on Thursday 15 January 2009, the Falmouth Maritime and Rescue Coordination Centre (FMRCC) received a satellite call. Leven had made his decision; with their attempt to repair the rudder overnight unsuccessful, he asked Falmouth to initiate a rescue.

'It was a remarkably easy decision to take. Faced with the option of going into the unknown for little more than heroism, or drawing a line through it and securing your crew, it didn't take me very long to come to a conclusion.'

Island Ranger was en route to Italy with a cargo of Brazilian soya bean when Captain Leonid Panamaryov received the call from the FMRCC. Although the bulk carrier was ill-equipped to carry out a rescue, she was the nearest ship to the stranded rowers. It was early evening when *Island Ranger* reached *La Mondiale* and by now the wind had increased to a force seven, whipping up the swell to fifteen feet. As the bulk carrier loomed into view, Leven sent up a flare to confirm his location. Once the huge, single-prop vessel had manoeuvred into position, with *La Mondiale* protected from the worst of the weather in the lee of the ship's hull, a rope ladder was thrown down. One by one, the crew scaled the forty-five-foot steel wall.

'The greatest concern was the sheer violence of the impact of *La Mondiale* against the *Island Ranger*. Should anyone have fallen off the ladder it's pretty unlikely they would have survived.'

With the boat disintegrating under their feet, they had to move quickly. Leven was the last to leave the stricken vessel. 'I remember poking my head over the side of *Island Ranger* and what I saw was thirteen other happy faces. It was all over.'

In the last of the light the crew watched as *La Mondiale* was cast off. Although battered and bruised, she was still riding high on the waves. Then, as *Island Ranger*'s propeller began to turn, the ropes attached to the rowing boat became tangled in it. For the next ten minutes the propeller was spun back and forth to snap the line and each time *La Mondiale* would smash into the back of the ship. Eventually her bows were split open. 'I remember very clearly looking over the stern of *Island Ranger* and watching something we had worked very hard for being utterly destroyed in front of our eyes.'

It's to learn more about what Leven did next that I'm here in the Scottish Borders on a grey afternoon in early spring. Despite being one of the legends of ocean rowing, Leven Brown is only thirty-eight. As he strode out of the back door of the farmhouse, over to where I'd parked beside the barn, I braced for a bear-hug; he has that sense about him. I was disappointed when he took my hand instead. When I showed him the bottle of Lagavulin single malt I'd brought, Leven's eyes lit up.

As a child, Leven was introduced to the idea of ocean rowing during a course at the John Ridgway School of Adventure in Ardmore. 'I heard that John Ridgway had rowed an ocean and my jaw dropped. I had never heard of this at the time.' Leven always relished physical challenges and was in his element at Ardmore – 'The colder and harder it was, the more of a thrill I got out of it.' After school Leven moved to Edinburgh to study mathematics, but hated the course and soon dropped out, taking a job in the post room of a stockbroker.

Over the next fifteen years Leven built a career at the firm, working his way steadily up from the post room to a management position. He felt content with his lot, and happy about the direction in which life had taken him, until in 2003 an otherwise unremarkable event caused him to question his life choices: a medic tried to pull him out of the Caledonian Challenge charity walk because of his badly blistered feet. Leven ducked out of the first-aid tent and eventually completed the fifty-four-mile route, but *almost* failing had a profound effect on him. Leven needed to prove himself, and the Atlantic was the benchmark set by his childhood hero.

Leven sold everything he owned and, during the 2005/6 season, rowed from the Spanish mainland to the West Indies in *Atlantic Wholff*, completing the solo crossing in 123 days. With one crossing under his belt, Leven wanted more. Six months later he put down a deposit on *La Mondiale*. Rowed by a French crew in 1992, she had completed the mid-Atlantic, Canaries–Caribbean route in thirty-five days – a record that still stood.

Leven set about modifying *La Mondiale*, trimming her weight and improving the gearing on the oars. To row across the Atlantic in less than thirty-five days he would need to squeeze every knot of performance from her. To select a crew, 200 hopefuls went through a two-stage process. The second stage was along the lines of the military-style survival course that Leven had enjoyed as a child at Ardmore.

The crew rowed out of Gran Canaria on 15 December 2007 and landed in Barbados on 17 January 2008, taking two days off the French record. With Leven's name in the record books and his reputation now established, Artemis Investments agreed to become the title sponsor for his next project. Leven's plan was to take *La Mondiale* into the North Atlantic, where, incredibly, Harbo and Samuelson's 1896 record of fifty-five days still stood. No rower in modern times had even come close to beating the two Norwegians in their open, cedar-clad fishing boat.

Knowing that the North Atlantic would present far greater challenges than the mid-Atlantic, Leven decided to first test the refurbished boat on a second mid-Atlantic crossing, and he set about selecting a new crew.

'I'm very into managing expectations,' explains Leven, whose advert for crew offered 'pain, fear and fatigue free of charge and part of the daily routine'. Some of those who had rowed *La Mondiale* during her record-breaking crossing the previous year signed up to this new team and Leven was particularly pleased to see fellow Scotsman Don Lennox, forty-one, in the line-up. 'Don's work rate I've never seen the likes of before on a boat.'

Amongst the new faces was Livar Nysted, thirty-nine, a Faroese sea-rowing champion, and 'pound for pound, one of the most powerful men I've ever met'. Livar had extensive experience in the North Atlantic, both as a fisherman and during two attempts to row the 200-mile passage from Faroe to the Shetland Islands in a traditional Faroese fishing boat.

On the first day of the selection process for the new team, Leven remembers Livar bounding up to him and taking his hand.

'Leven! I recognize your photograph off the internet. Although you looked much taller.' He paused. 'For years I thought I was the last one.'

'The last one of what?' asked Leven.

'For years I thought I was the last Neanderthal. Now I know I am not.'

Livar passed selection and became part of the ill-fated crew. On 14 January 2009, when disaster struck *La Mondiale*, he was amongst those who argued for staying with the stricken boat.

Given the pressure which Leven was under when he took the decision to abandon *La Mondiale*, I ask if he has any regrets about it. 'As a skipper, your boat means nothing compared to the safety of your guys. They fought very hard for ten days. My only regret is that the rudder didn't stay on the boat. We would have set a very good time.' At the moment she lost her rudder, *La Mondiale* had been on track to beat her previous record by almost three days. 'But fate dealt us those cards.'

Finding himself back in the UK in early 2009, with no boat and no equipment, Leven picked himself up and started over again. Before losing the boat his intention had been to go for the North Atlantic record and, with further support from Artemis Investments, he set about putting another expedition together.

'The upshot of it was that we had to tackle the North Atlantic in a much smaller boat and with a much smaller crew. But that was a great thing in that we were able to select the very best of our crew from the years gone by who had vast experience.'

Alongside Leven were just three others: Don Lennox, Livar Nysted and Ray Carroll, thirty-three, an Irish national rower who Leven describes as 'very focused, very determined, a perfectionist'. Ray had been a key member of *La Mondiale*'s record-breaking 2008 crossing. As another member of that crew told reporters at the time, 'Ray was the man who got us the record. He screamed at us and motivated us.'

Leven decided to squeeze the four-man team into a boat designed for two. In exchange for extremely cramped and difficult living conditions, the boat would have an exceptional power-to-weight ratio. He bought a fibreglass-and-Kevlar boat called *Flying Ferkins*, which had been rowed across the Indian Ocean earlier that year. With a few modifications, and renamed *Artemis Investments*, she was ready for the North Atlantic.

We're in the spare room which is the Ocean Rowing Events HQ

when the clock ticks past 6 PM. Leven's countdown to 'dram o'clock' is over. Back downstairs in the kitchen he brings out two tumblers, the top comes off the Lagavulin and we make ourselves comfortable for the evening.

Artemis Investments set off from Battery Park, New York, on Thursday 17 June 2010. It was their third attempt to leave New York – equipment failure, then illness, had foiled the first two. For the first five days they suffered from cross-winds and the effects of the tide, but still logged daily distances of seventy to eighty miles. An area of low pressure passed over them on Day 6, bringing headwinds and a short stint at sea anchor. By now the fog had also arrived, and it would stay with them for most of the crossing. After a few near misses, the crew became attuned to the sound of fishing boats hidden in the gloom.

On Day 8 a patch of 'sweet water' signalled that they had found the Gulf Stream, which increased their daily distance by around ten miles. In the log Leven noted, '. . . we suddenly accelerated from about 3 knots to 5 knots at times . . . this is fast moving oceanic current where the boat literally lifts 4 inches out of the water and goes like the clappers . . . always a reality check when you lose the sweet water!'

On board *Artemis Investments* the two shifts consisted of Leven and Livar, known collectively as the Neanderthals, and Ray and Don, who were the Beckhams ('they were more glamorous and certainly better rowers than us'). The pairings were decided on the basis of personality. 'Livar and Ray are very alpha male. They would never have worked together very well. Don and I are the two quieter characters and we sort of split it on that basis.' Competition between the Neanderthals and the Beckhams also helped to motivate the team, with Livar and Ray driving each other on.

The crew's twelfth day at sea was their fastest yet. With favourable currents, a fifteen-foot following swell and the wind on their stern, *Artemis Investments* covered 117 miles in twenty-four hours, setting a record for the North Atlantic. In these conditions a more cautious crew would have thrown out a drogue to slow and stabilize the boat, but with Harbo and Samuelson's record foremost in their minds, Leven's team took advantage of everything the ocean offered them. Conditions grew more challenging through the night and by morning the wind was gusting to forty-five knots, with thirty-foot waves swamping the boat. It was while Don and Ray were surfing down one of these large breakers that *Artemis Investments* capsized.

Caught awkwardly by the wave, she went into a barrel-roll, throwing Don into the water. Both men were wearing life jackets and were clipped on and Don was quickly back in the boat. Leven was pleased with how the team handled the situation. 'No one was fazed or frightened or undermined. We *knew* we were going to capsize, this is the North Atlantic. It was always going to happen and again it all comes down to managing expectations.'

A quick kit-check showed they had only lost a few water bottles and seat covers and, rather than throwing out the sea anchor and stopping to regroup, the crew decided to push on. Their perseverance was rewarded with a 102-mile day.

By the end of Day 14 they had already rowed more than 1,000 miles.

Just before midnight on their twenty-third day at sea, the crew passed the halfway point. They stopped for a ten-minute celebration, which involved each man wolfing down four Mars bars and an extra freeze-dried meal, before getting back on the oars. Here, as so often before, the extra calories were too much for them and the next morning they were all ill. At least, Leven noted in the log, being sick provided 'a distraction from our sore hands, legs and backsides and something else to chat about!' Despite this, *Artemis Investments* covered over a hundred miles that day too.

Even as conditions deteriorated, the crew continued to push the craft to its limits, and on their thirtieth day at sea they paid for this aggressive approach with a second capsize. This time it was Livar's turn to take a bath. With the wind on their stern gusting up to fifty knots, the crew had been on track for a 120-mile day. Leven remembers the wave that flipped them. From twenty metres it looked like any other, but the moment its shape started to change he knew that they were going over. As the crest of the wave broke over them, the boat veered sideways and began to barrel-roll, catapulting Livar from the stroke seat the full length of his thirty-foot safety line.

'He was thrown out like a golf ball, right over the top of the safety rail. One of my lasting memories is watching Livar's boots disappear. He flew through the air like Superman.'

Although far more violent than the capsize they had suffered a fortnight earlier, Livar took it in his stride.

'I was shouting, "Come on Livar! Come on, come on, come on, Livar!" And he swam back to the boat and got back in and he looked me in the eye and said, "I am not a fucking dog." Going overboard was in no way fazing him. He was more annoyed than anything.'

The team's resolve was unshaken, but the capsize caused the skipper to take stock. It wasn't safe to continue pushing *Artemis Investments* as hard as they had been, and despite the following wind Leven decided to throw out the sea anchor. With the seven-metre parachute off the bow, the boat swung round to face into the weather. Despite the sea anchor holding twelve tonnes of water, the ferocity of the conditions meant that the boat was still travelling at two knots *backwards*. That evening Livar sent a message to his wife. It was her birthday.

When the crew emerged the following morning it was clear that the decision to go to sea anchor had been a wise one. The violence of the storm that night had damaged the stainless-steel safety rail.

Ray and Leven were both suffering from ingrowing toenails, but by Day 33 Ray's toe was infected and swollen. He was in a great deal of pain. Concerned that the infection might spread, Leven tried to persuade Ray to let him cut the nail out. 'As the ship's surgeon I immediately recommended amputation. He wasn't too keen on that. So I offered to cut the nail out or pull it off.'

Ray wasn't sure about being put to the knife, so Leven demonstrated what he planned to do by cutting out his own ingrowing nail with the tools he had to hand: a penknife and a pair of pliers. After seeing the procedure, Ray agreed and he was pleased with the results. 'As you remove the offending toenail the fluid drains almost immediately from the toe, like toothpaste, and the pain relief is instantaneous,' explains Leven. In the ship's log he noted, 'Carroll agreed to proceed – and yes he will dance again!'

By Day 37 *Artemis Investments* was less than 600 miles from the Scilly Isles and the crew knew that the fifty-five-day record was well within reach. The previous week they had been contacted by the *Queen Mary 2*, which was preparing to leave New York on a six-day passage to Southampton. The largest vessel in the North Atlantic had requested a mid-ocean rendezvous with the smallest.

The crew had been listening to the ocean liner's horn for some time before her huge black hull started to emerge through the thick fog. At 1,100 feet long and with capacity for 3,900 passengers and crew, the *Queen Mary 2* is one of the world's largest cruise ships. Leven remembers gazing up at her in awe. 'She's one of the only ships in the modern era that wasn't built by an accountant. You've got a lovely flared bow, the accommodation block doesn't stick out like a great Roman nose. She's not a floating hotel, she's a liner.'

While they marvelled at the vessel that was coming into view, the VHF crackled to life.

'*Artemis Investment*, *Queen Mary 2*, channel six.'

'Hello *QM 2*, we can see you now, we have a visual on you, you're directly astern of us, about half a mile I would say.'

Up on the bridge Captain Nick Bates couldn't yet see the rowers through the fog, but he was tracking them on radar.

'We're going to come up and stop short of you.'

As *Artemis Investments* came into the lee of *Queen Mary 2*, the wind dropped and the sea flattened. Her presence in the water reduced the height of the swell by six feet. A thousand people lined the upper decks and on the lower decks they waved through the portholes; it was an overwhelming sight for the rowers. As the rowing boat drew close, people started shouting out questions and Captain Bates patched *Artemis Investments'* VHF through the ship's tannoy system so that everybody could hear their answers.

The *Queen Mary 2* lowered a RIB with the ship's cameramen on board to record the occasion. For the rowers it was one of the highlights of the crossing. 'It lifted our spirits no end. We were just grinding out the miles by that stage and it was a great morale booster.' Ray was particularly pleased to see the ship – by coincidence he had once worked on board as an engineer. But they had a record to beat, and so, after more waving, they rowed clear of the propellers and watched as her huge bulk disappeared once again into the fog.

The autohelm had been unreliable throughout the trip and the following day it stopped working again. The watermaker was also making some worrying noises and Leven wondered if they might soon have to ration water. With less than 500 miles to the finish line, the biggest risk now was equipment failure.

The influence of the tides was the first sign that they were approaching land. Next, as the fog began to clear, they started to notice aircraft and land birds. One night they found themselves surrounded by fishing boats, whose blinking lights reminded the crew that they were nearly home.

The Scilly Isles appeared on the AIS long before the crew could see them. Ten miles out, a press helicopter appeared, then boats carrying family and friends. Under a clear sky and bathed in the late July sunshine, the crew enjoyed their final few miles on the oars, followed by the growing flotilla of well-wishers. As they entered the harbour, Leven set off a hand flare, while Sinatra's 'New York, New York' played over the PA system.

At 14.56 GMT on 31 July 2010, Leven Brown, Don Lennox, Ray Carroll and Livar Nysted came ashore at St Mary's, following in the footsteps of Harbo and Samuelson, who had landed at that same spot on 1 August 1896, almost exactly 114 years before them.

The formal announcement was made by Ken Crutchlow, president of the Ocean Rowing Society. *Artemis Investments* had rowed from New York to the Scilly Isles in forty-three days, twenty-one hours; eleven days faster than Harbo and Samuelson. A cheer went up around the harbour. Leven, Don and Ray now held the rowing record for both the North and mid-Atlantic. Next on the microphone was the harbour master with a message from George Harbo's granddaughter:

> The Harbo families send our heartiest congratulations to team Artemis for a job well done. We know this is a true milestone since it took 114 years to beat our grandfather, George Harbo's 1896 Atlantic crossing, with his mate Frank Samuelson. The thirty-foot waves and capsizing are only part of their story. It is exhilarating to relive the excitement with your heroic journey . . . We applaud your courage and your spirit.

Leven had come a long way since watching *La Mondiale* being split apart on the stern of *Island Ranger* eighteen months earlier.

Today, his ambition is to broaden the appeal of ocean rowing and turn it into a high-profile, sponsored sport, like sailing. 'How fast you can go is directly proportional to the amount of money that's pumped into the sport. It determines the boat you buy and the information you get and the crew you select.' For those who are good enough, he wants to be able to take the financial burden out of rowing oceans by paying his crew.

Leven's next goal is to row the mid-Atlantic, Canaries–Caribbean route in under thirty days. It's the 'four-minute mile' of ocean rowing and, as Leven observes, that kind of story opens sponsors' chequebooks.

An empty bottle of Lagavulin sits on the kitchen table and next to it is my tape recorder. The red RECORD light is still flashing, but the wheels came off this interview hours ago. I'm carefully contemplating the half-full tumbler in my hand, when I become aware of a noise coming from the pantry. It's a sort of rummaging and clanking. Suddenly the door swings open and Leven, grinning, thrusts another bottle towards me. Before the whisky draws a curtain over the evening, he has one more thing to say.

'If ever there was an epitaph for those who rowed oceans or climbed mountains or went to the poles, instead of sitting down in front of a computer screen and becoming a servant, it is that we are much smaller and much less significant than we crack ourselves up to be. It's a wonderful thing to go through.'

Joy

Day 57
Date: 1 March 2010
Position: 16°55′N 49°20′W
750 nautical miles to Antigua

I trace familiar patterns between the stars, which recede in infinite layers into the darkness. I try to find a patch of pure black night, but in the emptiness between the furthest stars appear points of light tinier still. A thin white streak flashes in the sky then turns into half a dozen fiery fragments. One by one the falling embers burn out.

Somewhere between waking and sleeping I roll along the slide, only vaguely aware of time passing. And then a shrill noise pierces the silence. It takes a moment for me to realize that it's my mobile phone. I desperately look around the deck – who could be calling at this time of night? The ring is crisp and clear, but I can't see the phone anywhere. Then my conscious mind struggles back into control and I realize that there is no mobile phone.

I get a grip of myself and step up the tempo. But gradually my thoughts become hazy and dreamlike again. Now I imagine that there's a ghostly pirate ship, flames licking up its square rig, chasing us through the night. A jolt of adrenalin shakes me awake but the burning red object on the horizon remains vivid and real. My heart starts to pound; something is pursuing us across the black ocean. I take stock for a moment. *I am definitely awake, I'm not dreaming this.* I go to call Jimmy and a half-formed syllable escapes from my lips before I realize that the blazing spectre is the first glow of dawn.

At changeover I stand in the hatchway, enjoying the early sun and chatting with Jimmy. He had a tough night too.

*

We're rowing two-up. There is no wind and the late-morning heat is just becoming unpleasant. From over my shoulder Jimmy breaks the silence.

'Are you really *trying*, Adam?'

'What?'

'Are you really trying?'

'What do you mean? Of course I'm *trying*!'

Jimmy's tone is matter-of-fact. 'You're not driving with your legs and you're barely using the slide.'

I'm furious at the suggestion that I'm not pulling my weight, and channel this into my stroke, focusing on the drive and giving an extra flick of power through my shoulders at backstops. At the end of the shift I'm exhausted and slick with sweat.

'Where did that come from? If you'd been doing that for the last two months we'd be there by now.'

It's time for Jimmy to take an hour's break so I switch into the bow seat. Alone on deck I stew over the conversation and, knowing that although I can't see in, he can see out, I wonder if Jimmy is studying my stroke from the other side of the perspex hatch.

Since breaking below seventeen degrees north there's been a following wind and swell but the boat feels heavy in the water and watching the GPS at changeover confirms that we're fighting a south-westerly current. It's only two days since we met up with *Ocean Summit*, but already we're trailing them by twenty miles. Frustrated by the conditions, Jimmy's instinct is to throw everything he has into the oars, but the chafing and sores have returned and the time that he spends treating them means that there's even less left for sleep and recovery.

By the following morning it looks like we're free of the south-westerly currents and as the day draws on our speed increases. During his break Jimmy goes through the med kit and when he comes out for the afternoon shift a couple of padded burn dressings have been carefully taped to the infected sores on his bum. Just sitting in the rowing position is becoming an endurance exercise, but these dressings will help with the pain for now.

It's late afternoon and time to make dinner. Rationing means that I'm stretching every second freeze-dried meal over two sittings.

Tonight it's savoury mince with rice and, to make sure there's some left for breakfast, I bulk it up with BP-5 and peanuts. The pint of fresh water that I've just pumped goes in the Jetboil and two crushed BP-5 biscuits go into the foil pouch with the savoury mince. The boiling water is stirred in, peanuts added and the pouch resealed and left to rehydrate propped up beside the watermaker, to be eaten after my next shift.

I'm rowing across a long ocean swell, well over a hundred metres from peak to peak but less than ten metres peak to trough. We rise slowly, almost imperceptibly, up the face of the swell; its scale is majestic. The Marseilles flag flutters gently in the breeze and a sense of peace settles over me. I think about my parents and my sister and Alice; beneath everything that the sea has stripped away, I have found bedrock in the people that I love.

The hatch swings open and Jimmy comes out ready for the sunset shift.

'How are conditions?'

'Improving. Just short of a four-miler.'

'Good.'

Then I have a thought. 'I'm going to make a note of our mileage each shift, I reckon four miles will be a good challenge to go for.'

We do our changeover dance and back in the cabin I take the warm foil pouch from beside the watermaker and slowly scoop dinner into my mouth, savouring each spoonful. The texture of the rice is just about distinguishable and the peanuts give a satisfying crunch. I eat half and then reseal the pouch, putting it away in the netting for breakfast. After brushing my teeth I pop back out through the hatch to spit over the side. Although the sun hasn't quite set, the stars are already starting to appear. Back in the cabin, clean and with a full stomach, I settle down to sleep.

Ninety minutes later I'm out on deck again. Jimmy's working hard on the oars. I look at the mileage on the GPS and see that he's broken four miles. We're in a pocket of easterly currents and it's exhilarating to pull on the blades and feel the boat rip through the water. I put in a short sprint every twenty minutes to break up the shift. I find myself constantly recalculating our arrival date based on the current speed on the GPS, even though I know that this exercise will only end in disappointment. It's hard to imagine what landing in Antigua will be like; this little boat has been our world for so long.

I give a twenty-minute call and the cabin light comes on. Jimmy's out on deck in good time for his shift.

'How are conditions?'

'Great. Must be getting a knot from the current. Just broken four.'

'Four miles, that's great.'

Jimmy sits back down in the cabin and pours a sachet of EXTREME into his water bottle. He's keen to get on the oars. The new four-mile shift targets have given us a renewed focus.

While I sleep Jimmy pulls a 4.4 mile shift, which I try to match, but the increased tempo is taking its toll and my mileage slips to 3.9 and on the following shift, now out of the current, just 3.1.

It's mid-afternoon, the cabin hatch is open and Jimmy's sitting inside, looking at the shift log I've been keeping.

'How long do you plan on keeping this up for?' he asks.

'I thought I'd do twenty-four hours . . .'

'Well, there's an error.'

'There's an error?'

Jimmy doesn't reply so I try again. 'What's the error?'

'It doesn't matter.'

'Yeah, but what's the error?'

'It doesn't matter. It's pointless. A four-mile shift just isn't possible in these conditions.'

'The conditions are what they are, Jimmy.'

Jimmy's shaking his head. 'It's pointless . . . this whole thing is just pointless and it's not going to get us to Antigua any quicker.'

Back in the cabin I shut the log book and put it away in the netting. After checking our messages I watch Jimmy's most recent diary clip.

Well, Adam's finally managing to motivate himself. He's setting some targets which are a bit ambitious, but it's good that he's motivating himself because for the first two thousand miles he wasn't really rowing very hard, so after two thousand miles I had a chat with him and he's rowed a bit better and today's really the first day he's taken it upon himself to move things on. So that's a positive thing.

My jaw clenches in frustration. It feels like everything I've given over for the last nine weeks has just been dismissed. Out here Jimmy and I are the only ones who see how the other is dealing with the pressures of the environment. In this bare, vulnerable state, we alone bear witness to each other's character. Right now I'm not very happy with his assessment of mine.

I stare angrily at the ceiling for a while, then try to take a step back and look at things objectively. Perhaps Jimmy sees things more clearly than I do? Perhaps I haven't been pushing myself hard enough? And now I start to wonder what this whole experience will mean once we land in Antigua. What will be the legacy of these weeks and months on the ocean, the years of planning and training? What will it all have been for if we don't like what we've learnt out here?

After the big shifts of a couple of days ago, a building westerly means that we're heading onto sea anchor, again. To make headway in the deteriorating conditions we've been rowing two-up for most of the afternoon, with Jimmy in the bow seat and me at stroke. I spoke to Alice on the sat phone yesterday and have come to a decision that I've been thinking over for a long time.

'I'm going to propose to Alice.'

'You're going to propose . . . That's wonderful news! Congratulations.'

'She hasn't said yes yet!'

'Of course she'll say yes . . . how are you going to propose?'

'I'd like to do it when we step off the boat, but it might all be too much. I'll have to see if it's the right moment.'

'What are you going to do about a ring?' he asks.

'The ring will have to wait.'

'Or we could find something in the toolkit!'

'Yeah,' I say, 'a coil washer engagement ring!'

'I'm sure that would go down well!'

We're both quiet for a moment.

'So are you going to ask her dad?'

'I think that would be the right thing to do. I think he'd appreciate that. I'm going to call him when we're a few days out of Antigua.'

Rowing into the wind and swell is back-breaking work, but we know that when this shift ends we'll have an enforced break while the weather system passes over us. I glimpse across at the GPS and do a double-take, then spin round to look over my left shoulder. Jimmy stops rowing and follows my gaze.

'What the fuuuuu . . . ck?'

'SHIT!'

Three cranes are mounted along the deck of a huge dry bulk carrier. Everything is suddenly very vivid. The vessel's about a mile off the starboard bow and is moving quickly straight towards us.

'Fucking hell.'

I spring up from my seat and take a closer look at the GPS, which has a built-in collision alert system.

'Looks like they're going to pass in front of us . . . cargo ship P-O-L-Y-D-E-F-K-I-S. They're doing fifteen knots.'

I duck in through the hatch and pull the mic off the wall.

'*Polydefkis, Polydefkis, Polydefkis*, this is the ocean rowing boat *Spirit of Montanaro*, over.'

A Greek voice responds immediately. 'Hello, *Spirit of Montanaro* this is *Polydefkis*. Over.'

'*Polydefkis*, please be aware that we are a small ocean rowing boat, less than a mile directly ahead of you. Over.'

'*Spirit of Montanaro*, we have you on our AIS, we will be passing half a mile from you. Over.'

'Thanks, *Spirit of Montanaro*. Out.'

I hang the mic back on the wall and come back out on deck with the video camera to record 140 metres of dry bulk carrier glide past, a very short half-mile off our bow.

Over the next two hours the wind picks up and by late afternoon we've ground to a halt. We're disappointingly well practised at the sea-anchor drill and once it's been deployed, the deck tidied and oars secured, I retire to the cabin. Jimmy stays out to watch the sunset and to leave another entry on the video diary:

Considering we were on a roll a few days ago doing fifty-mile days, today we only did twenty miles and the going was so tough we were actually quite pleased with that. When we left La Gomera my mind was on thirty-foot waves and sixty-knot winds and braving the elements but it's not been like that at all, it's been a war of attrition, a war against the sea that's trying to push us in the wrong direction. When we think that we've done everything we can and given everything we've got, being on para-anchor again is incredibly frustrating.

Calculating our arrival date is becoming a perverse obsession. This turn in the weather means that despite two days of hard rowing our estimated arrival has been pushed back by another week and we're now in fifteenth place. I think back to the rush of excitement and expectation when we stepped off the ferry in La Gomera. That was four months ago; it has been too long.

In the morning we wake from a restless sleep desperate to make some miles. The conditions have barely improved, but the sea anchor comes in and we row two-up until nightfall before reverting to normal shifts. In the early hours of the morning Jimmy comes out to find me at the oars, struggling to keep my sense of humour. During the shift I've rowed 0.2 miles west and been pushed 0.5 miles north. At this rate we will never reach Antigua.

In the week following our close encounter with *Polydefkis* we average only twenty miles per day. The prevailing winds and swell are from the south and rowing at ninety degrees to them makes for awkward and uncomfortable progress. It's impossible to get into a rhythm and at night breaking waves hit the boat and snatch the oars from my hands, while the salt spray on Jimmy's sores compounds his pain and makes the chafing worse. A skirt that he's made out of plastic bags helps a little, as do the creams, dressings and painkillers which he is still carefully rationing. He no longer rests lying flat but instead crouches on his arms and knees, with his chest resting on the grab bag and his head in his hands. It's almost impossible to sleep in this position, but it stops his bum and crotch from coming into contact with the dried salt on our mattress. Despite all this, in his video diary Jimmy remains philosophical.

My feet are covered in sores and scars where sores have been. My arse has sores on it. My crotch is red raw where there's been a lot of chafing and my hands are stiff like claws. My body is telling me I've done enough. But the fact is we did come here for a challenge and I know that when I get to Antigua, as delighted as I'll be, I will miss being out here and miss the struggle of it.

Despite getting only a few hours of sleep each day, his hunger for the challenge means that he won't let me cover part of his shift. He must accept and overcome everything that the ocean throws at him.

I'm woken in the middle of the night by a scream of frustration. I look up through the perspex and see Jimmy crouching on deck with his head in his hands. He's just lost his last burn dressing.

It's there again, about ten metres away, just beneath the surface, moving slowly back and forth perpendicular to the boat. I can't make out what it is and I could just be imagining it, but this murky golden-brown presence brings only one thing to mind.

When Fairfax rowed across this stretch of ocean in 1969 he devoted a great deal of energy to killing sharks. In ten weeks at sea Jimmy and I hadn't seen a single one, but for days now this menacing spectre has been tracking the boat. It's about five metres long and always appears at a similar distance behind us. After a few sightings I mention it to Jimmy, who's noticed the same thing. I decide that it's just a trick of the light, some kind of reflection of the Coppercoat on our hull, projected into the water behind us, but I avoid swimming when it's around all the same.

We've been at sea for seventy-one days and with less than 300 miles to Antigua we're now building our shifts up to rowing flat out, two-up for the last twenty-four hours. I come in for an hour's break in the early afternoon to find a text on the sat phone from Rob and Stu on *Ocean Summit*.

DEAR ROWING MATES. SADLY, TIME HAS HAD THE BETTER OF
ME + I HAVE TO MAKE MY WAY TO NEPAL FOR EVEREST. STU
SADLY DOES NOT FEEL HE CAN SOLO IN CURRENT WEATHER

SCENARIO + FRANKLY WHO CAN BLAME HIM. TOO MUCH
TIME + MONEY HAS GONE INTO THIS + PRAGMATICALLY,
FINANCIALLY + PERSONALLY WE CAN GIVE NO MORE. THIS
IS OCEAN SUMMIT OUT. B SAFE

It takes a moment for the news to sink in. I read the message out
to Jimmy and we mull over *Ocean Summit*'s decision. In a way it puts
our own challenge into perspective. For us it's never been a question
of *if* but only *when* we will get to Antigua. But the more I think
about the choice that Rob and Stu have made the less I understand
it – after everything they've been through, and now so close to the
finish line, how can they just drop it all and walk away? I try to see
it from their perspective, but I can't. In the months and years to
come, in quiet moments of reflection, how will they stomach this
decision?

We row two-up for another hour before it's time for Jimmy to
take a break. After tending to his personal admin he has a little
time left, so picks up the video camera and watches my last diary
entry:

. . . when things are going well and we're overtaking other crews,
Jimmy's just a whirlwind of energy and enthusiasm and at times like
that it feels like a privilege to be out on this ocean. Sometimes
though when things are going badly, when we're not getting the
mileage or Jim's pain becomes excruciating, at times like that I feel
like I'm treading on eggshells because I feel like anything I say or do
can become a flashpoint. At times like that, this ocean is a very big
and lonely place.

I'm rowing from the bow position and studying the cloud base,
which has fallen in the last few days. These new formations are
quite different from the high cirrus we're used to, and they bring
frequent, localized downpours. The rain is clearly visible as a dark
patch moving across the surface of the ocean, and as it approaches
a gentle hum becomes audible, which quickly grows to a roar.
When the downpour hits it's pleasantly warm and lasts only a few
moments.

It's just past the hour and there's no sign of Jimmy, which is unusual.

'Hey, Jim, time for a bit of turbo.'

There's no sound from the cabin.

'Hey, Jim!'

'What?'

From his tone I know that something's wrong.

'Time for turbo!'

A few moments later the hatch swings open. Jimmy's sitting just inside with his sunglasses around his neck, glaring at me. I get up to move to the stroke position, so that he can take the bow seat. As we switch, he turns to me.

'I've got to tell you, I watched your video and I'm extremely pissed off.'

I'm now sat in the stroke seat and as I turn to face him I take my sunglasses off. I know the recording he's talking about.

'Why did it piss you off?'

'I'm finding it extremely hard to motivate myself now I know you're sat in the cabin whispering things about me behind my back.'

'I was just saying how I feel, getting it off my chest. It's a video diary, that's the whole point of it. You do just the same in your video diary.'

'The difference is if I've got something to say I'll say it to your face.'

He's right and now I feel defensive about not just telling him straight how I feel. If only I had the courage to tackle my frustrations straight on.

'Well . . . it wasn't a secret, I know you watch the recordings.'

'Oh, so you *wanted* me to see it.'

'I didn't care if you watched it or not!'

Perhaps my attempts to avoid conflict have really just fuelled it all along.

'The problem is, I just don't know if I can trust you any more, Adam.'

My anger turns to sadness. I don't know how to respond. I feel lost. What the hell are we doing out here? What's the point of all this? What are we left with if there's no trust? My face becomes hot and I feel tears welling in my eyes.

'But . . . but . . . all we've got out here is each other . . . each other and this little boat . . . we've got to trust each other.'

I try to keep it together, but a tear escapes from the corner of my eye and runs down my cheek.

For what feels like a long time we stare at each other in silence.

Jimmy's look softens. 'I can see that you're being sincere . . . and that means a lot to me . . . because you're the only person who knows what it's been like out here. You are the only person who will know how tough this really was.'

I take a deep breath and clear my throat.

Jimmy puts out his hand. 'Come on, let's shake hands.'

Suddenly my concerns about what this adventure will leave us with are swept away and the tension lifts. With just a few words and a handshake the air is cleared and it feels at last like things are coming together.

'How about you, Jim; what was your favourite day?'

'I think mine was when we saw Peter van Kets. It just made it apparent what we were doing, how unique it is. And seeing the look on his face was moving because it's hard to know how you're dealing with things when you're in the moment, but seeing how he was responding made me realize how demanding what we're doing really is.'

'I wonder if there will come a moment when we'll wish we had a little bit longer out here,' I ask.

'Yeah I'm pretty sure. It's like the last week at school in the last term of the last year and you're excited that you've got new horizons to look forward to but at the same time you know that it's your last chance to have time with your mates.'

I look out at the low cumulus dotted around us and try to spot where the rain is falling. The character of the ocean has changed over the last week; I can feel that land is near.

I come off my shift and Jimmy wishes me luck. It's time to call Alice's dad.

Alice's mum picks up the house phone and we have a chat, before I call her dad, Martin, on his mobile. He pulls into a lay-by and we chat for a while about the ocean before I come to my reason for calling.

'The thing is, you get a lot of thinking time out here . . . and actually the thing I've spent most of my time thinking about is Alice. And it's confirmed for me something that I've known for a few years . . . and that's that nothing would make me happier, and I hope Alice too, than for us to spend the rest of our lives together. So I'm calling you, Martin, because I want to ask for your daughter's hand in marriage.'

'I'm so glad that you called to ask me that . . . Alice is going to be so happy. You're going to be my son-in-law!'

We're both quite emotional, and talk about how I plan to propose.

'You know we're all going to have so much fun together,' he says.

I come off the phone with a grin across my face and pop my head out of the hatch to give Jimmy the thumbs-up.

Less than a hundred miles to go. I have to remind myself what this means. In two days I will be reunited with the people I care most about, and there will be fresh food, cold drinks and hot showers, clean clothes and soft beds. I consider all this while lying under the aft hatch, which is wide open.

There is no sound of warning as the wave approaches, but its angle is exactly such that it breaks through the hatch and onto my head. My hair is plastered to my face, and water is dripping from my nose. I crawl out onto the deck and the moment Jimmy sees me he erupts with laughter.

'It looks like you've taken a bath! What happened?'

'Hatch was open . . . didn't hear it coming . . . it was like someone threw a bucket of water in my face.'

'No, mate. More than a bucket!'

'Everything's soaked.'

'Everything?'

'Yeah. Everything.'

I turn back into the cabin to assess the situation. The foam mattress has acted like a sponge and soaked up most of the water. I drag it out on deck and wipe down the floor of the cabin with my towel, then come back to wring out the mattress. But it's no good, the whole thing is completely sodden. We leave it in the sun for a few hours, but it makes no difference.

'At least this didn't happen a month ago,' Jimmy points out.

We've had good easterlies for two days now – for once the wind is blowing right on our stern. This is probably the best bit of weather we've enjoyed all trip. A pregnant wave approaches and we put in a couple of hard strokes to catch it as the crest breaks. We surf down the tumbling face and spray flies over the cabin and across the deck.

'YEAH!'

'Six point eight knots! That's what I'm talking about!'

Back in the cabin it's time for the evening admin routine and it's bitter-sweet to think that I'm performing these rituals for the last time. There is a single freeze-dried pouch left in my netting and, spooning through it, I wonder what our next meal will be.

I lie on my back in the damp, filthy cabin, trying to grab a few hours of rest. I look up at the clock mounted over the main hatch and it fills me with urgency. I must soak up these final moments. In less than forty-eight hours this chapter of our lives will close.

The following afternoon, with fifty miles left, Jimmy puts on his plastic-bag skirt for the last time, we gather the remaining snacks from the cabin and settle into our rowing positions for the final push. With the surf up we're clipping along at three knots, twice our normal speed. As night descends over the ocean, the darkness is broken by an unfamiliar haze of light in the distance and a few hours later Jimmy catches the first glimpse of land.

'See that light?'

'Where?'

'It's gone . . . there, there it is again.'

'Seen. Must be the lighthouse.'

We turn back to the oars knowing that there are still seven hours of rowing ahead of us.

The wind continues to pick up but is now shifting round a little to the north, which means that we're taking some of it on the beam. We've been rowing two-up for almost twelve hours.

'How you doing, Adam?'

'I'm wiped! Not long to go now, though.'

'Do you want to take a break and have some food?'

'Good of you to offer, Jim, but I'm fine.'

'Why don't you put the Jetboil on and have some food?'

'I'm good, Jim, really. And I've finished my rations.'

'Look, I've got rations left and in these conditions, frankly it's easier to control the boat on my own. Why don't you have a break and take one of mine?'

'Are you sure? Do you want me to cook you something?'

'No, don't worry about me. I've got snacks. You have some food and I'll see you in an hour.'

I pull my oars across.

'Thanks, Jim. Sure you don't want anything?'

'Don't worry about me. I've had enough freeze-dried food for a lifetime.'

As I boil up water for a final spag bol, I text my parents and Alice, who landed in Antigua yesterday, to tell them that we'll be in English Harbour for breakfast. I also send our ETA to Simon Chalk, who'll come out on a RIB to mark us across the finish line, which is a mile from landfall.

I come back out on deck just as dawn is about to break. In the half light, the outline of land is visible on the horizon. I'm standing in the hatch when we're caught on the beam by a fat breaker. The boat flicks violently to port before the ballast swings us smartly back, and I grip firmly to the frame to avoid being thrown overboard.

Jim is tapping on the oars and flicking the steering line in and out of the cam cleats to keep the boat pointing in the right direction, while the swell rushes us towards land. His expression is one of contentment.

'Ironically after waiting months for the easterlies, we've now got gale force winds blowing us towards land. It's a cruel joke!'

'Of course the sea has the last laugh.'

I pull out the video camera.

'So, Jim, in a couple of hours this project, which has consumed the last three years of our lives, will be over! How do you feel?'

Jim shoots a grin. 'I can see Antigua behind me and I know I need to get there for the sake of repairing my mind and body, but . . .' he turns to look over his shoulder, '. . . it could be a little further away.'

'And when you're back in the office, looking out of the window, what'll you miss?'

Jimmy shakes his head, his voice is quiet. 'There's too much . . .'

He looks back to the east.

'Out here you get time to think about the important things and you get time to think about the things you miss. You're *forced* to think about the things you miss when you're out here and you quickly realize that the most important thing is the people. It makes you realize what's important.'

I look around and try to take it all in. I don't yet understand how, but I know that the life I'm about to return to won't be the same as the one I left.

'Think you'll do this again?' I ask.

'After seeing van Kets, I'd like to know what was going through his mind and there's no way of knowing without being in his shoes. But what I've really enjoyed is just being out here at sea and there are certainly more civilized ways of doing that than in a seven-metre rowing boat.'

The GPS ticks down through ten miles to Antigua.

As we row into the lee of the island, landmarks become visible.

'Look! Look at all the colours!'

Greens and reds are so vivid to eyes accustomed to a palette of blues. And there's the unfamiliar smell of land, and the way trees move in the wind.

We've got less than a mile to go and I call out from the stroke seat as we tick through each tenth of a mile. A RIB appears and circles us at a distance, it's Simon Chalk.

'How you doing, guys?'

'Simon! I can't believe we're actually here. It's so good to see you. Where are we going?'

Simon checks his hand-held GPS. 'Almost there, guys.'

The RIB circles us again then stops a couple of hundred metres off our bow. It takes us a few minutes to catch them up and as we come alongside Simon blasts an air horn.

'Congratulations, *Spirit of Montanaro*! You've crossed the finish line.'

A chapter of our lives has just closed. We drop our oars and from the bow seat Jim leans forwards and puts his hand on my shoulder.

'We've done it,' he shouts.

I turn round and we shake hands. This is the moment we've worked for day and night for the last eleven weeks.

'We've done it,' Jimmy says again.

'We've rowed across the Atlantic,' I say out loud to myself, without quite believing my own words.

I say it again, with more conviction. 'We've rowed across the Atlantic Ocean.'

Then Jim's expression changes. The tightly wound coil that's been holding his mind and body together has just snapped.

'I can't do it. I can't row any more.'

'Don't worry, Jim. No more rowing for you.'

Simon calls over. 'Follow us in.'

I get up from the stroke seat and for the last time we do the changeover dance. I settle into the bow seat and follow the RIB around the reef at the entrance to the bay. This last mile seems to take an age. Sitting on the battlements overlooking the entrance to the bay, I recognize four small figures, waving down at us. They're too far away to call to, but a day hasn't passed that I haven't thought about them. As we row past, they get up and walk down to the harbour.

Yachts are anchored across the bay and as we pass them, cheers and horns ring out. Now Jimmy settles back into the stroke seat and together we row the last of a million strokes. On the quayside a small crowd shouts encouragement and lets off flares. Peter van Kets, who finished overnight, is there with his wife, and greets us with a blast of Vuvuzela. It's overwhelming.

I follow Jimmy off the boat. The ground sways under my feet. A beer is thrust into one hand and a bottle of champagne into the other. I hug Alice and my parents and my sister and tell them that I love them. I hug Jimmy, there are tears on his cheeks.

We're shown over to a small gazebo where a table has been set for two. My legs aren't working properly, I can't walk straight, it feels like the earth is rocking. I'm handed a Coke. The intense sweetness and ice-cold fizzing sensation is exquisite. I savour it in small sips. My family stands by the table and asks us questions. Peter's wife pulls up a chair beside Jimmy, she's worried about his feet. Simon ushers us over to the scales. I've lost a stone, Jimmy one and a half, though many rowers have lost a lot more. We look around for Phil and Skippy; the last we heard they were a hundred miles ahead of us. We learn that they hit a reef last night as they were coming in to land and had to be rescued. They're both fine. We're told to get our passports and then we're shown to immigration, where two large cheerful women are stood behind the counter. I'm still clutching my Coke.

'And how did you enter the country?'

'We rowed.'

We amble around English Harbour talking to other rowers. We were the sixteenth boat home, so fifteen crews have already landed. Some have been here for days or weeks and look like healthy, clean-shaven tourists, while more recent arrivals, with unkempt beards and wild eyes, lurch around unsteadily like drunks. I walk hand in hand with Alice, looking for a quiet spot, wondering whether this is the right moment to propose. A RIB comes into the harbour, towing *Vision of Cornwall*. We go down to the pontoon to welcome Phil and Skippy. Except for a few cuts they're fine. They rolled and were grounded on a reef a couple of miles short of the finish, then stood on the reef in the darkness, clutching their EPIRB, until the rescue team spotted the flashing light. The cabin roof is smashed.

There are too many of us for the car, so my dad takes Mum and my sister Jenny back to the resort, then returns for Alice, Jimmy and me. We walk around the buffet finding it hard to take in all of the food on display. Nothing seems real. I eat plate after plate until I feel sick.

After lunch it feels strange to say goodbye to Jim as we go to our rooms to sleep. Alice shows me the way. I find stairs difficult; I need to approach them with momentum. I take a bath. Washing in fresh water is divine. Alice helps to scrub me down and when I get out the bathwater is black. The towels are thick and soft. I shave off my beard, lie down on the large soft bed and fall asleep. Alice wakes me for dinner. Word has got out and the hotel staff make us feel like celebrities.

After dinner I walk with Jimmy through the resort back to his room.

'I can't believe we were out there twelve hours ago.'

'Imagine the guys who are still out there.'

'Imagine Sean . . . !'[1]

We laugh, then Jimmy becomes serious. 'Adam. Did I push us too hard?'

'If it wasn't for you I'd still be out there on the ocean. You had to push us hard. It couldn't have been any other way.'

It will take time to understand what we've been through, how the ocean has changed us and how we've changed each other, but this is the first step.

We say goodnight. I'll see him at breakfast, it's the longest that we will have been apart for five months.

I wander through the warm tropical night, listening to the cicadas and the wind in the palms. The world is a wonderful and remarkable place. Tomorrow is Alice's birthday and on the balcony, looking out over the Atlantic, I will ask her to marry me.

Epilogue

Dear Friends,

On Tuesday 22 March, after seventy-six days at sea, we crossed the finish line at English Harbour, Antigua. Stepping ashore was overwhelming, and it will be some time before we have fully come to terms with the experience of the last eleven weeks. We are so happy to be back with the loved ones that filled our thoughts when we were at sea and we are finding joy in all of the little things that we missed on the ocean; the sights, sounds, smells and tastes that are part of everyday life back on dry land.

The crossing was tougher than we ever imagined it would be. Within a fortnight we were well adjusted to the sleep deprivation and the exertion of rowing for twelve hours/day, much of it in the searing heat. Managing our bodies was a constant battle, but the greatest challenge was mental. Even before the race started, adverse weather patterns would ensure that this was no 'normal' season for an Atlantic crossing and it soon became clear that our fifty-day target was completely unachievable. Eventually even our 'worst case' scenario of seventy days fell by the wayside. Including the delayed start, we have now been away from our lives back home for almost five months. We had hoped to be gone for little more than two. It has been too long.

Thank-you for all the support you have given us throughout the race and over the last three years. It has been a life changing experience for us and we return home with a different perspective on life and different priorities from those which we had when we left.

Jimmy & Adam
Antigua, 24 March 2010

Many different types of people choose to row oceans. Each takes a different motivation to sea with them, and each returns with a different answer. For Peter Bird, the rhythm of life on an ocean rowing boat exerted such a powerful draw that he was always ready to choose hardship and solitude at sea over laughter and companionship on land. Ocean rowing defined and then consumed him. As a young man, George Harbo had sailed across the North Atlantic in search of the American Dream, but once in New York, he believed that his fortune lay in rowing back the other way. Harbo and Samuelson never found what they were looking for, but where they failed, perhaps Sir Chay Blyth succeeded. Rowing the North Atlantic was his stepping stone to a decorated career as a sailor and businessman.

John Fairfax, the pirate, smuggler, gambler and shark hunter, is perhaps the most colourful character in these pages. He was from a period in the 1960s and 1970s that was a golden age for ocean rowing. Fairfax passed away while I was researching this book, and that era is now fading from living memory. In writing this book, I soon realized that the difficulty in constructing 'history' from fragile memory arises with respect not only to events that happened to someone else in 1896, or 1966, but also to the experiences Jimmy and I shared.

The best part of rowing an ocean is the feeling when it's over. For a time after our return, everyday life was far more *vivid* than the one that I remembered leaving behind five months earlier. But at the same time I was strangely detached from things around me; I was *witnessing* my own life rather than living it. Each week I looked back on how I had felt the week before and saw that, although I had thought I was 'normal' at the time, my head had still not been quite right.

I existed in this strange but not unpleasant bubble for several months, and although I wasn't quite back in the real world yet, I was already a very long way from our life on the ocean, which seemed like a distant dream. With my memories quickly slipping away, I began to write them down.

Thinking back to the period we spent planning and training was easy enough, but reliving our eleven weeks at sea was a difficult and emotional process. How quickly we forget those moments we would rather not remember. When Jimmy and I spoke about what I had written, he recalled some things differently, and so with my notes having grown into a book, I suggested that we add his perspective as a counterpoint to mine. But Jimmy didn't want to go back and pick apart what happened on the ocean; we each wanted to remember things a certain way. The personal narrative that we have built of the row forms part of the wider narrative of our lives; it's part of the journey that has brought us to this point, part of how we understand why we are who we are.

Jimmy and I met up often in the months after our return and one afternoon he appeared with a large brown envelope. The X-ray inside showed that Jimmy had rowed across the Atlantic with a broken wrist. He had suspected as much, but hadn't wanted to see a doctor who would certainly have stopped him from going. I was not surprised that Jimmy could row across an ocean with a broken wrist, or that we could spend eleven weeks at sea together without him mentioning it. What I've learnt about Jimmy has changed the way I understand myself.

We sold *Spirit of Montanaro* to Ben Stenning and James Adair and donated the proceeds to Save the Children. Ben and James went on to row her across the Indian Ocean, then sold her to a team who raced her around Britain. I wonder how many oceans she will see, and lives she will be part of, before her time is up.

The biggest change for me came back at work. I had an inkling of something when I was on the ocean, but it was impossible to know at the time if those thoughts were moments of clarity or confusion. Back behind the screen again, with the numbers flickering and emails, hundreds of them, pouring in, all I could think was: *another forty years of this*.

I see myself standing on the edge of a cliff; everything below is obscured by thick mist. I'm twenty-eight years old and it feels like I have no future. I tell myself to snap out of it. *You're a Fund Manager, you've just been promoted, you're on a ticket to the top.*

Months pass in this way, each day a greater struggle than the last. Charles Montanaro, the patron of both my adventure and my career, has noticed.

'Adam, you need to start setting an example, I'd like you to show your face in the office a little earlier.'

So I desperately try to summon the motivation to peel myself out of bed and make work for 8 AM. I sit and stare at the screen all day waiting for 5.30 to arrive. But after my first board meeting there's some feedback from the chairman. I didn't put on a good show. Even the chairman can see that my heart's not in it. I must draw a line under this. I can't pretend any longer. I need to get out. I write my resignation letter, swallow hard, and break the news to Charles. He's shocked, and initially sympathetic; he's hoping that I'll have a change of heart. When it's clear that I won't, he's furious; I've let him down. He's right, of course, I have let him down. But better that than let myself down.

Now the thick mist has cleared and from this vantage point I can see mountains and rolling hills, rivers meandering down to the sea, huge cities, barren deserts and impenetrable jungle. There are billions of people, all going about their daily lives; living, loving and *dreaming*. I see it all clearly and I understand what I need to do. When my time comes to an end, I need to know that I've made the most of the few precious years that I was given.

Notes

1. The American Dream, 1896

1 Unlike the traditional flat-sided Banks Dorys which were stacked on board schooners and launched to fish for cod over the Grand Banks, Harbo and Samuelson's Surf Dory was of a design widely used by fisherman launching from, and returning to, the beach.
2 Extracts throughout this chapter are taken from George Harbo's log book, a copy of which is contained in the archives of the Ocean Rowing Society.

3. The First Race, 1966

1 John Ridgway and Chay Blyth, *A Fighting Chance*, Pan Books, London, 1968, p. 14.
2 David Johnstone's diary, private papers of the Johnstone family and reproduced with their kind permission, entry for 5 April 1966.
3 John Ridgway, *The Road to Ardmore*, Hodder and Stoughton, London, 1971.
4 Ridgway and Blyth, *A Fighting Chance*, pp. 57–8.
5 David Johnstone's diary, entry for 7 June 1966.
6 Ridgway and Blyth, *A Fighting Chance*, p. 96.
7 Ibid., pp. 161–2.
8 David Johnstone's diary, entry for 31 July 1966.

5. The Pirate and the Paratrooper, 1969

1 From the archives of the Ocean Rowing Society.
2 From an interview by Kenneth Crutchlow, www.oceanrowing.com/ Oceanrowers/fairfax.htm

3 John Fairfax, *Britannia: Rowing Alone Across the Atlantic*, William Kimber, London, 1971, pp. 57–8.

4 Ibid., p. 63.

5 Ibid., p. 88.

6 Ibid., p. 176.

7 Tom McClean, *I Had to Dare*, Jarrolds, London, 1971, p. 27.

8 Ibid., p. 63.

9 Ibid., p. 69.

10 Fairfax, *Britannia*, p. 191.

11 McClean, *I Had to Dare*, p. 95.

12 Ibid., p. 103.

13 Ibid., p. 137.

14 Fairfax, *Britannia*, p. 221.

7. *The Loneliest Row, 1974–1996*

1 In 1971–2 John Fairfax and Sylvia Cook rowed *Britannia II* across the Pacific, from California to Australia, breaking their journey at a number of islands along the way.

2 Derek King and Peter Bird, *Small Boat Against the Sea*, Elek Books, London, 1976, p. 125.

3 Video recording transcribed with the kind permission of Louis Bird.

4 Ibid.

5 Personal interview. Andrew Golland is author of the screenplay *Beyond the Sea* about Peter's last row.

6 Peter Bird's 1992 newsletter from Vladivostok following his decision to abandon the row.

7 This note and those that follow are from Peter's final journal, retrieved from *Sector Two* and reproduced with the kind permission of Louis Bird.

8 Video recording retrieved from *Sector Two* and transcribed with the kind permission of Louis Bird.

9. The Challenge, 1997

1 Rob Hamill, *The Naked Rower*, Hodder Moa Beckett, Auckland, 2000, p. 204.

12. Joy

1 Sean McGowan arrived in Antigua on 2 May after 118 days at sea. Rob Casserley was collected by the support boat and successfully summitted Mount Everest twice that spring. Stu Burbridge changed his mind and continued with the row, joined by Ashley Baker, a member of the support boat crew. They rowed into Antigua ten days later.

Acknowledgements

In 2010, having rowed across the Atlantic from La Gomera in the Canary Islands to English Harbour in Antigua, I decided to write about the experience. When I looked at other ocean rows I was struck by the difference between the crossing that Jimmy and I made and those of the early pioneers, and I felt I needed to put our adventure in context. And so a book that began as the story of our crossing turned into a history of ocean rowing. Many remarkable characters have left their mark on this sport and I have been able to include only a handful of them here. I would like to thank the following for sharing their memories with me: Geoff Allum, Andrew Badenoch, Nic Bailey, Joan Bird, Louis Bird, Tony Bird, Chay Blyth, Leven Brown, Kenneth Crutchlow, Tatiana Rezva-Crutchlow, Tiffany Fairfax, Andrew Golland, Rob Hamill, James Johnstone, Tom McClean, Jill McClean, Teresa Page, Ivan Rezvoy, John Ridgway, Graham Walters and Polly Wickham.

Before we were ready to row an ocean, Jimmy and I needed to spend the best part of a thousand hours on the river and in the gym, learning to row, developing endurance and 'bulking up'; we had to take courses in sea survival, navigation, radios and seamanship, and raise £60,000 to buy and fit out a boat. Getting to the start line *really was* half the challenge, and we couldn't have done it without a lot of people. I would like to thank everyone at the Globe Rowing Club, including Phil Collins for teaching us to row, Gus Salcedo for helping me to migrate from one oar to two, Peter Jackson for getting us through our Ocean Yachtmaster and VHF courses and Ben Taylor for creating and continually updating the Pytheas Club website; also our sponsors, including Charles Montanaro, Janus Capital, Brewin Dolphin, IWOOT and Galleons Point Marina. Without Simon Chalk's tireless enthusiasm there would have been no race. Along with the team at Woodvale, Simon has helped hundreds of people make their dream of rowing an ocean a reality.

Acknowledgements

I have enjoyed the process of writing this book, but still, I would have been disappointed if no one ever had the chance to read it. For transforming my ream of paper into a book, I would like to thank Alex Christofi at Conville and Walsh, Joel Rickett at Penguin and David Llewelyn, the 'Gatekeeper' at Conville and Walsh who gave my manuscript a chance by plucking it from the pile of unsolicited submissions.

Above all, I'd like to thank my parents, Steve and Cristina, my sister, Jenny, my wife, Alice, and my rowing partner, Jimmy.

Jimmy, as you once said to me: 'You are the only person who will know how tough this really was.'

Chronology of successful and attempted ocean rows

The task of chronicling the history of ocean rowing would have been a great deal more difficult were it not for the work done over many years by Ken Crutchlow and the Ocean Rowing Society. Ken and his wife, Tatiana, maintain extensive records of the history of the sport and were my first port of call when trying to track down some of the more elusive ocean rowers, and the friends and relatives of those who are no longer with us.

The ocean rower's greatest reward is to come away understanding themselves a little better. It is fitting that *Nosce Te Ipsum* – 'Know Thyself' – is the motto of the Ocean Rowing Society. Ken founded the society in 1983, having been involved in the sport since reporting on John Fairfax's arrival in Miami for the *Daily Sketch* in 1969. He helped John Fairfax and Sylvia Cook plan their 1971 Pacific row and ran the support team for Peter Bird's Pacific rows and attempts, from 1980 until Peter was lost at sea in 1996. Over the years the Ocean Rowing Society has helped countless people to row oceans, established the Blue Riband Trophy for the fastest row across the Atlantic east to west along the 'Trade Winds' route, organized a permanent memorial to ocean rowers lost at sea in Kilkee, Northern Ireland, and maintained a database of every successful or attempted ocean row.

One hundred years after Harbo and Samuelson's first crossing, the 'database' still fitted comfortably on a small piece of paper – there had been only twenty-seven further ocean rows. But in 1997 all that changed when thirty boats arrived in Tenerife for the first Atlantic Rowing Race, organized by Chay Blyth. Twenty-four of those crews crossed the finish line in Barbados. Since then there has been an extraordinary growth in the sport with over 300 further successful ocean rows. Despite this, today almost ten times more people have climbed Mount Everest than have rowed an ocean.

I was delighted when the Ocean Rowing Society agreed to allow their database of ocean rowing statistics to be published – for the first time – as part of this book. The sport is richer thanks to the tireless work of Ken and Tatiana, Tatiana's son Theodore (himself an ocean rower) and a number of others who support their work.

ROW	OCEAN	NAME	COUNTRY	BOAT	DEPART	ARRIVE	DAYS AT SEA	NOTE
1	Atlantic	George Harbo & Frank Samuelsen	Norway	Fox	6 June 1896, New York, USA	1 August 1896, St Mary's, Scilly Isles, UK	55	
–	Atlantic	David Johnstone & John Hoare	UK	Puffin	21 May 1966, Virginia Beach, Virginia, USA	Lost at sea	(est.) 106	Lost at sea
2	Atlantic	John Ridgway & Chay Blyth	UK	English Rose III	4 June 1966, Cape Cod, Massachusetts, USA	3 September 1966, Aran Isles, Ireland	91	
3	Atlantic	John Fairfax	UK	Britannia	20 January 1969, San Agustín, Gran Canaria, Spain	19 July 1969, Hollywood Beach, Florida, USA	180	
4	Atlantic	Tom McClean	UK	Super Silver	17 May 1969, St John's, Newfoundland, Canada	27 July 1969, Blacksod Bay, County Mayo, Ireland	71	
–	Atlantic	Sidney Genders	UK	Khagga-visana	28 May 1969, Cape Wrath, Scotland, UK	15 June 1969	18	Incomplete
5	Atlantic	Sidney Genders	UK	Khagga-visana	11 September 1969, Sennen Cove, Cornwall, UK	8 March 1970, Miami, USA via Gran Canaria & Antigua	166	
–	Pacific	Arthur Hornby	UK	Yorkshire Rose	1 May 1970, Kamaishi, Japan	31 May 1970	30	Incomplete
–	Indian	Anders Svedlund	Sweden	Roslagena	15 September 1970, Perth, Australia	19 September 1970	3	Incomplete
6	Atlantic	Don Allum & Geoff Allum	UK	QE3	12 January 1971, Las Palmas, Gran Canaria, Spain	26 March 1971, Barbados	73	
7	Indian	Anders Svedlund	Sweden	Roslagena	21 April 1971, Kalbarri, Australia	23 June 1971, near Diego-Suarez, Madagascar	64	
–	Pacific	John Fairfax & Sylvia Cook	UK	Britannia II	10 April 1971, San Francisco, USA	10 April 1971	1	Incomplete
–	Pacific	John Fairfax & Sylvia Cook	UK	Britannia II	15 April 1971, San Francisco, USA	15 April 1971	1	Incomplete
–	Pacific	John Fairfax & Sylvia Cook	UK	Britannia II	20 April 1971, San Francisco, USA	20 April 1971	1	Incomplete
8	Pacific	John Fairfax & Sylvia Cook	UK	Britannia II	26 April 1971, San Francisco, USA	22 April 1972, Australia	361	
–	Pacific	Arthur Hornby	UK	Yorkshire Rose	16 March 1972, Kamaishi, Japan	20 March 1972	3	Incomplete
–	Atlantic	Don Allum & Geoff Allum	UK	QE3	5 June 1972, St John's, Newfoundland, Canada	19 August 1972	76	Geoff Allum rescued after 5 days, Don Allum rescued after 76 days at sea
–	Pacific	Patrick Quesnel & Peter Doorish	USA	Hawaiiki	18 May 1972, La Push, Washington State, USA	25 May 1972, Depoe Bay, Oregon, USA	7	Incomplete

ROW	OCEAN	NAME	COUNTRY	BOAT	DEPART	ARRIVE	DAYS AT SEA	NOTE
	Pacific	Patrick Quesnel & Peter Doorish	USA	*Hawaiiki*	2 June 1972, Depoe Bay, Oregon, USA	2 July 1972, San Francisco, USA	31	Incomplete
	Pacific	Patrick Quesnel & Steve Ewbanks	USA	*Hawaiiki*	28 August 1972, San Francisco, USA	3 September 1972, Half Moon Bay, California, USA	6	Incomplete
	Pacific	Patrick Quesnel & John Martineau	USA	*Hawaiiki*	3 October 1972, Half Moon Bay, California, USA	4 January 1973	93	John Martineau rescued after 5 days at sea, Patrick Quesnel rescued after 93 days at sea
9	Pacific	Anders Svedlund	Sweden	*Waka Moana*	27 February 1974, Huasco, Chile	6 September 1974, Apia, West Samoa via Papeete, Tahiti	191	
0	Atlantic	Derek King, Peter Bird & Carol Maystone	UK	*Britannia II*	24 March 1974, Gibraltar	10 August 1974, Vieux Fort, St Lucia, West Indies via Casablanca, Morocco	93	Carol Maystone left the voyage in Casablanca after 10 days at sea
1	Pacific	Patrick Quesnel	USA	*Hawaiiki*	14 July 1976, La Push, USA	2 November 1976, Hawaii	111	
	Pacific	Patrick Satterlee	USA	*Britannia II*	13 July 1978, San Diego, USA	13 July 1978	1	Incomplete
	Atlantic	Kenneth Kerr	UK	*Bass Conqueror*	1 May 1979, St John's, Newfoundland, Canada	26 June 1979	58	Incomplete
	Atlantic	Kenneth Kerr	UK	*Bass Conqueror*	21 May 1980, Corner Brook, Newfoundland, Canada	Lost at sea	(est.) 119	Lost at sea
	Atlantic	Andrew Wilson	UK	*Nautica*	25 June 1980, St John's, Newfoundland, Canada	Lost at sea	Unknown	Lost at sea
2	Atlantic	Gerard d'Aboville	France	*Capitaine Cook*	10 July 1980, Cape Cod, Massachusetts, USA	20 September 1980, Lizard Meridian	71	
	Pacific	Peter Bird	UK	*Britannia II*	1 October 1980, San Francisco, USA	26 February 1981, Maui, Hawaii via San Quintin, Mexico	147	
	Atlantic	Curtis Saville & Kathleen Saville	USA	*Excalibur*	18 March 1981, Casablanca, Morocco	10 June 1981, English Harbour, Antigua via Hierro, Canary Islands, Spain	89	
	Pacific	Peter Bird	UK	*Hele-on-Britannia*	23 August 1982, San Francisco, USA	14 June 1983, Great Barrier Reef, Australia	294	
	Atlantic	Hugh King-Fretts	UK	*Hulu*	30 January 1984, Los Cristianos, Tenerife, Spain	8 May 1984, Conset Bay, Barbados	100	

(Continued)

ROW	OCEAN	NAME	COUNTRY	BOAT	DEPART	ARRIVE	DAYS AT SEA	NOTE
17	Atlantic	Amyr Khan Klink	Brazil	I. A. T.	9 June 1984, Luderitz Bay, Namibia	18 September 1984, Praia de Espera, Brazil	101	
18	Pacific	Curtis Saville & Kathleen Saville	USA	Excalibur	4 July 1984, Callao, Peru	31 July 1985, Cairns, Australia via Galapagos Islands, Marquises Islands, American Samoa and Vanuatu	189	
19	Atlantic	Sean Crowley & Mike Nestor	UK	In Finne-gans Wake	30 January 1986, Pasito Blanco, Gran Canaria, Spain	14 April 1986, Georgetown, Guyana	73	
20	Atlantic	Don Allum	UK	QE3	30 January 1986, Pasito Blanco, Gran Canaria	23 May 1986, Nevis, West Indies	114	
–	Atlantic	Geoff Cooper	UK	My Annette	27 August 1986	Unknown	100	Incomplete
–	Atlantic	Geoff Cooper	UK	Water Rat	1986	Unknown	Un-known	Incomplete
21	Atlantic	Tom McClean	UK	Skoll 1080	16 June 1987, St John's, Newfoundland, Canada	10 August 1987, Bishops Light, Ireland	55	
–	Atlantic	Guy Lemonier	France	Jacquet Enterprises	16 June 1987, Cape Cod, Massachusetts, USA	17 June 1987	1	Incomplete
–	Atlantic	Guy Lemonier	France	Jacquet Enterprises	21 June 1987, Cape Cod, Massachusetts, USA	21 August 1987	57	Incomplete
22	Atlantic	Don Allum	UK	QE3	21 June 1987, St John's, Newfoundland, Canada	5 September 1987, Achill Island, Ireland	76	
23	Atlantic	Sean Crowley	UK	Finn Again	17 June 1988, Halifax, Canada	21 September 1988, Galway, Ireland	92	
–	Atlantic	Frederic Guerin	France	Ramereve	27 June 1991, Cape Cod, Massachu-setts, USA	22 September 1991	87	Incomplete
24	Pacific	Gerard d'Aboville	France	Sector	11 July 1991, Choshi, Japan	21 November 1991, Ilawaco, Washington State, USA	135	
25	Atlantic	Gerard Seibel (skipper), Jaques Busson, Jean-Claude Coucardon, Herve Douard, Patrick Gollnisch, Thierry Judet, Jean Juras, Charles-Henry De La Moynerie, Jean-Louis Landry, Francisco Sanchez, Philippe Piriou, Alexander Smurgis	France	La Mondiale	25 March 1992, Santa Cruz, La Palma, Spain	29 April 1992, Martinique, West Indies	35	

ROW	OCEAN	NAME	COUNTRY	BOAT	DEPART	ARRIVE	DAYS AT SEA	NOTE
	Pacific	Peter Bird	UK	Sector Two	6 June 1992, Vladivostok, Russia	25 June 1992	19	Incomplete
26	Arctic	Eugene Smurgis & Alexander Smurgis	Russia	Max-4	20 July 1992, Tiksi, Russia	1 September 1993, London, UK	131	
	Atlantic	Eugene Smurgis	Russia	Max-4	29 September 1993, London, UK	19 November 1993	52	Lost at sea
	Pacific	Peter Bird	UK	Sector Two	12 May 1993, Vladivostok, Russia	12 March 1994	304	Incomplete
	Atlantic	Jean Lukes	France	Luxior Assurances	31 July 1994, Cape Cod, Massachusetts, USA	8 August 1994	8	Incomplete
	Pacific	Peter Bird	UK	Sector Two	12 June 1995, Nakhodka, Russia	13 June 1995	1	Incomplete
27	Atlantic	Joseph Le Guen	France	Pour les Sauveteurs en Mer	13 June 1995, Cape Cod, Massachusetts, USA	24 September 1995, Ile Molene, France	103	
	Pacific	Peter Bird	UK	Sector Two	14 June 1995, Nakhodka, Russia	15 June 1995	1	Incomplete
	Atlantic	Jean Lukes	France	Luxior Assurances	24 June 1995, Cape Cod, Massachusetts, USA	27 June 1995	3	Incomplete
	Atlantic	Jean Lukes	France	Luxior Assurances	3 July 1995, Cape Cod, Massachusetts, USA	6 July 1995	3	Incomplete
	Atlantic	Roger Montandon	Switzerland	Exodus	23 February 1996, Pasito Blanco, Gran Canaria, Spain	22 April 1996, Jipioca Island, Brazil	59	
	Pacific	Peter Bird	UK	Sector Two	27 March 1996, Nakhodka, Russia	3 June 1996	69	Lost at sea
	Pacific	Mick Bird	USA	Reach	4 August 1996, Monterey, USA	14 August 1996	10	Incomplete
	Atlantic	Andrew Halsey	UK	Brittany Rose	28 April 1997, Santa Cruz, Tenerife, Spain	23 August 1997, St Lucia, West Indies	117	
	Pacific	Mick Bird	USA	Reach	19 August 1997, Fort Bragg, USA	1 August 1999, Cairns, Australia via Hawaii & Marshall Islands & Solomon Islands	186	
	Atlantic	Rob Hamill & Phil Stubbs	NZ	Kiwi Challenge	12 October 1997, Los Gigantes, Tenerife, Spain	22 November 1997, Port St Charles, Barbados	41	
	Atlantic	Pascal Blond & Joseph Le Guen	France	Atlantik Challenge	12 October 1997, Los Gigantes, Tenerife, Spain	30 November 1997, Port St Charles, Barbados	49	
	Atlantic	David Rice & Nadia Rice	UK	Hannah Snell	12 October 1997, Los Gigantes, Tenerife, Spain	6 December 1997, Port St Charles, Barbados	55	
	Atlantic	Ian Blandin & Rob Cassin	UK	Spirit of Jersey	12 October 1997, Los Gigantes, Tenerife, Spain	8 December 1997, Port St Charles, Barbados	58	

(Continued)

ROW	OCEAN	NAME	COUNTRY	BOAT	DEPART	ARRIVE	DAYS AT SEA	NOTE
35	Atlantic	Eamonn Kavanagh & Peter Kavanagh	Ireland	Christina	12 October 1997, Los Gigantes, Tenerife, Spain	9 December 1997, Port St Charles, Barbados	58	
36	Atlantic	Steve Isaacs & Mark Stubbs	UK	Toc H Phoenix	12 October 1997, Los Gigantes, Tenerife, Spain	9 December 1997, Port St Charles, Barbados	58	
37	Atlantic	Peter Hogden & Neil Hitt	UK	Hospiscare	12 October 1997, Los Gigantes, Tenerife, Spain	9 December 1997, Port St Charles, Barbados	59	
38	Atlantic	John Searson & Carl Clinton	UK	Commodore Shipping	12 October 1997, Los Gigantes, Tenerife, Spain	11 December 1997, St Charles, Barbados	60	Carl Clinton rescued after 7 days at sea
39	Atlantic	Wayne Callaghan & Tim Welford	UK	Ryvita	12 October 1997, Los Gigantes, Tenerife, Spain	11 December 1997, Port St Charles, Barbados	60	
40	Atlantic	Steven Lee & John Bryant	UK	Kielder Atlantic Warrior	12 October 1997, Los Gigantes, Tenerife, Spain	12 December 1997, Port St Charles, Barbados	61	
41	Atlantic	Danniel Innes & Peter Lowe	UK	Golden Fleece	12 October 1997, Los Gigantes, Tenerife, Spain	12 December 1997, Port St Charles, Barbados	61	
42	Atlantic	Graham Walters & Keith Mason-Moore	UK	George Geary	12 October 1997, Los Gigantes, Tenerife, Spain	13 December 1997, Port St Charles, Barbados	62	
43	Atlantic	Duncan Nicoll & Jock Wishart	UK	Mount Gay Rum Runner	12 October 1997, Los Gigantes, Tenerife, Spain	14 December 1997, Port St Charles, Barbados	63	
44	Atlantic	Andrew Watson & Russell Reid	UK	Bitzer	12 October 1997, Los Gigantes, Tenerife, Spain	15 December 1997, Port St Charles, Barbados	64	
45	Atlantic	Simon Chalk & George Rock	UK	Cellnet Atlantic Challenger	12 October 1997, Los Gigantes, Tenerife, Spain	15 December 1997, Port St Charles, Barbados	64	
46	Atlantic	John Van Katwyck & Geoff Gavey	UK	Endeavour	12 October 1997, Los Gigantes, Tenerife, Spain	15 December 1997, Port St Charles, Barbados	64	
47	Atlantic	Jim Shekhdar & Dave Jackson	UK	Boatcom Wave-rider	12 October 1997, Los Gigantes, Tenerife, Spain	16 December 1997, Port St Charles, Barbados	65	
48	Atlantic	Michael Elliot & Louis Hunkin	UK	Cornish Challenger	12 October 1997, Los Gigantes, Tenerife, Spain	17 December 1997, Port St Charles, Barbados	65	
49	Atlantic	Charles Street & Roger Gould	UK	Sam Deacon	12 October 1997, Los Gigantes, Tenerife, Spain	17 December 1997, Port St Charles, Barbados	65	

ROW	OCEAN	NAME	COUNTRY	BOAT	DEPART	ARRIVE	DAYS AT SEA	NOTE
	Atlantic	David Immelman & David Mossman	South Africa	Key Challenger	12 October 1997, Los Gigantes, Tenerife, Spain	18 December 1997, Port St Charles, Barbados	67	David Mossman rescued after 5 days at sea
	Atlantic	Stein Hoff & Arvid Benston	Norway	Star Atlantic	12 October 1997, Los Gigantes, Tenerife, Spain	20 December 1997, Port St Charles, Barbados	69	
	Atlantic	Martin Bellamy & Mark Mortimer	UK	Salamanca	12 October 1997, Los Gigantes, Tenerife, Spain	25 December 1997, Port St Charles, Barbados	74	
	Atlantic	Isabel Fraser & Richard Duckworth	UK	Stylus Mistral Endeavour	12 October 1997, Los Gigantes, Tenerife, Spain	4 January 1998, Port St Charles, Barbados	83	
	Atlantic	Jan Meek & Daniel Byles	UK	Carpe Diem	12 October 1997, Los Gigantes, Tenerife, Spain	21 January 1998, Port St Charles, Barbados	101	
	Atlantic	Boris Renzelmann & Nikolai Wedemeye	Germany	Wabun	12 October 1997, Los Gigantes, Tenerife, Spain	22 October 1997	10	Incomplete
	Atlantic	Jean Marc Meunier & Marie Christine Meunier	France	La Baleine	12 October 1997, Los Gigantes, Tenerife, Spain	29 October 1997	17	Incomplete
	Atlantic	Peter Haining & David Riches	UK	Walter Scott Partners	12 October 1997, Los Gigantes, Tenerife, Spain	14 October 1997	2	Incomplete
	Atlantic	Tori Murden & Louise Graff	USA	American Pearl	12 October 1997, Los Gigantes, Tenerife, Spain	13 October 1997	1	Incomplete
	Atlantic	Ian Chater & Nigel Garbett	UK	This Way Up	12 October 1997, Los Gigantes, Tenerife, Spain	13 October 1997	1	Incomplete
	Atlantic	Edward Boreham & Matthew Boreham	UK	Spirit of Spelthorne	12 October 1997, Los Gigantes, Tenerife, Spain	13 November 1997	32	Incomplete
	Atlantic	Tori Murden & Louise Graff	USA	American Pearl	22 October 1997, Los Gigantes, Tenerife, Spain	24 October 1997	2	Incomplete
	Atlantic	Peggy Bouchet	France	Sector No Limits	10 March 1998, Puerto de Mogán, Gran Canaria, Spain	28 May 1998	79	Capsized and rescued 120 miles from Guadeloupe
	Atlantic	Tori Murden	USA	American Pearl	14 June 1998, Nag's Head, North Carolina, USA	7 September 1998	85	Incomplete
	Atlantic	Matthew Boreham	UK	Spirit of Spelthorne II	17 August 1998, Los Gigantes, Tenerife, Spain	25 August 1998	9	Incomplete
	Atlantic	Richard Jones	USA	Brother of Jared	24 September 1998, Lisbon, Portugal	27 September 1998	3	Incomplete
	Atlantic	Roy Finlay & crew of 15	UK	Atlantic Endeavour	1 November 1998, Puerto de Mogán, Gran Canaria, Spain	16 November 1998	16	Incomplete

(Continued)

ROW	OCEAN	NAME	COUNTRY	BOAT	DEPART	ARRIVE	DAYS AT SEA	NOTE
–	Atlantic	Arnaud Guiot	Belgium	*Koloss*	6 December 1998, Tenerife, Spain	13 December 1998	7	Incomplete
–	Atlantic	Elisabeth Hoff	Norway	*Star Atlantic*	17 February 1999, Los Gigantes, Tenerife, Spain	27 February 1999	10	Incomplete
–	Pacific	Andrew Halsey	UK	*Brittany Rose*	15 July 1999, San Diego, USA	5 April 2000	266	Incomplete
–	Atlantic	Matthew Boreham	UK	*Spirit of Spelt-horne II*	22 July 1999, St John's, Newfoundland, Canada	22 July 1999	1	Incomplete
55	Atlantic	Tori Murden	USA	*American Pearl*	13 September 1999, Los Gigantes, Tenerife, Spain	3 December 1999, Guadeloupe	81	
56	Atlantic	Diana Hoff	UK	*Star Atlantic II*	13 September 1999, Los Gigantes, Tenerife, Spain	5 January 2000, Port St Charles, Barbados	113	
57	Atlantic	Peggy Bouchet	France	*SFR*	18 November 1999, Cape Verde Islands	5 January 2000, Martinique	48	
58	Atlantic	Patrick Lihurt	France	*Lune de Mer*	9 December 1999, Pasito Blanco, Gran Canaria, Spain	14 February 2000, Petit-Bourg, Guadeloupe	68	
–	Atlantic	Dominic Pichon	France	*Les enfants de la terre-Crédit Mutuel*	23 January 2000, Dakar, Senegal	9 February 2000	17	Incomplete
–	Pacific	Joseph Le Guen	France	*www. Keepitblue.com*	3 February 2000, Wellington, New Zealand	2 April 2000	59	Incomplete
59	Pacific	Jim Shekhdar	UK	*Le Shark*	29 June 2000, Ilo, Peru	30 March 2001, North Stradbroke, Australia	274	
–	Atlantic	Roy Finlay & Colleen Cronin	UK	*Celtic Crossing*	28 July 2000, St John's, Newfoundland, Canada	24 August 2000	26	Incomplete
–	Indian	Mick Bird	USA	*Reach*	20 September 2000, Thursday Island, Australia	24 November 2000	65	Incomplete
60	Atlantic	Richard Jones	USA	*Brother of Jared*	10 October 2000, Los Gigantes, Tenerife, Spain	20 February 2001, Ragged Island, Bahamas	133	
–	Atlantic	Vyatcheslav Kavtchenko	Russia	*Rostov-on-Don*	31 March 2001, Los Gigantes, Tenerife, Spain	8 April 2001	8	Incomplete
61	Atlantic	Emmanuel Coindre	France	*Ville de Dinard*	15 April 2001, Puerto de Mogán, Gran Canaria, Spain	11 June 2001, Guadeloupe	57	
–	Pacific	Tim Welford & Dom Mee	UK	*Pacific Odyssey*	5 May 2001, Choshi, Japan	17 September 2001	135	Incomplete
–	Atlantic	Nenad Belic	USA	*LUN*	11 May 2001, Cape Cod, Massachu-setts, USA	30 September 2001	142	Lost at sea

ROW	OCEAN	NAME	COUNTRY	BOAT	DEPART	ARRIVE	DAYS AT SEA	NOTE
–	Atlantic	Jean Lukes	France	Les Sauveteurs en Mer	21 June 2001, Cape Cod, Massachusetts, USA	30 June 2001	9	Incomplete
52	Atlantic	Matt Goodman & Steve Westlake	NZ	Telecom Challenge 1	7 October 2001, Playa San Juan, Tenerife, Spain	18 November 2001, Port St Charles, Barbados	42	
53	Atlantic	Paul McCarthy & Patrick Weinrauch	Australia	Freedom	7 October 2001, Playa San Juan, Tenerife, Spain	21 November 2001, Port St Charles, Barbados	45	
54	Atlantic	Alain Lewuillon & Bruno Lewuillon	Belgium	Win.Belgium	7 October 2001, Playa San Juan, Tenerife, Spain	25 November 2001, Port St Charles, Barbados	49	
5	Atlantic	Stephanie Brown & Jude Ellis	NZ	Telecom Challenge 25	7 October 2001, Playa San Juan, Tenerife, Spain	26 November 2001, Port St Charles, Barbados	50	
6	Atlantic	Andrew Chapple & Ian Anderson	UK	Comship.com	7 October 2001, Playa San Juan, Tenerife, Spain	27 November 2001, Port St Charles, Barbados	51	
7	Atlantic	Will Mason & Tim Thurnham	UK	Bright Spark	7 October 2001, Playa San Juan, Tenerife, Spain	27 November 2001, Port St Charles, Barbados	51	
8	Atlantic	Pascal Hanssen & Serge van Cleve	Belgium	Bruxelles-Challenge	7 October 2001, Playa San Juan, Tenerife, Spain	1 December 2001, Port St Charles, Barbados	56	
9	Atlantic	Christian Havrehed & Sun Haibin	Denmark, China	Yantu	7 October 2001, Playa San Juan, Tenerife, Spain	3 December 2001, Port St Charles, Barbados	57	
0	Atlantic	Richard White & Ian Roots	UK	DLE GlobalStar	7 October 2001, Playa San Juan, Tenerife, Spain	3 December 2001, Port St Charles, Barbados	57	
1	Atlantic	Rory Shannon & Alex Wilson	UK	Atlantic Warrior	7 October 2001, Playa San Juan, Tenerife, Spain	3 December 2001, Port St Charles, Barbados	57	
2	Atlantic	John Zeigler & Tom Mailhot	USA	American Star	7 October 2001, Playa San Juan, Tenerife, Spain	4 December 2001, Port St Charles, Barbados	58	
3	Atlantic	Istvan Hajdu & Simon Walpole	Hungary, UK	UniS Voyager	7 October 2001, Playa San Juan, Tenerife, Spain	4 December 2001, Port St Charles, Barbados	58	
4	Atlantic	Pierre Deroi & Jean Jacques Gautier	France	Esprit PME	7 October 2001, Playa San Juan, Tenerife, Spain	5 December 2001, Port St Charles, Barbados	59	
5	Atlantic	Scott Gilchrist & Peter Moore	UK	Carphone Warehouse	7 October 2001, Playa San Juan, Tenerife, Spain	6 December 2001, Port St Charles, Barbados	61	
	Atlantic	Pedro Ripol & Francisco Korff	Spain	Project Martha 2	7 October 2001, Playa San Juan, Tenerife, Spain	8 December 2001, Port St Charles, Barbados	62	

(Continued)

ROW	OCEAN	NAME	COUNTRY	BOAT	DEPART	ARRIVE	DAYS AT SEA	NOTE
77	Atlantic	Kerry Blandin & Paul Perchard	UK	Spirit of Jersey	7 October 2001, Playa San Juan, Tenerife, Spain	8 December 2001, Port St Charles, Barbados	62	
78	Atlantic	Tim Humfrey & Jo Lumsdon	UK	Keltec Challenger	7 October 2001, Playa San Juan, Tenerife, Spain	9 December 2001, Port St Charles, Barbados	63	
79	Atlantic	Dominic Marsh & Gary Fooks	UK	Onward Atlantic	7 October 2001, Playa San Juan, Tenerife, Spain	9 December 2001, Port St Charles, Barbados	63	
80	Atlantic	Julian McHardy & Mark Williams	UK	McLlaid	7 October 2001, Playa San Juan, Tenerife, Spain	10 December 2001, Port St Charles, Barbados	64	
81	Atlantic	Dominic Comonte & Crispin Comonte	UK	Team Nutri-Grain	7 October 2001, Playa San Juan, Tenerife, Spain	10 December 2001, Port St Charles, Barbados	64	
82	Atlantic	Benjamin Marty & Olivier Villian	France	La Gironde	7 October 2001, Playa San Juan, Tenerife, Spain	10 December 2001, Port St Charles, Barbados	65	
83	Atlantic	Alistair Smee & Chris Marett	UK	Linda	7 October 2001, Playa San Juan, Tenerife, Spain	15 December 2001, Port St Charles, Barbados	69	
84	Atlantic	Steve Dawson & Mick Dawson	UK	Mrs D	7 October 2001, Playa San Juan, Tenerife, Spain	16 December 2001, Port St Charles, Barbados	70	
85	Atlantic	Dugald Macdonald & David Mitchell	South Africa, Australia	Brunetto	7 October 2001, Playa San Juan, Tenerife, Spain	18 December 2001, Port St Charles, Barbados	72	
86	Atlantic	Denis Bribosia & Gregory Loret	Belgium, France	Embar-quons les Droits de l'Homme	7 October 2001, Playa San Juan, Tenerife, Spain	18 December 2001, Port St Charles, Barbados	72	
87	Atlantic	Graham Walters & Michael Ryan	UK	George Geary	7 October 2001, Playa San Juan, Tenerife, Spain	24 December 2001, Port St Charles, Barbados	78	
88	Atlantic	Damian West & Alex Hinton	UK	43° West	7 October 2001, Playa San Juan, Tenerife, Spain	26 December 2001, Port St Charles, Barbados	80	
89	Atlantic	Ian Chater & Tony Day	UK	This Way Up	7 October 2001, Playa San Juan, Tenerife, Spain	31 December 2001, Port St Charles, Barbados	85	
90	Atlantic	Niclas Mardfelt & Rune Larsson	Sweden	Uppsala.com	7 October 2001, Playa San Juan, Tenerife, Spain	10 January 2002, Port St Charles, Barbados	95	
91	Atlantic	Malcolm Atkinson & Ben Martell	UK	Kaos	7 October 2001, Playa San Juan, Tenerife, Spain	23 January 2002, Port St Charles, Barbados	109	
92	Atlantic	Andrew Veal & Debra Veal	UK	Troika Transatlantic	7 October 2001, Playa San Juan, Tenerife, Spain	26 January 2002, Port St Charles, Barbados	111	Andrew Ve rescued after 13 da at sea

ROW	OCEAN	NAME	COUNTRY	BOAT	DEPART	ARRIVE	DAYS AT SEA	NOTE
–	Atlantic	Rik Knoop & Michael Tuijn	Netherlands	Domani 2	7 October 2001, Playa San Juan, Tenerife, Spain	8 October 2001	1	Incomplete
–	Atlantic	Xabier Agote & Urko Mendiburu	Spain	Euskadi	7 October 2001, Playa San Juan, Tenerife, Spain	10 October 2001, El Hierro, Canary Islands, Spain	3	Incomplete
–	Atlantic	Richard Wood & Rob Ringer	UK	Spirit of Worcestershire	7 October 2001, Playa San Juan, Tenerife, Spain	13 October 2001	6	Incomplete
–	Atlantic	Jason Hart & David Hart	UK	Dartmothian	7 October 2001, Playa San Juan, Tenerife, Spain	14 October 2001	7	Incomplete
–	Atlantic	Jonathan Gornall & Dominic Biggs	UK, Hong Kong	Star Challenger	7 October 2001, Playa San Juan, Tenerife, Spain	23 November 2001	47	Incomplete, Dominic Biggs rescued after 12 days at sea
93	Atlantic	Norman Butler & Phil Scuntlebury	UK	Spirit of Swindon	8 October 2001, San Sebastián, La Gomera, Spain	29 December 2001, Port St Charles, Barbados	83	Phil Scuntlebury rescued after 73 days at sea
–	Atlantic	Rik Knoop & Michael Tuijn	Netherlands	Domani 2	8 October 2001, Playa San Juan, Tenerife, Spain	9 October 2001	1	Incomplete
94	Atlantic	Rik Knoop & Michael Tuijn	Netherlands	Domani 2	9 October 2001, Playa San Juan, Tenerife, Spain	18 January 2002, Port St Charles, Barbados	101	
95	Atlantic	Theodore Rezvoy	Ukraine	Odessa	12 October 2001, San Sebastián, La Gomera, Spain	18 December 2001, Port St Charles, Barbados	67	
96	Atlantic	Urko Mendiburu	Spain	Euskadi	22 October 2001, El Hierro, Canary Islands, Spain	30 December 2001, Port St Charles, Barbados	81	
–	Indian	Simon Chalk & Bill Greaves	UK	Elssea	15 May 2002, Kalbarri, Australia	17 May 2002	2	Incomplete
–	Atlantic	Mark Stubbs, Robert Munslow, Nigel Morris, George Rock	UK	Skandia	11 June 2002, St John's, Newfoundland, Canada	3 July 2002	21	Incomplete
97	Atlantic	Emmanuel Coindre	France	Lady Bird	29 July 2002, Cape Cod, Massachusetts, USA	25 October 2002, Ile d'Ouessant, France	88	
98	Atlantic	Stein Hoff	Norway	Star Atlantic II	10 August 2002, Lisbon, Portugal	14 November 2002, Georgetown, Guyana	97	
99	Atlantic	Fedor Konyukhov	Russia	Uralaz	16 October 2002, San Sebastián, La Gomera, Spain	1 December 2001, Port St Charles, Barbados	46	
100	Atlantic	Ray Jardine & Jenny Jardine	USA	Caper	7 November 2002, San Sebastián, La Gomera, Spain	30 December 2002, Port St Charles, Barbados	53	
–	Pacific	Andrew Halsey	UK	Brittany Rose	25 November 2002, Callao, Peru	3 April 2003	129	Incomplete

(Continued)

ROW	OCEAN	NAME	COUNTRY	BOAT	DEPART	ARRIVE	DAYS AT SEA	NOTE
–	Atlantic	Anne Quéméré	France	Le Connetable	5 December 2002, San Sebastián, La Gomera, Spain	13 December 20029		Incomplete
101	Atlantic	Anne Quéméré	France	Le Connetable	26 December 2002, San Sebastián, La Gomera, Spain	21 February 2003, Guadeloupe	57	
102	Atlantic	Martin Wood	UK	Pacific Pete	16 January 2003, San Sebastián, La Gomera, Spain	25 March 2003, Port St Charles, Barbados	68	
103	Indian	Simon Chalk	UK	True Spirit	27 February 2003, Kalbarri, Australia	15 June 2003, Longitude of Rafael Island	107	
–	Indian	Mike Noel-Smith & Rob Abernethy	UK	TRANS-Venture	19 April 2003, Carnarvon, Australia	4 June 2003	46	Incomplete
–	Pacific	Mick Dawson	UK	Mrs D	2 June 2003, Choshi, Japan	14 June 2003	13	Incomplete
104	Atlantic	Maud Fontenoy	France	Pilot	13 June 2003, St Pierre et Miquelon, Canada	9 October 2003, La Coruña, Spain	118	
–	Atlantic	Theodore Rezvoy	Ukraine	Ukraine	2 July 2003, New York, USA	10 July 2003	8	Incomplete
–	Atlantic	Emanuel Coindre	France	Lady Bird	26 July 2003, Cape Cod, Massachusetts, USA	28 July 2003	2	Incomplete
–	Pacific	Jim Shekhdar	UK	Hornette	16 October 2003, Bluff, New Zealand	16 October 2003	1	Incomplete
105	Atlantic	James Fitzgerald & Kevin Biggar	NZ	Holiday Shoppe Challenge	19 October 2003, San Sebastián, La Gomera, Spain	28 November 2003, Port St Charles, Barbados	40	
106	Atlantic	Matt Goodman & Steve Westlake	NZ	Team CRC	19 October 2003, San Sebastián, La Gomera, Spain	29 November 2003, Port St Charles, Barbados	41	
107	Atlantic	Philip Als & Randal Valdez	Barbados	Rowing Home	19 October 2003, San Sebastián, La Gomera, Spain	1 December 2003, Port St Charles, Barbados	44	
108	Atlantic	Jason McKinlay & Phillip Carrington	UK	Pura Vida	19 October 2003, San Sebastián, La Gomera, Spain	9 December 2003, Port St Charles, Barbados	51	
109	Atlantic	Alan Watson & Miles Barnett	UK	Bright Spark	19 October 2003, San Sebastián, La Gomera, Spain	10 December 2003, Port St Charles, Barbados	52	
110	Atlantic	Alasdair MacGregor & Andrew Vinsen	UK	Huntswood Atlantic Challenge	19 October 2003, San Sebastián, La Gomera, Spain	13 December 2003, Port St Charles, Barbados	55	
111	Atlantic	Andy Giles & Faye Langham	UK	Bluebell	19 October 2003, San Sebastián, La Gomera, Spain	17 December 2003, Port St Charles, Barbados	59	
112	Atlantic	Guy Quilter & Hugo Ambrose	UK	Atlantic Wholff	19 October 2003, San Sebastián, La Gomera, Spain	17 December 2003, Port St Charles, Barbados	59	

ROW	OCEAN	NAME	COUNTRY	BOAT	DEPART	ARRIVE	DAYS AT SEA	NOTE
13	Atlantic	Adam Murfitt & Paul Nelson	UK	Spirit of Lancashire	19 October 2003, San Sebastián, La Gomera, Spain	17 December 2003, Port St Charles, Barbados	59	
14	Atlantic	Christopher Hall & Richard Pullan	UK	Team Altitude	19 October 2003, San Sebastián, La Gomera, Spain	18 December 2003, Port St Charles, Barbados	61	
15	Atlantic	John Williams & Michael Burke	UK	Two Blokes, No Smokes	19 October 2003, San Sebastián, La Gomera, Spain	29 December 2003, Port St Charles, Barbados	71	
16	Atlantic	David Pearse & Sjaak De Jong	UK, Netherlands	Petrel	19 October 2003, San Sebastián, La Gomera, Spain	3 January 2004, Port St Charles, Barbados	76	
17	Atlantic	George Lambert-Porter Jnr & George Lambert-Porter	South Africa	Brunetto	19 October 2003, San Sebastián, La Gomera, Spain	5 January 2004, Port St Charles, Barbados	78	
18	Atlantic	Mark Jacklin & Mathew Stowers	UK	Per Ardua	19 October 2003, San Sebastián, La Gomera, Spain	5 January 2004, Port St Charles, Barbados	78	
	Atlantic	Gregory Loret & Sebastien Lefebvre	France	Mardine Meuse Lorraine	19 October 2003, San Sebastián, La Gomera, Spain	21 October 2003	2	Incomplete
	Atlantic	Marcus Thompson & Sally Kettle	UK	Calderdale: The Yorkshire Challenger	19 October 2003, San Sebastián, La Gomera, Spain	24 October 2003	5	Incomplete
19	Atlantic	Jeremy Hinton & Sebastien Lefebvre	UK, France	Mardine Meuse Lorraine	23 October 2003, San Sebastián, La Gomera, Spain	18 January 2004, Port St Charles, Barbados	91	
20	Atlantic	Graham Walters	UK	George Geary	29 October 2003, Playa de Santiago, La Gomera, Spain	26 January 2004, Port St Charles, Barbados	89	
	Pacific	Jim Shekhdar	UK	Hornette	4 November 2003, Bluff, New Zealand	18 November 2003	14	Incomplete
21	Atlantic	Stuart Boreham	UK	Macmillan Spirit	15 November 2003, Playa de Santiago, La Gomera, Spain	3 March 2004, Port St Charles, Barbados	109	
	Atlantic	Emmanuel Coindre	France	Lady Bird	4 January 2004, San Sebastián, La Gomera, Spain	5 January 2004	2	Incomplete
22	Atlantic	Emmanuel Coindre	France	Lady Bird	7 January 2004, El Hierro, Canary Islands, Spain	19 February 2004, Guadeloupe	43	
23	Atlantic	Jason Hart, Phil Langman, Yorkie Lomas & Shaun Barker	UK	Queensgate	20 January 2004, San Sebastián, La Gomera, Spain	26 February 2004, Port St Charles, Barbados	36	
24	Atlantic	Christopher Morgan & Michael Perrens	UK	Carpe Diem	20 January 2004, San Sebastián, La Gomera, Spain	8 March 2004, Port St Charles, Barbados	48	
25	Atlantic	James Doust & Nige Gower	UK	Linda	20 January 2004, San Sebastián, La Gomera, Spain	14 March 2004, Port St Charles, Barbados	54	

(Continued)

ROW	OCEAN	NAME	COUNTRY	BOAT	DEPART	ARRIVE	DAYS AT SEA	NOTE
126	Atlantic	Sam Knight	UK	Pacific Pete TNT	20 January 2004, San Sebastián, La Gomera, Spain	19 March 2004, Port St Charles, Barbados	59	
127	Atlantic	Pavel Rezvoy	Ukraine	Marion Lviv	20 January 2004, San Sebastián, La Gomera, Spain	9 June 2004, Port Chivirico, Cuba via Port St Charles, Barbados	88	
128	Atlantic	William Stableforth & Nathaniel Spring	UK	Sea Slug	20 January 2004, San Sebastián, La Gomera, Spain	23 March 2004, Port St Charles, Barbados	63	
129	Atlantic	John Peck & Fraser Dodds	UK	New Horizons	20 January 2004, San Sebastián, La Gomera, Spain	28 March 2004, Port St Charles, Barbados	68	
130	Atlantic	Matthew Boreham	UK	Alison May	20 January 2004, San Sebastián, La Gomera, Spain	13 April 2004, Port St Charles, Barbados	84	
131	Atlantic	Richard Wood	UK	NaJoJo	20 January 2004, San Sebastián, La Gomera, Spain	1 May 2004, Port St Charles, Barbados	102	
132	Atlantic	Sally Kettle & Sarah Kettle	UK	Calderdale: The Yorkshire Challenger	20 January 2004, San Sebastián, La Gomera, Spain	5 May 2004, Port St Charles, Barbados	106	
133	Atlantic	Henry Dale & Justin Coleman	UK	Kenneth C	20 January 2004, San Sebastián, La Gomera, Spain	18 May 2004, Port St Charles, Barbados	118	Justin Coleman rescued after 19 day at sea
134	Atlantic	Louis Ginglo	Canada	Moose on the Move	20 January 2004, San Sebastián, La Gomera, Spain	20 May 2004, Port St Charles, Barbados	120	
–	Atlantic	Mark Mortimer	UK	Acorn Atlantic Warrior	20 January 2004, San Sebastián, La Gomera, Spain	23 February 2004	33	Incomplete
135	Atlantic	Scott Wonenberg & Brett Sparrow	Zimbabwe	Against All Odds	22 January 2004, San Sebastián, La Gomera, Spain	9 March 2004, Port St Charles, Barbados	47	
–	Pacific	Mick Dawson	UK	Mrs D's Viking Spirit	6 May 2004, Choshi, Japan	23 August 2004	109	Incomplete
136	Atlantic	Anne Quéméré	France	Le Connetable	3 June 2004, Cape Cod, Massachusetts, USA	30 August 2004, Meridian of Ile d'Ouessant, France	88	
–	Atlantic	Jean Lukes	France	SOJASUN	26 June 2004, Cape Cod, Massachusetts, USA	11 July 2004	15	Incomplete
–	Atlantic	Mark Stubbs, Peter Bray, John Wills & Jonathan Gornall	UK	Pink Lady	30 June 2004, St John's, Newfoundland, Canada	8 August 2004	38	Incomplete
137	Atlantic	Emmanuel Coindre	France	Lady Bird	9 July 2004, Cape Cod, Massachusetts, USA	10 September 2004, Meridian of Ile d'Ouessant, France	63	
–	Atlantic	Andreas Rommel	Germany	Lady Georgia	16 July 2004, Cape Cod, Massachusetts, USA	2 September 2004	47	Incomplete

ROW	OCEAN	NAME	COUNTRY	BOAT	DEPART	ARRIVE	DAYS AT SEA	NOTE
–	Atlantic	Alex Bellini	Italy	Rosa d'Ata- cama	21 October 2004, Genoa, Italy	12 November 2004	22	Incomplete
–	Atlantic	Daniel Serenelli	Argentina	Vamos Argentina!!!	2 November 2004, San Sebastián, La Gomera, Spain	4 November 2004	2	Incomplete
138	Atlantic	Michael Perrens & Frank Gargan	UK	Britannia Endeavour	12 November 2004, San Sebastián, La Gomera, Spain	23 December 2004, St Charles, Barbados	41	
139	Atlantic	Thierry Dagues	France	Lune de Mer	15 November 2004, Las Palmas, Gran Canaria, Spain	22 January 2005, Guadeloupe	68	
–	Atlantic	Daniel Serenelli	Argentina	Vamos Argentina!!!	3 December 2004, Las Palmas, Gran Canaria, Spain	14 December 2004	12	Incomplete
140	Pacific	Maud Fontenoy	France	OCÉOR	12 January 2005, Callao, Peru	26 March 2005, Marquesas Islands, Polynesia, France	72	
141	Atlantic	Tiny Little	UK	Womble	21 January 2005, San Sebastián, La Gomera, Spain	17 May 2005, Antigua	116	Towed 51 miles
–	Indian	Alexander Sinelnik & Sergey Sinelnik	Russia	Rus	22 April 2005, Carnarvon, Australia	16 May 2005	24	Incomplete
142	Atlantic	Gijs Groeneveld, Robert Hoeve, Jaap Koomen & Maarten Staarink	Netherlands	Vopak Victory	27 May 2005, Atlantic Highlands, New Jersey, USA	27 July 2005, Bishop's Rock, UK	61	
143	Atlantic	Oliver Hicks	UK	Miss Olive	27 May 2005, Atlantic Highlands, New Jersey, USA	28 September 2005, St Mary's, Scilly Isles, UK	124	
144	Atlantic	George Rock, Robert Munslow, Nigel Morris & Steve Dawson	UK	Naturally Best	31 May 2005, St John's, Newfoundland, Canada	10 July 2005, Longitude of Bishop's Rock, UK	40	
145	Pacific	Emmanuel Coindre	France	Somewhere	24 June 2005, Choshi, Japan	31 October 2005, Coos Bay, Oregon, USA	130	
146	Indian	Theodore Rezvoy	Ukraine	Ukraine	3 August 2005, Carnarvon, Australia	23 August 2005, Cocos Islands, Australia	20	
–	Atlantic	Leven Brown	UK	Atlantic Wholff	14 August 2005, Cadiz, Spain	18 August 2005	4	Incomplete
147	Atlantic	Leven Brown	UK	Atlantic Wholff	26 August 2005, Rota, Spain	27 January 2006, Trinidad	123	
148	Indian	Pavel Rezvoy	Ukraine	Ukraine	13 September 2005, Cocos Islands, Australia	9 November 2005, Mahé, Seychelles	57	
149	Atlantic	Alex Bellini	Italy	Rosa d'Ata- cama II	18 September 2005, Genoa, Italy	30 April 2006, Fortaleza, Brazil	224	

(Continued)

ROW	OCEAN	NAME	COUNTRY	BOAT	DEPART	ARRIVE	DAYS AT SEA	NOTE
150	Atlantic	Julie Wafaei & Colin Angus	Canada	*Ondine*	23 September 2005, Lisbon, Portugal	19 January 2006, St Lucia	118	
151	Atlantic	Tim Harvey & Erden Eruç	Canada, Turkey	*Around-n-Over*	9 November 2005, Lisbon, Portugal	5 May 2006, Guadeloupe via Gran Canaria, Spain	177	Tim Harvey left the voyage in Gran Canaria after 32 days at sea
152	Atlantic	Justin Adkin, James Green, Robert Adkin & Martin Adkin	UK	*All Relative*	30 November 2005, San Sebastián, La Gomera, Spain	8 January 2006, Antigua	39	
153	Atlantic	George Simpson, David Martin, Neil Wightwick & Glynn Coupland	UK	*Atlantic4*	30 November 2005, San Sebastián, La Gomera, Spain	19 January 2006, Antigua	50	
154	Atlantic	Ben Fogle & James Cracknell	UK	*Spirit of EDF Energy*	30 November 2005, San Sebastián, La Gomera, Spain	19 January 2006, Antigua	50	
155	Atlantic	Chris Andrews & Clint Evans	UK	*C²*	30 November 2005, San Sebastián, La Gomera, Spain	19 January 2006, Antigua	51	
156	Atlantic	Franck Bruno & Dominique Benassi	France	*Bout de Vie*	30 November 2005, San Sebastián, La Gomera, Spain	23 January 2006, Antigua	54	
157	Atlantic	Dan Darley & Richard Dewire	UK	*Atlantic Prince*	30 November 2005, San Sebastián, La Gomera, Spain	28 January 2006, Antigua	59	
158	Atlantic	Christian Petersen & Soren Sprogoe	Denmark	*Team Scandlines*	30 November 2005, San Sebastián, La Gomera, Spain	28 January 2006, Antigua	59	
159	Atlantic	Richard Mayon-White & Liz O'Keeffe	UK	*Row 4 Cancer*	30 November 2005, San Sebastián, La Gomera, Spain	30 January 2006, Antigua	61	
160	Atlantic	Charles Woodward-Fisher & Philip Harris	UK, Australia	*Row 4 Life*	30 November 2005, San Sebastián, La Gomera, Spain	30 January 2006, Antigua	61	
161	Atlantic	Charles Bairsto & Tom Bright	UK	*Atlantic Warrior*	30 November 2005, San Sebastián, La Gomera, Spain	30 January 2006, Antigua	61	
162	Atlantic	Andrew Barnett & Juan Carlos Sagastume Bendana	UK, Guatemala	*Mayabrit*	30 November 2005, San Sebastián, La Gomera, Spain	3 February 2006, Antigua	65	
163	Atlantic	Al Howard & Nick Rowe	UK	*Gurkha Spirit*	30 November 2005, San Sebastián, La Gomera, Spain	5 February 2006, Antigua	67	

ROW	OCEAN	NAME	COUNTRY	BOAT	DEPART	ARRIVE	DAYS AT SEA	NOTE
164	Atlantic	Paula Evemy, Kathy Tracey, Sarah Day & Lois Rawlins-Duquemin	Guernsey	*Mission Atlantic*	30 November 2005, San Sebastián, La Gomera, Spain	5 February 2006, Antigua	67	
165	Atlantic	Robert Eustace & Peter Williams	UK	*Mark 3*	30 November 2005, San Sebastián, La Gomera, Spain	6 February 2006, Antigua	68	
166	Atlantic	Chris Martin	UK	*Pacific Pete*	30 November 2005, San Sebastián, La Gomera, Spain	7 February 2006, Antigua	69	
167	Atlantic	Rebecca Thorpe & Stephanie Temperton	UK	*Marion*	30 November 2005, San Sebastián, La Gomera, Spain	13 February 2006, Antigua	75	
168	Atlantic	Sally Kettle, Claire Mills, Sue McMillan & Jo Davies	UK	*Shelterbox*	30 November 2005, San Sebastián, La Gomera, Spain	15 February 2006, Antigua	77	Jo Davies rescued after 45 days at sea
169	Atlantic	Paul Gleeson & Victoria Holmes	Ireland, Canada	*Christina*	30 November 2005, San Sebastián, La Gomera, Spain	23 February 2006, Antigua	85	
170	Atlantic	Roz Savage	UK	*Sedna Solo*	30 November 2005, San Sebastián, La Gomera, Spain	13 March 2006, Antigua	103	
–	Atlantic	Andrew Morris & Stephane Portes	UK	*1 Life*	30 November 2005, San Sebastián, La Gomera, Spain	30 November 2005	1	Incomplete
–	Atlantic	Gearoid Towey & Ciaran Lewis	Ireland	*Digicel Atlantic Challenge 1*	30 November 2005, San Sebastián, La Gomera, Spain	8 January 2006	39	Incomplete
–	Atlantic	Tara Remington & Iain Rudkin	NZ	*Team Sun Latte*	30 November 2005, San Sebastián, La Gomera, Spain	15 January 2006	46	Incomplete
	Atlantic	Sarah Kessans & Emily Kohl	USA	*American Fire Atlantic Challenge*	30 November 2005, San Sebastián, La Gomera, Spain	15 January 2006	46	Incomplete
	Atlantic	Bobby Prentice & Colin Briggs	UK	*Moveahead*	30 November 2005, San Sebastián, La Gomera, Spain	19 January 2006	49	Incomplete
	Atlantic	Chris Barrett & Bob Warren	UK	*Spirit of Cornwall*	30 November 2005, San Sebastián, La Gomera, Spain	23 January 2006	54	Incomplete
	Atlantic	Duncan Pearson & Gareth Pearson	UK	*Serenity Now*	30 November 2005, San Sebastián, La Gomera, Spain	24 January 2006	55	Incomplete

(Continued)

ROW	OCEAN	NAME	COUNTRY	BOAT	DEPART	ARRIVE	DAYS AT SEA	NOTE
171	Atlantic	Andrew Morris & Mick Dawson	UK	*Charmed Life*	6 December 2005, San Sebastián, La Gomera, Spain	5 February 2006, Antigua	61	
–	Southern Ocean	Colin Yeates	UK	*Charlie Rossiter*	2 January 2006, Port Stanley, Falkland Islands	3 January 2006	1	Incomplete
172	Atlantic	Mike Norman & Tim Bradbury	UK	*Fraser's Boat*	29 January 2006, San Sebastián, La Gomera, Spain	21 May 2006, Antigua	112	
–	Atlantic	Graham Walters	UK	*Puffin*	30 January 2006, San Sebastián, La Gomera, Spain	5 February 2006	6	Incomplete
173	Atlantic	Serge Jandaud	France	*Diogène*	13 February 2006, Pasito Blanco, Gran Canaria, Spain	30 April 2006, Saint François, Guadeloupe	76	
–	Southern Ocean	Colin Yeates	UK	*Charlie Rossiter*	16 February 2006, Port Stanley, Falkland Islands	18 February 2006	2	Incomplete
–	Atlantic	Bhavik Gandhi	India	*Miss Olive*	11 April 2006, San Sebastián, La Gomera, Spain	15 April 2006	4	Incomplete
–	Atlantic	Victor Mooney	USA	*John Paul the Great*	7 May 2006, Goree Island, Senegal	7 May 2006	1	Incomplete
174	Atlantic	Brad Vickers, Dylan Le Valley, Greg Spooner & Jordan Hanssen	USA	*James Robert Hanssen*	10 June 2006, Jersey City, USA	20 August 2006, Falmouth, UK	71	
175	Atlantic	Andrew Unwin, Carl Powell, Mick Cataldo & Paul Tetlow	UK	*Yorkshire Warrior*	10 June 2006, Jersey City, USA	25 August 2006, Longitude of Bishop's Rock, UK	76	
176	Atlantic	Ben Fouracre, Charlie Martell, Mark Waterson & Pete Rowlands	UK	*Team Hesco*	10 June 2006, Jersey City, USA	3 September 2006, Mevagissey, Cornwall, UK	85	
–	Atlantic	Alasdair MacGillivray, Andy Clark, Peter Stevenson & Steve Hayson	UK	*Team Sevenoaks*	10 June 2006, Jersey City, USA	11 June 2006	1	Incomplete
177	Atlantic	Rob Munslow	UK	*Carnegie X-Stream*	27 June 2006, St John's, Newfoundland, Canada	30 August 2006, Rosevear Island, UK	64	
178	Atlantic	Michael Tuijn & Ralph Tuijn	Netherlands	*Zeeman Challenger*	27 September 2006, San Sebastián, La Gomera, Spain	22 December 2006, Curaçao, Dutch Antilles	86	
179	Atlantic	Romain Vergé	France	*Parrainez un Enfant*	19 November 2006, Saint-Louis, Senegal	29 December 2006, Cayenne, French Guiana	40	
180	Atlantic	Jean-Pierre Lasalarié	French Guiana	*Crokignol*	19 November 2006, Saint-Louis, Senegal	4 January 2007, Saint-Laurent, French Guiana	46	
181	Atlantic	Jean-François Tardiveau	France	*Saco*	19 November 2006, Saint-Louis, Senegal	5 January 2007, Saint-Laurent, French Guiana	47	

ROW	OCEAN	NAME	COUNTRY	BOAT	DEPART	ARRIVE	DAYS AT SEA	NOTE
182	Atlantic	Patrick Favre	France	*Adreanlines II*	19 November 2006, Saint-Louis, Senegal	5 January 2007, Saint-Laurent, French Guiana	47	
183	Atlantic	Christophe Henry	France	*Le Macaque*	19 November 2006, Saint-Louis, Senegal	7 January 2007, Saint -Laurent, French Guiana	49	
184	Atlantic	Sophie Macé	France	*Le Koonak*	19 November 2006, Saint-Louis, Senegal	7 January 2007, Saint -Laurent, French Guiana	49	
185	Atlantic	Jean Pierre Lacroix	French Guiana	*Ibis Rouge*	19 November 2006, Saint-Louis, Senegal	10 January 2007, Saint-Laurent, French Guiana l	52	
–	Atlantic	Philippe Malapert	France	*Paulimber*	19 November 2006, Saint-Louis, Senegal	19 November 2006	1	Incomplete
–	Atlantic	Patrick Deixonne	French Guiana	*Groupe Oceanic*	19 November 2006, Saint-Louis, Senegal	19 November 2006	1	Incomplete
–	Atlantic	Joseph Le Guen	France	*Rames Guyane*	19 November 2006, Saint-Louis, Senegal	19 November 2006	1	Incomplete
–	Atlantic	Jean Jacques Gauthier	France	*Rame en Coeur*	19 November 2006, Saint-Louis, Senegal	19 November 2006	1	Incomplete
–	Atlantic	Emmanuel Coindre	France	*Lady Génie*	19 November 2006, Saint-Louis, Senegal	5 December 2006	16	Incomplete
–	Atlantic	Philippe Soetaert	Belgium	*Celine*	19 November 2006, Saint-Louis, Senegal	19 December 2006	30	Incomplete
	Atlantic	Jacques DJeddi	France	*Defi Retais*	19 November 2006, Saint-Louis, Senegal	–		Incomplete
	Atlantic	Didier Lemoine	France	*Mercator II*	19 November 2006, Saint-Louis, Senegal			Incomplete
	Atlantic	Patrick Deixonne	French Guiana	*Groupe Oceanic*	21 November 2006, Saint-Louis, Senegal	25 November 2006	4	Incomplete
	Atlantic	Jean Jacques Gauthier	France	*Rame en Coeur*	21 November 2006, Saint-Louis, Senegal	27 November 2006	6	Incomplete
	Atlantic	Joseph Le Guen	France	*Rames Guyane*	21 November 2006, Saint-Louis, Senegal	8 January 2007	50	Incomplete
186	Atlantic	Gábor Rakonczai & Andrea Pálos	Hungary	*Tüzh-angya*	27 November 2006, Rota, Spain	1 March 2007, Antigua via Morocco and Gran Canaria	94	
187	Atlantic	Andreu Mateu	Spain	*Isidoro Arias*	2 December 2006, San Sebastián, La Gomera, Spain	7 March 2007, Martinique	95	
	Atlantic	Victor Gavrishev	Kyrgyzstan	*Solar Wind*	13 December 2006, San Sebastián, La Gomera, Spain	13 December 2006	1	Incomplete
188	Atlantic	Charles Hedrich	France	*Respectons la Terre*	18 December 2006, Dakar, Senegal	23 January 2007, Guara Point, Brazil	36	

(Continued)

ROW	OCEAN	NAME	COUNTRY	BOAT	DEPART	ARRIVE	DAYS AT SEA	NOTE
189	Atlantic	Stu Turnbull & Ed Baylis	UK	Memory of Zayed	20 December 2006, San Sebastián, La Gomera, Spain	21 February 2007, Antigua	64	
190	Atlantic	Wendel Rontgen & Gijs Koning	Netherlands	Optiver	20 December 2006, Puerto Mogán, Gran Canaria, Spain	22 February 2007, Antigua	64	
191	Atlantic	Olivier Bertonnier & Bruno Froideval	France	Oceanite	7 January 2007, Pasito Blanco, Gran Canaria, Spain	27 February 2007, Guadeloupe	52	
192	Atlantic	Dom Mee, Peter Bird, Ed James & Tom Rendell	UK	Atlantic Quest	14 January 2007, Porto Tazacorte, La Palma, Spain	19 February 2007, Barbados	37	
193	Atlantic	Graham Walters	UK	Puffin	3 February 2007, San Sebastián, La Gomera, Spain	13 May 2007, St Barts, Leeward Islands, France	99	
–	Atlantic	Bhavik Gandhi	India	Miss Olive	12 February 2007, San Sebastián, La Gomera, Spain	18 February 2007	6	Incomplete
194	Atlantic	Bhavik Gandhi	India	Miss Olive	28 February 2007, El Hierro, Canary Islands, Spain	14 June 2007, Antigua	106	
195	Pacific	Ralph Tuijn	Netherlands	Zeeman Challenger	14 March 2007, Callao, Peru	16 July 2008, New Britain, Papua New Guinea via Atafu Atoll & Fiji	281	
196	Indian	Glenn Edwards & John Williams	Canada, UK	Atlantic Warrior	24 March 2007, Fremantle, Australia	10 July 2007, Longitude of Rodrigues	108	Glenn Edwards rescued after 89 days at sea
–	Pacific	Erden Eruc	Turkey	Around-n-Over	5 June 2007, San Francisco, USA	5 June 2007	1	Incomplete
–	Atlantic	Andy Clark & Weston Miller	UK	Team Sevenoaks	16 June 2007, New Jersey, USA	17 June 2007	1	Incomplete
–	Atlantic	Charlie Girard	France	Caliste	30 June 2007, Cape Cod, Massachusetts, USA	30 June 2007	1	Incomplete
–	Atlantic	Charlie Girard	France	Caliste	4 July 2007, Cape Cod, Massachusetts, USA	6 July 2007	2	Incomplete
197	Pacific	Erden Eruc	Turkey	Around-n-Over	10 July 2007, Bodega Bay, California, USA	9 January 2010, Thursday Island, Australia via Papua New Guinea	364	
–	Pacific	Roz Savage	UK	Brocade	12 August 2007, Crescent City, California, USA	22 August 2007	11	Incomplete
198	Atlantic	Carl Theakston, John Cecil-Wright, Robbie Grant & Tom Harvey	UK	Pura Vida	2 December 2007, San Sebastián, La Gomera, Spain	19 January 2008, English Harbour, Antigua	48	
199	Atlantic	Bill Godfrey & Peter van Kets	South Africa	Gquma Challenger	2 December 2007, San Sebastián, La Gomera, Spain	22 January 2008, English Harbour, Antigua	51	

ROW	OCEAN	NAME	COUNTRY	BOAT	DEPART	ARRIVE	DAYS AT SEA	NOTE
200	Atlantic	Jon Csehi & Nick Histon	UK	No Fear	2 December 2007, San Sebastián, La Gomera, Spain	22 January 2008, English Harbour, Antigua	51	
201	Atlantic	Emily Kohl, Sarah Kessans, Tara Remington & Jo Davies	USA, NZ, UK	UnFinished Business	2 December 2007, San Sebastián, La Gomera, Spain	23 January 2008, English Harbour, Antigua	52	
202	Atlantic	Ben Gaffney & Orlando Rogers	UK	Go Commando	2 December 2007, San Sebastián, La Gomera, Spain	26 January 2008, English Harbour, Antigua	55	
203	Atlantic	Paul Harris & Steve Gardner	UK	The Reason Why	2 December 2007, San Sebastián, La Gomera, Spain	27 January 2008, English Harbour, Antigua	56	
204	Atlantic	Ian Andrews & Joss Elliot	UK	Pendovey Swift	2 December 2007, San Sebastián, La Gomera, Spain	3 February 2008, English Harbour, Antigua	63	
205	Atlantic	Andy Ehrhart, Justin Ellis, Mark Hefford & Nick Young	UK	Mission Atlantic	2 December 2007, San Sebastián, La Gomera, Spain	5 February 2008, English Harbour, Antigua	65	
206	Atlantic	Andrew Jordon-White & Joseph Jordon-White	UK	Jaydubyoo	2 December 2007, San Sebastián, La Gomera, Spain	7 February 2008, English Harbour, Antigua	67	
207	Atlantic	Angela Madsen & Franck Festor	USA	Row of Life	2 December 2007, San Sebastián, La Gomera, Spain	7 February 2008, English Harbour, Antigua	67	
208	Atlantic	Neil Hunter & Scott McNaughton	UK	Ocean Summit	2 December 2007, San Sebastián, La Gomera, Spain	7 February 2008, English Harbour, Antigua	67	
209	Atlantic	Benoit Dusser & Fabien Decourt	France	Pygram	2 December 2007, San Sebastián, La Gomera, Spain	13 February 2008, English Harbour, Antigua	73	
210	Atlantic	Catherine Allaway & Margaret Bowling	UK	Atlantic Jack	2 December 2007, San Sebastián, La Gomera, Spain	13 February 2008, English Harbour, Antigua	73	
211	Atlantic	Andy Watson & Ian McGlade	UK & Ireland	C2	2 December 2007, San Sebastián, La Gomera, Spain	14 February 2008, English Harbour, Antigua	74	
212	Atlantic	Clair Desborough, Fiona Waller, Rachel Flanders & Sarah Duff	UK	Silver Cloud	2 December 2007, San Sebastián, La Gomera, Spain	14 February 2008, English Harbour, Antigua	74	
213	Atlantic	Peter Collett	UK & Australia	1 Charmed Life	2 December 2007, San Sebastián, La Gomera, Spain	16 February 2008, English Harbour, Antigua	76	
214	Atlantic	Paul Attalla	Canada	Spirit of Fernie	2 December 2007, San Sebastián, La Gomera, Spain	16 February 2008, English Harbour, Antigua	76	
215	Atlantic	Linda Griesel & Rachel Smith	UK	Barbara Ivy	2 December 2007, San Sebastián, La Gomera, Spain	16 February 2008, English Harbour, Antigua	76	
216	Atlantic	Elin Haf Davies & Herdip Sidhu	UK	Dream Maker	2 December 2007, San Sebastián, La Gomera, Spain	17 February 2008, English Harbour, Antigua	77	

(Continued)

ROW	OCEAN	NAME	COUNTRY	BOAT	DEPART	ARRIVE	DAYS AT SEA	NOTE
–	Atlantic	Andrew Lothian & Jim Hook	UK	Titanic Challenge	2 December 2007, San Sebastián, La Gomera, Spain	3 December 2007	1	Incomplete
–	Atlantic	Billy Blunden, Bobby Prentice, Colin Briggs & Ted Manning	UK	Move Ahead II	2 December 2007, San Sebastián, La Gomera, Spain	13 December 2007	11	Incomplete
217	Atlantic	James Burge & Niall McCann	UK	Komale	4 December 2007, San Sebastián, La Gomera, Spain	5 February 2008, English Harbour, Antigua	65	
–	Atlantic	Simon Chalk (skipper), Ben Thackwray, Mike Martin, George Oliver, Ian Couch & Andrew Morris	UK	Oyster Shack	5 December 2007, San Sebastián, La Gomera, Spain	6 December 2007	1	Incomplete
218	Atlantic	Peter Raab & Tim Wilks	Germany	Martha Dos	8 December 2007, Puerto Colón, Tenerife, Spain	5 February 2008, Antigua	59	
219	Atlantic	Frederic Blond	France	Lune de Mer	11 December 2007, Pasito Blanco, Gran Canaria, Spain	16 February 2008, Guadeloupe	68	
220	Atlantic	Leven Brown (skipper), Peter Donaldson, Mike Tooth, Julian Barnwell, Reinhardt von Hof, Ray Carroll, Charlie Taylor, Stuart Kershaw, Don Lennox, Oliver Dudley, Rob Loder-Symonds, PJ Luard, Jamie Walker & Liam Hughes	UK, Ireland	La Mondiale	15 December 2007, Puerto de Mogán, Gran Canaria, Spain	17 January 2008, Port St Charles, Barbados	33	
221	Atlantic	Roy Finlay (skipper), Denis Richardson, Chris Cuddihy & Ronnie Desiderio	USA	ORCA	15 December 2007, Puerto de Mogán, Gran Canaria, Spain	20 February 2008, Port St Charles, Barbados	36	
222	Atlantic	Simon Chalk (skipper), Ben Thackwray, Mike Martin, George Oliver & Ian Couch	UK	Oyster Shack	23 December 2007, San Sebastián, La Gomera, Spain	29 January 2008, Antigua	37	
223	Atlantic	Alan Lock & Matt Boreham	UK	Gemini	11 January 2008, San Sebastián, La Gomera, Spain	5 April 2008, Port St Charles, Barbados	85	.
224	Atlantic	David Clarke	UK	Positive Outcomes	12 January 2008, San Sebastián, La Gomera, Spain	2 April 2008, Antigua	81	
225	Atlantic	Anthony Taylor	UK	Albatross	12 January 2008, San Sebastián, La Gomera, Spain	30 March 2008, Antigua	78	
226	Atlantic	Sam Williams	UK	Pacific Pete	12 January 2008, San Sebastián, La Gomera, Spain	27 March 2008, Antigua	75	
–	Atlantic	Pieter Hennipman	Netherlands	Atlantic Wholff	24 January 2008, Sagres, Portugal	15 February 2008	22	Incomplete

ROW	OCEAN	NAME	COUNTRY	BOAT	DEPART	ARRIVE	DAYS AT SEA	NOTE
227	Pacific	Alex Bellini	Italy	Rosa d'Atacama II	21 February 2008, Callao, Peru	12 December 2008, Coral Sea, Australia	294	
–	Atlantic	Jose Toledo	France	Oceanite	18 April 2008, Dakar, Senegal	16 May 2008	28	Incomplete
228	Pacific	Roz Savage	UK	Brocade	25 May 2008, San Francisco, USA	3 June 2010, Madang, Papua New Guinea via Hawaii & Kiribati	251	
–	Atlantic	Andy Clarke & Pete Lumley	UK	Sevenoaks	1 June 2008, Jersey City, USA	2 June 2008	1	Incomplete
–	Atlantic	Chris Jenkins, Tim Garratt, Wayne Davey & Joby Newton	UK	Scilly Boys	1 June 2008, Jersey City, USA	14 June 2008	12	Incomplete
–	Indian	Sergey Sinelnik & Alexander Sinelnik	Russia	Rus	16 June 2008, Carnarvon, Australia	18 June 2008	2	Incomplete
–	Atlantic	Aldo Diana & Ken Maynard	UK	Rita	12 December 2008, Puerto de Mogán, Gran Canaria	6 January 2009	25	Incomplete
–	Atlantic	Leo Rosette	USA	Halcyon	1 January 2009, San Sebastián, La Gomera, Spain	3 January 2009	2	Incomplete
–	Atlantic	Paul Ridley	USA	Liv	1 January 2009, San Sebastián, La Gomera, Spain	29 March 2009, Antigua	87	Incomplete
–	Atlantic	Leven Brown (skipper), Don Lennox, James Mouland, Danny Longman, Matt Craughwell, Gareth Wilson, George Kitovitz, Breffny Morgan, Peter Williams, Ryan Corcoran, Robert Byrne, Ian McKeever, Livar Nysted & Yaacov Mutnikas	UK, Ireland, Faroe Islands, Canada	La Mondiale	4 January 2009, Puerto de Mogán, Gran Canaria, Spain	15 January 2009	11	Incomplete
	Atlantic	Eddy Lesage	France	Martha Dos	14 January 2009, Puerto Colón, Tenerife, Spain	19 January 2009	5	Incomplete
	Atlantic	Victor Gavrishev	Kyrgyzstan	Solar Wind	22 January 2009, Pasito Blanco, Gran Canaria, Spain	23 January 2009	1	Incomplete
	Southern Ocean	Oliver Hicks	UK	Flying Carrot	23 January 2009, Recherche Bay, Tasmania, Australia	28 April 2009	95	Incomplete
	Atlantic	Victor Gavrishev	Kyrgyzstan	Solar Wind	27 February 2009, Pasito Blanco, Gran Canaria, Spain	28 February 2009	1	Incomplete
29	Atlantic	Patrick Hoyau	French Guiana	SDVI	8 March 2009, Saint-Louis, Senegal	19 April 2009, Saint-Laure	42	
30	Atlantic	Mathieu Bonnier	France	Hil's SanteVet	8 March 2009, Saint-Louis, Senegal	20 April 2009, Saint-Laurent, French Guiana	43	

(Continued)

ROW	OCEAN	NAME	COUNTRY	BOAT	DEPART	ARRIVE	DAYS AT SEA	NOTE
231	Atlantic	Charles Bergère	French Guiana	Le Brigandin	8 March 2009, Saint-Louis, Senegal	21 April 2009, Saint-Laurent, French Guiana	44	
232	Atlantic	Patrick Favre	France	Victoria Patrimoine	8 March 2009, Saint-Louis, Senegal	22 April 2009, Saint-Laurent, French Guiana	45	
233	Atlantic	Eric Lainé	France	Twinea	8 March 2009, Saint-Louis, Senegal	22 April 2009, Saint-Laurent, French Guiana	45	
234	Atlantic	Patrick Deixonne	French Guiana	Matoury	8 March 2009, Saint-Louis, Senegal	23 April 2009, Saint-Laurent, French Guiana	47	
235	Atlantic	Jean Luc Torre	France	Dago Vera	8 March 2009, Saint-Louis, Senegal	23 April 2009, Saint-Laurent, French Guiana	47	
236	Atlantic	Gilles Ponthieux	France	Ram Atao	8 March 2009, Saint-Louis, Senegal	24 April 2009, Saint-Laurent, French Guiana	47	
237	Atlantic	Pascal Vaudé	French Guiana	Marine & Loisirs	8 March 2009, Saint-Louis, Senegal	24 April 2009, Saint-Laurent, French Guiana	47	
238	Atlantic	Jean Pierre Lacroix	French Guiana	Ibis Rouge	8 March 2009, Saint-Louis, Senegal	27 April 2009, Saint-Laurent, French Guiana	50	
239	Atlantic	Pierre Katz	France	Le Quinze	8 March 2009, Saint-Louis, Senegal	29 April 2009, Saint-Laurent, French Guiana	52	
240	Atlantic	Jean Pierre Habold	France	La Rebelle	8 March 2009, Saint-Louis, Senegal	30 April 2009, Saint-Laurent, French Guiana	53	
241	Atlantic	Karl Barranco	French Guiana	Alea Jacta Est	8 March 2009, Saint-Louis, Senegal	2 May 2009, Saint-Laurent, French Guiana	55	
–	Atlantic	Victor Gavrishev	Kyrgyzstan	Solar Wind	8 March 2009, Pasito Blanco, Gran Canaria, Spain	8 March 2009	1	Incomplete
–	Atlantic	Jean Jacques Gauthier	France	Ram en Coeur	8 March 2009, Saint-Louis, Senegal	16 March 2009	7	Incomplete
–	Atlantic	Henri Deboulonge	France	Innovatys	8 March 2009, Saint-Louis, Senegal	18 March 2009	10	Incomplete
–	Atlantic	Christophe Lemur	France	Triskell	8 March 2009, Saint-Louis, Senegal	3 April 2009	26	Incomplete
–	Atlantic	Patricia Lemoine	France	Mercator III	8 March 2009, Saint-Louis, Senegal	11 April 2009	34	Incomplete

ROW	OCEAN	NAME	COUNTRY	BOAT	DEPART	ARRIVE	DAYS AT SEA	NOTE
–	Atlantic	Rémy Alnet	France	*Areva*	8 March 2009, Saint-Louis, Senegal	18 April 2009	41	Incomplete
–	Atlantic	Jean Pierre Vennat	France	*Oytech*	8 March 2009, Saint-Louis, Senegal	21 April 2009	43	Incomplete
–	Atlantic	Bertrand de Gaullier	France	*Easy Dentici*	8 March 2009, Saint-Louis, Senegal	28 April 2009	51	Incomplete
–	Atlantic	Didier Lemoine	France	*Mercator II*	8 March 2009, Saint-Louis, Senegal	6 May 2009	58	Incomplete
–	Atlantic	Henri-Georges Hidair	French Guiana	*Defi Nofrayane*	8 March 2009, Saint-Louis, Senegal	6 May 2009	58	Incomplete
–	Indian	Sarah Outen	UK	*Serendipity*	13 March 2009, Fremantle, Australia	24 March 2009	10	Incomplete
242	Indian	Sarah Outen	UK	*Serendipity*	1 April 2009, Fremantle, Australia	3 August 2009, Mauritius	125	
–	Atlantic	Victor Mooney	USA	*The Spirit of Zayed*	1 April 2009, Goree Island, Senegal	15 April 2009	15	Incomplete
243	Indian	Phil McCorry, Nick McCorry, Matt Hellier & Ian Allen	UK	*Bexhill Trust Challenger*	19 April 2009, Geraldton, Australia	26 June 2009, Port Louis, Mauritius	69	
244	Indian	Sarah Duff, Fiona Waller, Jo Jackson & Elin Haf Davies	UK	*Pura Vida*	19 April 2009, Geraldton, Australia	6 July 2009, Port Louis, Mauritius	78	
245	Indian	Tom Wigram, Billy Gammon, Mat Hampel & Pete Staples	UK, NZ	*Rowing for Prostate*	19 April 2009, Geraldton, Australia	9 July 2009, Port Louis, Mauritius	81	
46	Indian	Guy Watts & Andrew Delaney	UK	*Flying Ferkins*	19 April 2009, Geraldton, Australia	30 July 2009, Port Louis, Mauritius	103	
47	Indian	James Thysse & James Facer-Childs	UK	*Southern Cross*	19 April 2009, Geraldton, Australia	31 July 2009, Port Louis, Mauritius	103	
	Indian	Mick Moran	UK	*Hoppipolla*	19 April 2009, Geraldton, Australia	21 April 2009	1	Incomplete
	Indian	Roger Haines & Tom Lee	UK	*Dream It Do It*	19 April 2009, Geraldton, Australia	21 April 2009	1	Incomplete
	Indian	Matt Hort, Andrew Taylor, Peter Tomic & David Louw	Australia	*Whatever It Takes*	19 April 2009, Geraldton, Australia	22 April 2009	3	Incomplete
	Indian	Ben Steadman & Mark Davis	UK	*Doing Time*	19 April 2009, Geraldton, Australia	30 April 2009	11	Incomplete
	Indian	Simon Prior	UK	*Old Mutual Endurance*	19 April 2009, Geraldton, Australia	11 June 2009	53	Incomplete

(Continued)

ROW	OCEAN	NAME	COUNTRY	BOAT	DEPART	ARRIVE	DAYS AT SEA	NOTE
248	Indian	Simon Chalk (skipper), Angela Madsen, Helen Taylor, Bernard Fissett, Doug Tumminello, Brian Flick, Paul Cannon & Ian Couch	UK, USA, Belgium	Aud Eamus	28 April 2009, Geraldton, Australia	25 June 2009, Port Louis, Mauritius	59	
249	Pacific	Mick Dawson & Chris Martin	UK	Bojangles	8 May 2009, Choshi, Japan	13 November 2009, San Francisco, USA	189	
–	Atlantic	Charlie Girard	France	Caliste	19 May 2009, Cape Cod, Massachusetts, USA	29 May 2009	10	Incomplete
–	Atlantic	John Mollison	UK	Shepherd Purple Heart	5 July 2009, Cape Cod, Massachusetts, USA	28 July 2009	22	Incomplete
–	Atlantic	Peter Bray	UK	Black Knight	8 July 2009, St John's, Canada	19 August 2009	42	Incomplete
250	Atlantic	Katie Spotz	USA	Liv	3 January 2010, Dakar, Senegal	14 March 2010, Georgetown, Guyana	70	
251	Atlantic	Ian Couch (skipper), David Hosking, Linda Brewer, James Scott, James Nettleton, Peter Gadiot, Lee Fudge, Robert Prentice, Neil Ward, Anne Miltenberger, Lise Kronborg & Allan Lyngholm	UK, USA, Denmark	Britannia III	4 January 2010, San Sebastián, La Gomera, Spain	11 February 2010, Port St Charles, Barbados	38	
252	Atlantic	Charlie Pitcher	UK	Insure & Go	4 January 2010, San Sebastián, La Gomera, Spain	25 February 2010, English Harbour, Antigua	52	
253	Atlantic	James Croome & Oliver Back	UK	QBE Insurance Challenger	4 January 2010, San Sebastián, La Gomera, Spain	5 March 2010, English Harbour, Antigua	59	
254	Atlantic	François Lamy & Benoît Dusser	France	Karukera	4 January 2010, San Sebastián, La Gomera, Spain	8 March 2010, English Harbour, Antigua	63	
255	Atlantic	Catherine Remy, Quitterie Marque, Laurence Grand Clement & Laurence De Rancourt	France	Vivaldi	4 January 2010, San Sebastián, La Gomera, Spain	9 March 2010, English Harbour, Antigua	64	
256	Atlantic	Charlie Marlow & Matthew Mackaness	UK	Roberto Coin	4 January 2010, San Sebastián, La Gomera, Spain	13 March 2010, English Harbour, Antigua	68	
257	Atlantic	Nick Jackson & Jonathan Miller	UK	Patience	4 January 2010, San Sebastián, La Gomera, Spain	13 March 2010, English Harbour, Antigua	68	
258	Atlantic	Joe Thompson & Chris Brooks	UK	HCL Workforce 1	4 January 2010, San Sebastián, La Gomera, Spain	16 March 2010, English Harbour, Antigua	70	
259	Atlantic	Thomas Barnes & Richard Hume	UK	Red Arrow	4 January 2010, San Sebastián, La Gomera, Spain	17 March 2010, English Harbour, Antigua	72	

ROW	OCEAN	NAME	COUNTRY	BOAT	DEPART	ARRIVE	DAYS AT SEA	NOTE
260	Atlantic	Mick Birchall & Lia Ditton	UK	Dream Maker	4 January 2010, San Sebastián, La Gomera, Spain	18 March 2010, English Harbour, Antigua	73	
261	Atlantic	Neil Gyllenship & Dean Jagger	UK	Spirit of MA	4 January 2010, San Sebastián, La Gomera, Spain	20 March 2010, English Harbour, Antigua	74	
262	Atlantic	Kiley Trehoral-Daly, Sarah Medland, Karen Radband & Jo Langmead	UK	Mission Atlantic	4 January 2010, San Sebastián, La Gomera, Spain	20 March 2010, English Harbour, Antigua	74	
263	Atlantic	Dominic Marsh, Andrew Mallinson, Paul Williams & Benjy Thomasson	UK	Limited Intelligence	4 January 2010, San Sebastián, La Gomera, Spain	20 March 2010, English Harbour, Antigua	74	Benjy Thomasson rescued after 4 days at sea
264	Atlantic	Mike Arnold & Simon Evans	UK	Pendovey Swift	4 January 2010, San Sebastián, La Gomera, Spain	21 March 2010, English Harbour, Antigua	76	
265	Atlantic	Peter van Kets	South Africa	Nyamezela	4 January 2010, San Sebastián, La Gomera, Spain	21 March 2010, English Harbour, Antigua	76	
266	Atlantic	Phil Pring & Benjamin Cummings	UK	Vision of Cornwall	4 January 2010, San Sebastián, La Gomera, Spain	21 March 2010, Antigua	76	
267	Atlantic	Stephen Coe & Richard Hoyland	UK	No Fear	4 January 2010, San Sebastián, La Gomera, Spain	22 March 2010, English Harbour, Antigua	76	
268	Atlantic	Adam Rackley & James Arnold	UK	Spirit of Montanaro	4 January 2010, San Sebastián, La Gomera, Spain	22 March 2010, English Harbour, Antigua	76	
269	Atlantic	Melanie King & Anne Januszewski	UK	Explore	4 January 2010, San Sebastián, La Gomera, Spain	22 March 2010, English Harbour, Antigua	77	
270	Atlantic	Paul Milnthorpe & Jim Houlton	UK	Reason Why	4 January 2010, San Sebastián, La Gomera, Spain	22 March 2010, English Harbour, Antigua	77	
271	Atlantic	David Brooks	UK	Team Panasonic	4 January 2010, San Sebastián, La Gomera, Spain	23 March 2010, English Harbour, Antigua	78	
272	Atlantic	Tom Heal & Will Smith	UK	Heritage Explorer	4 January 2010, San Sebastián, La Gomera, Spain	25 March 2010, English Harbour, Antigua	80	
273	Atlantic	Stuart Burbridge & Rob Casserley	UK	Ocean Summit	4 January 2010, San Sebastián, La Gomera, Spain	27 March 2010, English Harbour, Antigua	82	Rob Casserley rescued after 68 days at sea
274	Atlantic	Norman Beech & James Beech	UK	Beech Boys Atlantic	4 January 2010, San Sebastián, La Gomera, Spain	27 March 2010, English Harbour, Antigua	82	
275	Atlantic	Luke Grose & Alex MacDonald	UK	Yorkshire Challenger	4 January 2010, San Sebastián, La Gomera, Spain	29 March 2010, English Harbour, Antigua	84	

(Continued)

ROW	OCEAN	NAME	COUNTRY	BOAT	DEPART	ARRIVE	DAYS AT SEA	NOTE
276	Atlantic	James Dennistoun & Sam Langmead	UK	Heart of the Warrior	4 January 2010, San Sebastián, La Gomera, Spain	30 March 2010, English Harbour, Antigua	85	
277	Atlantic	Roger Haines	UK	Dream It Do It	4 January 2010, San Sebastián, La Gomera, Spain	6 April 2010, English Harbour, Antigua	92	
278	Atlantic	Ole Elmer & Brian Heron	Canada	Boogie Woogie	4 January 2010, San Sebastián, La Gomera, Spain	11 April 2010, English Harbour, Antigua	97	
279	Atlantic	Leo Rossette	USA	Halcyon	4 January 2010, San Sebastián, La Gomera, Spain	14 April 2010, Les Saintes, off Guadeloupe	101	
280	Atlantic	James Ketchell	UK	Speedo	4 January 2010, San Sebastián, La Gomera, Spain	25 April 2010, English Harbour, Antigua	110	
281	Atlantic	Sean McGowan	Ireland	Tess	4 January 2010, San Sebastián, La Gomera, Spain	2 May 2010, English Harbour, Antigua	118	
–	Atlantic	Matt Craughwell (skipper), Peter Williams, Mylene Paquette, Pedro Cunha, Mike Jones & James Kenworthy	UK, Ireland, Canada & Portugal	Sarah G	7 January 2010, Agadir, Morocco	7 January 2010	1	Incomplete
–	Atlantic	Eddy Lesage	France	Martha Dos	10 January 2010, El Hierro, Canary Islands, Spain	20 January 2010	10	Incomplete
282	Atlantic	Matt Craughwell (skipper), Peter Williams, Mylene Paquette, Pedro Cunha, Mike Jones & James Kenworthy	UK, Ireland, Canada & Portugal	Sarah G	12 January 2010, Agadir, Morocco	11 March 2010, Port St Charles, Barbados	58	
–	Atlantic	Anthony Titcombe	UK	Help for Heroes	19 January 2010, San Sebastián, La Gomera, Spain	3 February 2010	14	Incomplete
283	Atlantic	Christophe Sepot & Bart Verboven	Belgium	Zeeman Challenger	26 January 2010, Ar- guineguín, Gran Canaria, Spain	15 May 2010, Kourou, French Guiana	109	
–	Atlantic	Julian Bellido & Sigurd Haveland	Gibraltar	Herkules	5 March 2010, Gibraltar	6 March 2010	1	Incomplete
–	Atlantic	Leven Brown (skipper), Ray Carroll, Don Lennox & Livar Nysted	UK, Ireland & Faroe Islands	Artemis Investments	30 May 2010, Liberty Harbor Marina, New York	1 June 2010	3	Incomplete
284	Pacific	Serge Jandaud	France	Clinique Pasteur Toulouse	12 June 2010, Callao, Peru	25 June 2011, Vanuatu Islands via Wallis Island	190	
–	Atlantic	Leven Brown (skipper), Ray Carroll, Don Lennox & Livar Nysted	UK, Ireland & Faroe slands	Artemis Investments	12 June 2010, Liberty Harbor Marina, New York	12 June 2010	1	Incomplete
285	Atlantic	Leven Brown (skipper), Ray Carroll, Don Lennox & Livar Nysted	UK, Ireland & Faroe Islands	Artemis Investments	17 June 2010, Battery Park, New York	31 July 2010, St Mary's, Scilly Isles, UK	44	

ROW	OCEAN	NAME	COUNTRY	BOAT	DEPART	ARRIVE	DAYS AT SEA	NOTE
286	Indian	Erden Eruc	Turkey	Around-n-Over	13 July 2010, Carnarvon, Australia	20 April 2011, Cidade de Angoche, Mozambique via Madagascar	163	
–	Atlantic	Barbara Schwarz-mann & Anton Weikmann	Germany	Santa Maria	25 December 2010, Agadir, Morocco	29 December 2010	4	Incomplete
287	Atlantic	Chris Cleghorn & Matthew Cleghorn	UK	Papa Delta	3 January 2011, Puerto de Mogán, Gran Canaria, Spain	9 March 2011, Antigua	65	
288	Atlantic	Matt Craughwell (skipper), Graham Carlin, Thomas Cremona, Rob Byrn, Adam Burke & Flann Paul	UK, Malta, Ireland & Iceland	Sara G	5 January 2011, Tarfaya, Morocco	8 February 2011, Port St Charles, Barbados	33	
289	Atlantic	David Hosking (skipper), Chris Covey, Paddy Thomas, Naomi Hoogesteger, Justin Johanneson & Jack Stonehouse	UK	Hallin Marine	6 January 2011, Marina San Miguel, Tenerife, Spain	7 February 2011, Port St Charles, Barbados	32	
290	Atlantic	Angela Madsen, David Davlianidze, Ernst Fiby, Ryan Worth, Elizabeth Koenig, Aleksandra Klimas-Mikalauskas, Louise Graff, Steve Roedde, Nigel Roedde, Dylan White, Zach Scher, Charles Wilkins, Sylvain Croteau, Tom Butscher, Margaret Bowling & Liam Flynn	USA, Georgia, Austria, Canada, Switzerland, Australia	Big Blue	15 January 2011, Tarfaya, Morocco	4 March 2011, Port St Charles, Barbados	48	
291	Atlantic	Simon Chalk (skipper), Guy Griffiths, Ben Gothard, Mike Palmer, Colin Gray, Anna Lewis, Roger Gould, Shaun Pedley, Jonathan Paine, Dan Munier, Suzanne Pinto, Beth O'Kain, Jennifer Weterings & Nabs El-Busaidy	UK, Antigua, USA, Canada, Oman	Britannia III	31 January 2011, Puerto de Mogán, Gran Canaria, Spain	15 March 2011, Port St Charles, Barbados	43	
292	Atlantic	Ole Elmer & Serge Roetheli	Canada	Progress Amigo	2 February 2011, San Sebastián, La Gomera, Spain	5 April 2011, Port St Charles, Barbados	62	
	Atlantic	Kamel Chaabane	France	Karukera	2 February 2011, Tazacorte, La Palma, Spain	13 March 2011	39	Incomplete
	Atlantic	Victor Mooney	USA	Never Give Up	26 February 2011, Port of Mindelo, Cape Verde	27 February 2011	1	Incomplete
	Indian	Roz Savage	UK	Sedna	12 April 2011, Fremantle, Australia	25 April 2011	13	Incomplete

(Continued)

ROW	OCEAN	NAME	COUNTRY	BOAT	DEPART	ARRIVE	DAYS AT SEA	NOTE
–	Indian	Rob Eustace	UK	*2 Hopes*	13 April 2011, Geraldton, Australia	15 April 2011	2	Incomplete
293	Indian	James Kayll, Edward Wells, Oliver Wells & Tom Kelly	UK	*Indian Runner 4*	21 April 2011, Geraldton, Australia	6 July 2011, Port Louis, Mauritius	75	
294	Indian	Ben Stenning & James Adair	UK	*Indian Runner 2*	21 April 2011, Geraldton, Australia	14 August 2011, Port Louis, Mauritius	115	
295	Indian	Roz Savage	UK	*Sedna*	30 April 2011, Geraldton, Australia	4 October 2011, Mauritius via Abrolhos Islands	157	
–	Indian	Keith Whelan	Ireland		7 May 2011, Geraldton, Australia	19 May 2011	12	Incomplete
–	Indian	Keith Whelan	Ireland		4 June 2011, Abrolhos Islands, Australia	7 June 2011	3	Incomplete
–	Atlantic	Sean Moriarty	Ireland	*Positive Outcome*	11 June 2011, St John's, Newfoundland, Canada	13 June 2011	2	Incomplete
296	Atlantic	Erden Eruc	Turkey	*Around-n-'Over*	10 October 2011, Luderitz, Namibia	27 May 2012, Cameron, Louisiana, USA via Venezuela	220	
297	Atlantic	John Beeden	UK		23 November 2011, Puerto de Mogán, Gran Canaria, Spain	15 January 2012, Barbados	53	
298	Atlantic	Janice Jakait	Germany	*Bifröst*	23 November 2011, Portimão, Portugal	21 February 2012, Barbados	90	
299	Atlantic	Tom Dignum & Christian Howard	UK	*Oar Raisers*	25 November 2011, Puerto de Mogán, Gran Canaria, Spain	7 March 2012, Barbados	103	
300	Atlantic	Toby Iles & Nick Moore	UK	*Box Number 8*	5 December 2011, San Sebastián, La Gomera, Spain	14 January 2012, Port St Charles, Barbados	40	
301	Atlantic	Andrew Brown	UK	*JJ*	5 December 2011, San Sebastián, La Gomera, Spain	14 January 2012, Port St Charles, Barbados	40	
302	Atlantic	Ross Turner, Hugo Turner, Adam Wolley & Greg Symondson	UK	*Atlantic 4*	5 December 2011, San Sebastián, La Gomera, Spain	16 January 2012, Port St Charles, Barbados	42	
303	Atlantic	Jamie Windsor & John Haskell	UK	*Pendovey Swift*	5 December 2011, San Sebastián, La Gomera, Spain	20 January 2012, Port St Charles, Barbados	46	
304	Atlantic	Julia Immonen (skipper), Debbie Beadle, Katie Pattison-Hart, Helen Leigh & Kate Richardson	Finland, UK, Ireland	*The Guardian*	5 December 2011, San Sebastián, La Gomera, Spain	22 January 2012, Port St Charles, Barbados	48	

ROW	OCEAN	NAME	COUNTRY	BOAT	DEPART	ARRIVE	DAYS AT SEA	NOTE
305	Atlantic	Chris Walters, Elliot Dale, Tony Short & Brian Fletcher	UK	Spirit of Corinth	5 December 2011, San Sebastián, La Gomera, Spain	22 January 2012, Port St Charles, Barbados	48	
306	Atlantic	Ed Janvrin, Alex Mackenzie, Daniel Whittingham, Will Dixon, Neil Heritage & Carl Anstey	UK	Row2Recovery	5 December 2011, San Sebastián, La Gomera, Spain	25 January 2012, Port St Charles, Barbados	51	
307	Atlantic	Sonya Baumstein, Jonathan Crane, Oliver Levick & Chris Crane	USA	Limited Intelligence	5 December 2011, San Sebastián, La Gomera, Spain	30 January 2012, Port St Charles, Barbados	56	
308	Atlantic	Emil Eide Eriksen & Trond Bratland Erichsen	Norway	Njord	5 December 2011, San Sebastián, La Gomera, Spain	2 February 2012, Port St Charles, Barbados	59	
309	Atlantic	Bertie Portal & James Cash	UK	Patience	5 December 2011, San Sebastián, La Gomera, Spain	7 February 2012, Port St Charles, Barbados	64	
310	Atlantic	Helena Smalman-Smith & Richard Smalman-Smith	UK	Dream It Do It	5 December 2011, San Sebastián, La Gomera, Spain	18 February 2012, Port St Charles, Barbados	75	
–	Atlantic	Ole Elmer & Michael Majgaard	Canada	Amigo	5 December 2011, San Sebastián, La Gomera, Spain	8 December 2011	3	Incomplete
–	Atlantic	Tommy Tippetts	UK	KED Endeavour	5 December 2011, San Sebastián, La Gomera, Spain	10 December 2011	5	Incomplete
–	Atlantic	Tom Fancett & Tom Sauer	UK, Netherlands	PS Vita	5 December 2011, San Sebastián, La Gomera, Spain	14 December 2011	9	Incomplete
–	Atlantic	James Dennistoun & Wayne Dueck	UK, Canada	Boogie Woogie	5 December 2011, San Sebastián, La Gomera, Spain	18 December 2011	13	Incomplete
–	Atlantic	John Higson & Barnaby Mabbs	UK	Go Commando	5 December 2011, San Sebastián, La Gomera, Spain	19 December 2011	14	Incomplete
–	Atlantic	Viktor Matteson & Fredrik Albelin	Sweden	Two Friends	5 December 2011, San Sebastián, La Gomera, Spain	30 December 2011	25	Incomplete
311	Atlantic	Aldo Diana, Ken Maynard, Graham Witham & Jason Howard-Ady	UK	HM& S Twiggy	14 December 2011, Puerto de Mogán, Gran Canaria, Spain	17 February 2012, Barbados	65	
312	Atlantic	David Whiddon & Lloyd Figgins	UK	Atlantic Calling	19 December 2011, Agadir, Morocco	18 February 2012, Port St Charles, Barbados	61	
	Atlantic	Matt Craughwell (skipper), Ian Rowe, Aodhan Kelly, Mark Beaumont, Simon Brown & Yaacov Mutnikas	UK, Ireland	Sara G	2 January 2012, Tarfaya, Morocco	30 January 2012	28	Incomplete
313	Atlantic	Marin Medak, Alastair Humphreys, Simon Osborne & Stephen Bowens	Slovenia	Tusmobile	12 January 2012, Puerto de Mogán, Gran Canaria, Spain	27 February 2012, Port St Charles, Barbados	46	

(Continued)

ROW	OCEAN	NAME	COUNTRY	BOAT	DEPART	ARRIVE	DAYS AT SEA	NOTE
314	Atlantic	Tommy Tippetts	UK	KED Endeavour	21 January 2012, San Sebastián, La Gomera, Spain	12 April 2012, Port St Charles, Barbados	82	
315	Atlantic	Nicolas Carvajal	UK	Pito	26 January 2012, Puerto de Mogán, Gran Canaria, Spain	19 April 2012, Georgetown, Guyana	84	
316	Atlantic	Pascal Vaude	French Guiana	Marine & Loisirs	29 January 2012, Dakar, Senegal	6 March 2012, Cayenne, French Guiana	37	
317	Atlantic	Julien Besson	French Guiana	Cariacou Boto	29 January 2012, Dakar, Senegal	8 March 2012, Cayenne, French Guiana	39	
318	Atlantic	Jean-Emmanuel Alein	French Guiana	Sapro Point Bois	29 January 2012, Dakar, Senegal	8 March 2012, Cayenne, French Guiana	39	
319	Atlantic	Henri-Georges Hidair	French Guiana	Montsi-néry-Tonne-grande	29 January 2012, Dakar, Senegal	9 March 2012, Cayenne, French Guiana	39	
320	Atlantic	Christophe Dupuy	France	D.O.C.	29 January 2012, Dakar, Senegal	9 March 2012, Cayenne, French Guiana	40	
321	Atlantic	Pierre Verdu	French Guiana	La Fileuse	29 January 2012, Dakar, Senegal	9 March 2012, Cayenne, French Guiana	40	
322	Atlantic	Remi Dupont	French Guiana	Le Brigandin	29 January 2012, Dakar, Senegal	9 March 2012, Cayenne, French Guiana	40	
323	Atlantic	Benoît Soulies	France	Bel O	29 January 2012, Dakar, Senegal	10 March 2012, Cayenne, French Guiana	41	
324	Atlantic	Eric Laine	France	Solirames	29 January 2012, Dakar, Senegal	10 March 2012, Cayenne, French Guiana	41	
325	Atlantic	Christophe Letendre	France	Thermience	29 January 2012, Dakar, Senegal	11 March 2012, Cayenne, French Guiana	42	
326	Atlantic	Pierre Mastalski	France	Mauvilac	29 January 2012, Dakar, Senegal	12 March 2012, Cayenne, French Guiana	43	
327	Atlantic	Alan Pinguet	France	Lilo	29 January 2012, Dakar, Senegal	16 March 2012, Cayenne, French Guiana	47	
328	Atlantic	Marc Chailan	France	Grain de Sel	29 January 2012, Dakar, Senegal	17 March 2012, Cayenne, French Guiana	49	
329	Atlantic	Said Ben Amar	France	Le Champion-net	29 January 2012, Dakar, Senegal	20 March 2012, Cayenne, French Guiana	51	
–	Atlantic	Pascal Tesnière	France	Charlotte 76	29 January 2012, Dakar, Senegal	1 February 2012	3	Incomplete
–	Atlantic	Frederic Devilliers	France	Cocta	29 January 2012, Dakar, Senegal	–	–	Incomplete
–	Atlantic	Jean-Christophe Lagrange	France	La Quenelle Magique	29 January 2012, Dakar, Senegal	–	–	Incomplete

ROW	OCEAN	NAME	COUNTRY	BOAT	DEPART	ARRIVE	DAYS AT SEA	NOTE
–	Atlantic	Jean-Jacques Gauthier	France	*Echo-Mer*	29 January 2012, Dakar, Senegal	–	–	Incomplete
–	Atlantic	Rémy Alnet	France	*Areva*	29 January 2012, Dakar, Senegal	–	–	Incomplete
–	Atlantic	Olivia La Hondé	France	*Bleu Citron*	29 January 2012, Dakar, Senegal	8 February 2012	10	Incomplete
–	Atlantic	Francis Cerda	France	*Moana*	29 January 2012, Dakar, Senegal	–	–	Incomplete
–	Atlantic	Guillaume Bodin	France	*Pink Boat*	29 January 2012, Dakar, Senegal	–	–	Incomplete
–	Atlantic	Didier Lemoine	France	*Mercator II*	29 January 2012, Dakar, Senegal	–	–	Incomplete
330	Atlantic	Simon Chalk (skipper), Liam Stevenson, Paul Williams, Franck Festor, Patrick Favre, Bryan Fuller & Noel Watkins	UK, France, USA, NZ	*Titan*	26 February 2012, Puerto de Mogán, Gran Canaria, Spain	31 March 2012, Port St Charles, Barbados	35	
331	Indian	Laurence Grand Clement & Laurence De Rancourt	France	*Spirit of MA*	19 April 2012, Geraldton, Australia	13 July 2012, Mauritius	85	
–	Pacific	Charlie Martell	UK	*Blossom*	4 May 2012, Choshi, Japan	8 June 2012	35	Incomplete
–	Pacific	Sarah Outen	UK	*Gulliver*	12 May 2012, Choshi, Japan	8 June 2012	26	Incomplete
–	Atlantic	Bruno Froideval	France	*Caouanne*	20 June 2012, Cape Cod, Massachusetts, USA	29 June 2012	8	Incomplete
–	Atlantic	Mathieu Bonnier	France	*Liteboat*	20 June 2012, Cape Cod, Massachusetts, USA	2 July 2012	12	Incomplete
–	Indian	Ralph Tuijn	Netherlands	*Me Inc*	28 June 2012, Geraldton, Australia	3 July 2012	5	Incomplete
332	Atlantic	Charles Hedrich	France	*Respectons la Terre*	9 July 2012, Saint Pierre and Miquelon (off Newfoundland, Canada), France	2 December 2012, Petite Anse d'Arlet, Martinique	145	Double Atlantic crossing; west-to-east, down the European and African coasts, then east-to-west
333	Arctic	Paul Ridley, Collin West, Neal Mueller & Scott Mortensen	USA	–	17 July 2012, Inuvik, Northwest Territories, Canada	26 August 2012, Point Hope, Alaska	40	
–	Indian	Ralph Tuijn	Netherlands	*Me Inc*	1 August 2012, Geraldton, Australia	8 October 2012	68	Incomplete
334	Atlantic	Patrick Favre & Julien Bahain	France	*SOLVEO Energy*	8 January 2013, Tarfaya, Morocco	26 February 2013, Martinique	49	
–	Atlantic	Geoff Allum	UK	*Pacific Pete*	10 January 2013, Puerto de Mogán, Gran Canaria, Spain	11 January 2013	1	Incomplete

(Continued)

ROW	OCEAN	NAME	COUNTRY	BOAT	DEPART	ARRIVE	DAYS AT SEA	NOTE
335	Atlantic	Simon Chalk (skipper), Rufus Bostock, Mikey Buckley, Andrew Berry, Kez Bostock & Paul Gerritsen	UK, NZ	*Titan*	15 January 2013, Puerto de Mogán, Gran Canaria, Spain	19 February 2013, Port St Charles, Barbados	36	
336	Atlantic	Leven Brown (skipper), Calum McNicol, Benno Rawlinson, Jan Öner, James Cowan, Peter Fleck, Livar Nysted, Tim Spiteri	UK, Australia & Faeroe Islands	*Avalon*	17 January 2013, Puerto de Mogán, Gran Canaria, Spain	22 February 2013, Port St Charles, Barbados	36	
–	Atlantic	Jordan Hanssen, Pat Fleming, Adam Kreek, Markus Pukonen	USA, Canada	*James Robert Hanssen*	23 January 2013, Dakar, Senegal	6 April 2013	73	Incomplete
–	Atlantic	Charlie Pitcher	UK	*Soma*	2 February 2013, San Sebastián, La Gomera, Spain	3 February 2013	1	Incomplete
337	Atlantic	Charlie Pitcher	UK	*Soma*	6 February 2013, San Sebastián, La Gomera, Spain	13 March 2013, Barbados	35	
–	Atlantic	Ole Elmer, Fraser Sinclair	Canada	*Deep Blue*	7 February 2013, San Sebastián, La Gomera, Spain	14 February 2013	6	Incomplete
–	Atlantic	Jose Tavares	Portugal	*Paraguaçú*	1 March 2013, Tarfaya, Morocco	27 March 2013	26	Incomplete
–	Pacific	Sarah Outen	UK	*Happy Socks*	27 April 2013, Choshi, Japan	In progress		In progress

The period that each crew spent at sea has been rounded to the nearest day, so in some cases crews that landed on the same day will have spent a different number of days at sea and crews that landed on different days will have spent the same number of days at sea, depending on precisely when on that day they landed. Where crews have made a stopover en route to their final destination, the 'days at sea' do not include any days that they spent on land during the stopover. In many cases this means a difference of months between the departure and final arrival date and the number of days at sea. In the case of Erden Eruc's Pacific row in the boat *Around-n-Over*, the result is that the period between the start and the finish of the crossing is eighteen months longer than the number of days that he spent at sea.

For updates to the Chronology, see www.oceanrowing.com.

He just wanted a decent book to read ...

Not too much to ask, is it? It was in 1935 when Allen Lane, Managing Director of Bodley Head Publishers, stood on a platform at Exeter railway station looking for something good to read on his journey back to London. His choice was limited to popular magazines and poor-quality paperbacks – the same choice faced every day by the vast majority of readers, few of whom could afford hardbacks. Lane's disappointment and subsequent anger at the range of books generally available led him to found a company – and change the world.

'We believed in the existence in this country of a vast reading public for intelligent books at a low price, and staked everything on it'
Sir Allen Lane, 1902–1970, founder of Penguin Books

The quality paperback had arrived – and not just in bookshops. Lane was adamant that his Penguins should appear in chain stores and tobacconists, and should cost no more than a packet of cigarettes.

Reading habits (and cigarette prices) have changed since 1935, but Penguin still believes in publishing the best books for everybody to enjoy. We still believe that good design costs no more than bad design, and we still believe that quality books published passionately and responsibly make the world a better place.

So wherever you see the little bird – whether it's on a piece of prize-winning literary fiction or a celebrity autobiography, political tour de force or historical masterpiece, a serial-killer thriller, reference book, world classic or a piece of pure escapism – you can bet that it represents the very best that the genre has to offer.

Whatever you like to read – trust Penguin.

read more
www.penguin.co.uk